Modernism/Postmodernism

Longman Critical Readers

General Editor

STAN SMITH, Professor of English, University of Dundee

Published Titles

MODERNISM/POSTMODERNISM

Edited and Introduced by

PETER BROOKER

Routledge
Taylor & Francis Group

LONDON AND NEW YORK

First published 1992 by Pearson Education Limited

Published 2014 by Routledge
2 Park Square, Milton Park, Abingdon, Oxfordshire OX14 4RN
711 Third Avenue, New York, NY 10017, USA

First issued in hardback 2016

Routledge is an imprint of the Taylor & Francis Group, an informa business

British Library Cataloguing-in-Publication Data

A catalogue record for this book is
available from the British Library

Library of Congress Cataloging-in-Publication Data
Modernism/Postmodernism/edited and introduced by Peter Brooker.
    p. cm. - (Longman critical readers)
    Includes bibliographical references and index.
ISBN 0-582-06358-2 (csd.). - ISBN-0582-06357- 4
(pbk.)
        1. Modernism (Literature)   2. Postmodernism (Literature)
    3. Literature, Modern–20th century–History and critcism.
    I. Brooker, Peter.   II. Series.
    PN771.M6175 1992
    809'.91 – dc20   91-24537
                                                          CIP

Set by 9K in 9 / 11.5 Palatino

ISBN 13: 978-1-138-14465-1 (hbk)
ISBN 13: 978-0-582-06357-0 (pbk)

Contents

General Editors' Preface

The outlines of contemporary critical theory are now often taught as a standard feature of a degree in literary studies. The development of particular theories has seen a thorough transformation of literary criticism. For example, Marxist and Foucauldian theories have revolutionised Shakespeare studies, and 'deconstruction' has led to a complete reassessment of Romantic poetry. Feminist criticism has left scarcely any period of literature unaffected by its searching critiques. Teachers of literary studies can no longer fall back on a standardised, received, methodology.

Lectures and teachers are now urgently looking for guidance in a rapidly changing critical environment. They need help in understanding the latest revisions in literary theory, and especially in grasping the practical effects of the new theories in the form of theortetically sensitised new readings. A number of volumes in the series anthologise important essays on particular theories. However, in order to grasp the full implications and possible uses of particular theories it is essential to see them put to work. This series provides substantial volumes of new readings, presented in an accessible form and with a significant amount of editorial guidance.

Each volume includes a substantial introduction which explores the theoretical issues and conflicts embodied in the essays selected and locates areas of disagreement between positions. The pluralism of theories has to be put on the agenda of literary studies. We can no longer pretend that we all tacitly accept the same practices in literary studies. Neither is a *laissez-faire* attitude any longer tenable. Literature departments need to go beyond the mere toleration of theoretical differences: it is not enough merely to agree to differ; they need actually to 'stage' the differences openly. The volumes in this series all attempt to dramatise the differences, not necessarily with a view to resolving them but in order to foreground the choices presented by different theories or to argue for a particular route through the impasses the differences present.

The theory 'revolution' has had real effects. It has loosened the grip of traditional empiricist and romantic assumptions about language and literature. It is not always clear what is being proposed as the new agenda for literary studies, and indeed the very notion of 'literature' is questioned by the post-structuralist strain in theory. However, the uncertainties and obscurities of contemporary theories appear much less worrying when we see what the best critics have been able to do with them in practice. This series aims to disseminate the best of recent criticism, and to show that it is possible to re-read the canonical texts of literature in new and challenging ways.

RAMAN SELDEN AND STAN SMITH

The Publishers and fellow Series Editor regret to record that Raman Selden died after a short illness in May 1991 at the age of fifty-three. Ray Selden was a fine scholar and a lovely man. All those he has worked with will remember him with much affection and respect.

Acknowledgements

We are grateful to the following for permission to reproduce copyright material:
Art and Text for an extract from the article 'Discussing Modernity, "Third World" and *The Man Who Envied Women*' by Laleen Jayamanne from *Art and Text* Vol 23, Part 4 (1987); Associated University Presses for the chapter 'Postmodernism?' by Julia Kristeva from *Bucknell Review: Romanticism, Modernism, Postmodernism* ed by Harry R. Garvin (1980), © Bucknell Review; Basil Blackwell Ltd for chapters 19, 20 and 27 from *The Condition of Postmodernity* by David Harvey (1989); California Institute of the Arts, Division of Critical Studies, for extracts from *Simulations* by Jean Baudrillard (Semiotext(e), Foreign Agents Series, 1983); University of Chicago Press and the author, Houston A. Baker, Jnr, for chapter 10 from *Modernism and the Harlem Renaissance* (1987); the author's agent for the article 'Words Apart' by Carlos Fuentes, first published in *The Guardian* 24.2.89, copyright © 1989 by Carlos Fuentes; HarperCollins Publishers for the poem 'Ma Rainey' by Sterling A. Brown from *The Collected Poems of Sterling A Brown*. Copyright 1932 by Harcourt Brace Jovanovich, Inc, copyright renewed by Sterling A Brown. Copyright © 1980 by Sterling A Brown; University of Illinois Press & the author, Iain Chambers for the chapter 'Contamination, Coincidence, and Collusion: Pop Music, Urban Culture, and the Avant-Garde' from *Marxism and the Interpretation of Culture* ed by Cary Nelson and Lawrence Grossberg (1988), © Board of Trustees of University of Illinois 1988; Manchester University Press for the article 'The Metropolis and the Emergence of Modernism' by Raymond Williams from *Unreal City, Urban Experience in Modern European Literature and Art* ed by Edward Timms and David Kelley (1985); Manchester University Press, University of Minnesota Press and Suhrkamp Verlag for the chapter 'Avant-Garde and Engagement' from *Theory of the Avant-Garde* by Peter Bürger, translated by Michael Shaw, © 1984 University of Minnesota; Martin Secker & Warburg Ltd & Harcourt Brace Jovanovich, Inc for the chapter 'Postmodernism, Irony, the Enjoyable' from *Reflections on the Name of the Rose*, US title *Postscript to the Name of the Rose* by Umberto Eco, translated by William Weaver, copyright © 1983 by Umberto Eco, English translation copyright © 1984 by Harcourt Brace Jovanovich, Inc; The Merlin Press Ltd for an extract from *The Meaning of Contemporary Realism* by Georg Lukács, translated by John and Necke Mander (1962); Methuen London, Octopus Publishing Group Ltd, and Hill & Wang, a division of Farrar, Straus and Giroux, Inc for an extract from *Brecht and the Theatre*, US title *Brecht on Theatre* by Bertolt Brecht, translated by John Willett. Translation copyright © 1964 by

Editor's Preface

Both modernism and postmodernism are phenomena, primarily, of twentieth-century Anglo-American and European culture, though with a changing relation to that culture. For while the novelty of the first fades out of favour and into the grey orthodoxies of the Western tradition, the second abandons the conformities of museum, gallery and library (taking some texts and images along with it) for the fluid potential of hands-on home technologies and the rich adventure of cross-cultural forms and mobile subjectivities. At least that is one view of postmodernism. In fact the word sketches a culture as superficial and monotonous as it is multi-accented, as derivative as it is new; a society, in sum, with all the variety and flatness of its favourite icon, the television screen. Is postmodernism modernism reborn, the second time as soap opera? Is it a mere fashion (and already outmoded)? Does it describe a now permanent mass uniformity, or a new diversity and way forward?

Only in the recesses of one of those museums (talking of Michelangelo) can anyone have failed to hear some of these questions and the answers to them. By the end of the eighties a quickening stream of studies and commentary had become a cascade – which this book tries to catch but of course also joins – by literary and social critics, sociologists and philosophers, geographers, art historians, Rock critics and style-watchers. Inevitably postmodernism became what it described; for the cycle of more books and articles and late-night TV programmes about other books and TV programmes about films and buildings and TV programmes could only demonstrate the dynamic of mass production and consumption at the heart of post-war, postmodern societies. And this destabilising self-reflexiveness, or, from another view, instant weariness, even despair, at a culture that can only out-clone itself, are among the most commonly recognised features of postmodern tone and style. Some find new hope in this end to old certainties, a redeeming fall into everyday life from the heights of intellectual, artistic and political élitism. Others struggle against postmodernism's smooth surfaces aiming to recover a lost critical distance and rational perspective upon past and future.

These positions have been adopted on a very wide front within academic disciplines and in different spheres of the arts and cultural production. In turn they have provoked questionings about major changes and continuities in twentieth-century criticism and culture as a whole; that is to say, about modernity and modernism as well as postmodernism. In my view these earlier and later movements are intimately connected and comprise a network of dominant and marginalised forms and practices. One book, however, is not enough to represent the many-sided cultural history in which these relationships have been acted out. The cross-currents in literary and cultural criticism alone, to which in the main this Reader confines itself, themselves run wide and deep. I have assumed that most readers will appreciate having well-known essays on postmodernism made available, and have given more space to these. On modernism, where the earlier main debates in Anglo-American and German Marxist criticism are of considerable interest but too extensive for equal inclusion here, my solution has been to give the first more attention in the Introduction and to present the second, with commentary, in the book's contents. The Introduction continues this emphasis in relation to postmodernism; basically because I see postmodernism as closely associated with developments in post-war Western capitalist societies and because the United States remains the paradigm case for these.

It is true too, I believe, that both modernism and postmodernism have been interpreted according to Western intellectual, ideological and aesthetic models. Though it has become easier to acknowledge this with respect to modernism – indeed this might comprise a postmodern perspective upon modernism – postmodernist debate, for all its claims to a new pluralism, has also exercised a hegemonic pull towards selective topics and modes of enquiry. I have wanted to present these 'traditions', as they might be termed, in both movements, in the commentary and contents which follow. But I have wanted also to set them with essays which broaden, redefine and challenge their assumptions, from positions within feminism, or from black or Third World perspectives. This dual purpose, presentational and polemical, has determined the selection of extracts and the overall shape of the volume.

For The Walkers – a band for all isms.

Introduction: Reconstructions

'Somebody' said Frank Kermode in the mid-sixties, 'should write the history of the word "modern"'.[1] He suggests it has implied 'a serious relationship with the past . . . that requires criticism and indeed radical re-imagining' (p. 27), and as such is a weightier term than 'the new' or 'the contemporary'. Stephen Spender had used this second term in *The Struggle of the Modern* in 1963 to distinguish one group of 'modernist' writers, committed to the new and a break with the past, from another, the 'moderns' of his title. Kermode terms this 'traditionalist modernism', but warns that it is open to ideological distortion and can seem academicist and out of date in a world where shops label popular lines in furniture and curtains 'contemporary'. This 'modern', he points out moreover, is not the same as the 'avant-garde', and he ends the essay, 'But somebody should write a history of that word, too' (p. 32).

Kermode raises many familiar problems here; of periodisation, of academic and popular usage, of ideological and critical position and taste, and so of definition. There is plainly more than one modernism, and not all modernisms are equal. Kermode's essay is indeed titled 'Modernisms', and though he plots and queries some of its versions, he is ready to take some things for granted: 'On the whole, everybody knows what is meant by modern literature, modern art, modern music. The words suggest Joyce, Picasso, Schoenberg, or Stravinsky – the experiments of two or more generations back' (p.28). Unfussy and trouble-free though this seems, it suavely disguises the double sleight-of-hand by which a literary orthodoxy, at least, came into being; by shuffling 'traditionalist modernism' and 'the modern' together to produce what was taken as *the* modernist tradition. This is the modernism of Peter Faulkner's more recent *A Modernist Reader* (1986). With enviable conviction Faulkner pegs the dates for modernism in England at 1910–30 and looks again to Spender for a definition of what it was (modernism appears as interchangeable with 'modern art' in this discussion). Modern art, says Spender, 'reflects awareness of an unprecedented modern situation in its form and idiom'.[2] This simple and

1

blandly reflectionist formula somehow authorises the view that the early twentieth century produced a series of unparalleled 'masterpieces' which still command attention. Faulkner names Picasso, Stravinsky, Proust, and of literary modernists in England, Pound, Eliot, Lawrence, Woolf, Joyce and Yeats (aside from other quarrels and complications, the fact that only two of this list were English by birth decides his sub-title 'Modernism in England'). Faulkner's assumptions are remarkably unflustered and for that reason now exceptional, at least in print. What is more, his account is without the tension shaping many of the earlier studies, including Spender's significantly titled volume. Kermode presents his own discriminations, between 'neo' and 'paleo-modernism', by way of a series of reviews of contemporary studies. His three-part discussion breaks in mid-decade (1965–66) across accepted terms and groupings (what 'On the whole, everybody knows') and signs of change in art and criticism. Immediately following the statement quoted above, he writes:

> The fact that defining the modern is a task that now imposes itself on many distinguished scholars may be a sign that the modern period is over. We need a language to argue about it, as we argue about Renaissance. The formula devised will, in the same way, vary with time. A documentary history of the modern would have been different twenty years ago, and will be different twenty years hence.
>
> (Kermode, 'Modernisms', p. 28)

Kermode's is still a relaxed, common-room sense of an ending, but he rightly links matters of definition with broader historical change. In America where the post-war period saw an earlier and accelerating shift into the features of 'mass culture', there was a more vexed and more campaigning sense of cultural change, and hence a flurry of critical activity to meet the new paradigm. The terms 'postmodern' and 'postmodernism' surfaced briefly in the forties and fifties and were then employed, still earlier than is usually supposed, in the next decade as organising terms in critical essays registering tremors in cultural values. From the first, postmodernism presented an argument for sensuous response and the languages of the body over intellectual analysis. It declared itself for open, randomised, and popular forms and looked to an alliance with the counter-culture of youth, drugs, Rock-and-Roll and a new erotics in a deliberate affront to the decorums and hierarchies of the literary establishment.

The broad and contrary directions ascribed to postmodernism since this early post-war period in America, towards an aesthetics of consumption and stylistic eclecticism or a politics of cultural subversion energised by the new social movements, might be already discovered in embryo in this earlier constellation. As with modernism, however, the important question is less what postmodernism 'is' or 'means', in any absolute sense, than how and for whom it has functioned. There is a level of understanding, no doubt, at which 'everybody knows' what 'it' is – postmodernism, we can say, splices high with low culture, it raids and parodies past art, it questions all absolutes, it swamps reality in a culture of recycled images, it has to do with deconstruction, with consumerism, with television and the information society, with the end of communism – but already this sketches a quite different 'knowledge' from the way modernism is 'known' through the citation of major works of art or artists. Rather than pursue a description of this kind, however, we need to see how postmodernism is first of all a name for the series of social and cultural tendencies provoking the definition of modernism. Kermode talks of a documentary history of the 'modern' twenty years before his own essay. Definitions then would have been very thin on the ground, however, precisely because, as Kermode is aware, it was the sense that the modern period was *over* which produced its definition. The more usual understanding that postmodernism came into being as a reaction to an institutionalised modernism follows from this, since it was this particular construction of modernism which was then made explicit. Beyond this point of reciprocal definition, while traditional critics have continued to define and study modernism in traditional ways, postmodernism has functioned to further 'undefine' its supposed unitary identity, itself often collaborating in the construction of that very identity as fit only for deconstruction.

Kermode is right therefore to call for a 'history of the word "modern"' and of the avant-garde, rather than for their definition. And the same is true of modernism of course, and of postmodernism. Their meanings lie in their uses and function, their rise and fall in a history of dominant, receding, emergent, and always selective evaluations. These meanings, as I suggest, have taken shape in relation to each other, in culturally specific histories, especially in the major example of post-war America, itself increasingly engaged through this period in a complex exchange and dialogue with other cultures.

It is the first purpose of this Reader to present the broad materials of this intellectual and cultural history. Yet a book such as this cannot itself be free from the problems of definition and appraisal it raises. Is this commentary and selection postmodern because it is produced in the present postmodern period? Is it postmodernist in its assumptions, approach and tone? Fredric Jameson has argued that we cannot view postmodernism as an historical situation and present a critique of it from a position on the outside – for how can we be outside history? It follows that we cannot view modernism from outside postmodernism either. In which case this discussion, like every other, is on the inside looking in.

3

But does this mean it is trapped there, a replicant under a world-embracing geodesic dome of postmodernism which only sounds like or thinks itself a free agent? Is there nothing outside, before or after, the postmodern bubble? And if there is, is it modernity and modernism? My argument is initially that there are postmodernisms as well as modernisms, that between them there is the dialogic traffic of collage and argument, the building and unbuilding of orthodoxies. There is no absolute singular cultural entity or absolute historical break, therefore, and no absolute inside or outside part from the ideological constructions requiring them.

Already to put things this way is to combine a modernist discourse (of 'collage', dominant and emergent tendencies and so on) with an anti-essentialism, a scepticism towards fixed positions and meanings associated with postmodernism. At the same time it implies the rejection of a second postmodern perspective in which difference is endless and unstoppable, the ever-new confirming the ever-same. For my purpose a better (perhaps modernist) image than this recurring vision of the postmodern world as a bountiful hell of unrelieved, unhampered flatness (the desert, the prairie, the highway, the shopping mall) is of different maps, showing differently arranged seas and islands and continents which purport to be true representations of the same world. A map which shows the South of England, the Eastern seaboard of North America, and which marks in Paris, Trieste, perhaps Berlin and Vienna but not Moscow, Petrograd or Milan is not an acceptable map of 'the' world, but might be the map of a certain cultural mentality, and is, as it turns out, the 'map' of an Anglo-American construction of modernism. The same general point applies to postmodernism. However internally different its main versions, their common geography stretches to the American West, Canada and Australia, and until recently would show little else, even of Europe, beyond Paris and Frankfurt.

These maps which 'distort' the world, centring portions of it through the filter of aesthetic value and the force of sheer cultural dominance, also focus on particular periods or years. The book-ends of 1910 and 1930 for example, which Faulkner erects on a very narrow stretch of island, are widened in other versions to anywhere between 1880 and 1950, though the first quarter of the twentieth century is commonly regarded as the period of most intense modernist activity. Some critics (Spender, Graham Hough) would then give priority to the pre-war years, others to the post-war period; some again (Harry Levin, Julian Symons) favour one year, 1922, as the *annus mirabilis* of modernism.[3] As for postmodernism, Arnold Toynbee detected its beginnings in the 1870s; Charles Olson and Irvin Howe, though they mean different things by it, saw it as emerging in the 1950s; Fredric Jameson, in one account, 'in the late 1940s and early 1950s', in other, around 'the end of the 1950s or the early 1960s'; Charles

4

Jencks's as beginning on 15 July 1972 at 3.32 p.m.[4] For others, postmodernism is a phenomenon of the eighties. The heroes and villains of either movement can similarly shift about and change places.

The point is an obvious one. What you get is what you see from where you stand. What is more, these different perspectives and informing criteria do not add up. They do not together form a complete picture so much as cancel, subsume or contend with each other. A chronology of modernism would identify a range of artistic movements, decisive meetings, individual works and events, and would, for all its inevitable superficialities, underline these disparities. To realise, for example, that T.S. Eliot and H.D. (Hilda Doolittle) and Mayakovsky and Langston Hughes were contemporaries, that Leon Trotsky's *Literature and Revolution* and Eliot's *The Waste Land* were produced within a year of each other, does not so much round out orthodoxies as unfix them. A fuller picture would only confirm the plurality of modernisms, across their several divergent and contrary formations. The proper approach therefore must be one which reveals and questions hegemonic structures by bringing marginalised figures and movements into a fuller dialogue, in a fuller and more argumentative artistic and cultural history.

Making it old: 'Traditionalist Modernism'

Behind the starting date of 1910 and the 'clear cultural identity' Faulkner ascribes to modernism there no doubt lies Virginia Woolf's famous remark of 1924 that 'in or about December, 1910, human character changed'.[5] Virginia Woolf went on to suggest this had to do with a perception of changed social relations and attitudes, but did not explore this further, perhaps because her concern was precisely with a new interiorising treatment of character and consciousness in the novel: to present 'Mrs Brown' 'herself', not as a factoring out of class and environment in the way of an Arnold Bennett or of naturalism. By her own reckoning, however, her method was not the method of modernism, for in the same essay she finds the 'modernists' Joyce and Eliot indecent and obscure. We might choose to see her metonymic substitution of the part for the whole, of individual consciousness for 'life itself' as equivalent to Joyce's 'epiphany' or Eliot's 'objective correlative' or the Imagist 'doctrine or the image', but Woolf was not consciously contributing to a 'modernist aesthetic'. Nor were these other ideas recognised as new outside a small circle, and far less as dominant until the late twenties and thirties.

None of this points especially either to 1910. If there was any reason for this date for Virginia Woolf it was presumably less a matter of life

5

itself in the round – which would have something to do, say, with the death of liberal England, with suffrage, Home Rule, trade union militancy, as well as changing domestic relations in the middle-class household – than of the first Post-Impressionist exhibition of that year at the Grafton Gallery. As interpreted by Roger Fry this exhibition, showing work by Picasso, Matisse, Braque and Derain, signalled not so much a new direct address to the modern world as an assertion of artistic autonomy. To complicate matters it revealed 'a markedly classic spirit', and classicism was 'completely free and pure'; it recorded 'a positive and disinterestedly passionate state of mind'.[6] There were cross-references for this new classicism in literature, in Hulme, Eliot, Joyce, as well as Virginia Woolf, but again the claims and tendencies they pursued (for non-representationalism, impersonality of form and design, analogies across the arts or between art and science) were not in their own terms 'modernist'. The classicist temper of this modernism was directly opposed, moreover, to the tradition of 'modernist' liberal or radical political thought. Eliot, for example, recommended T.E. Hulme as 'classical, reactionary and revolutionary . . . the antipodes of the eclectic, tolerant and democratic mind of the last century'.[7] The spectrum of reactionary ideas occupied by Pound, Lewis, Eliot, Yeats and Lawrence is well known and a long-time embarrassment to modernism's liberal defenders. What these 'modernists' came to prescribe was a 'modern' art which would administer to and correct 'the modern world', not collaborate with it. This is the suggestion in Eliot's famous remark on Joyce's 'mythical method', a nodal point in discussions of literary modernism: 'It is simply a way of controlling, of ordering, of giving a shape and a significance to the immense panorama of futility and anarchy which is contemporary history . . . It is, I seriously believe, a step toward making the modern world possible for art.'[8] Following Spender, Faulkner writes of how modernist art reflected a rapidly changing social world, but here Eliot, as we can see, saw modern art and the contemporary world as drastically at odds; related (a weak term but less weak than the erroneous 'reflects' or 'expresses') as order is to anarchy.

What this history also tells us is that the term 'modernist' was a construction after the event. Its first sustained but isolated usage in English appeared in Graves and Riding's *A Survey of Modernist Poetry* in 1927. Here modernism signified an impersonal attention to art as composition ('in the interests of the poem itself'), a use of language and level of obscurity well in advance of the expectations and sensibilities of plain readers.[9] 'Genuine modernism' – contrasted with the commercially manufactured newness, the 'merely modernized advertisements' of such 'dead movements' as Imagism and Georgianism (p. 116) – could appear equally at any age, the vehicle of creative invention and insight not topicality. Evidently again, this had little to do with the new or modern age other than in a neo-Arnoldian sense that it might unsettle and uplift it. Here was a 'modernist' poetry not so much *of* the modern age as *for* that age and all time, an emphatically creative endeavour given to *making* it new rather than making it *new*.

Eliot was fairly clearly an influence on Graves and Riding's avantgardist formulations, though they saw him too as an example of modernism's inevitable fate. 'Already its most "correct" writers such as T.S. Eliot' they say, 'have become classics over the heads of the plain reader' (p. 264). Eliot comes to represent modernism's telescoped high point and end, its self-creation and auto-destruction; prematurely institutionalised and out of reach. In fact, however, these were the very terms of this modernism's selective absorption and continued life as an 'un-popular' élite tradition, a process to which Eliot's rapid elevation was quite crucial. In the twenties and thirties, I.A. Richards, F.R. Leavis, and then through the forties the American New Critics, Ransom, Tate and Brooks installed an Eliotic aesthetic of self-reflexive dislocation, allusion and impersonality at the centre of established literary taste. For Delmore Schwartz in 1945, Eliot was an international 'culture hero', whose poetry 'has a direct relationship to modern life . . . concerned with the whole world and all history'.[10] This, when arguably, Joyce's indispensable 'mythic method' had led Eliot even further away from contemporary history, towards notions of the eternal in art and religion. What Schwartz's 'direct relationship' and historical relevance entailed then, was, characteristically, a reaction *against* modernity; poetic testimony of its crises and tribulations and of their transcendence.

Eliot's mature project of cultural and religious redemption further suited the anti-industrialism and conservative Christianity of the Southern New Critics, if it did not suit all his English admirers. The effect, as F.R. Leavis, one early champion since persuaded to transfer his allegiance to D.H. Lawrence, commented in 1950, was to make Eliot 'a public institution, a part of the establishment'.[11] Thus the particular post-symbolist trajectory Eliot had discovered for himself came to represent 'modernist', and simultaneously 'modern' poetry, pulling a carriage of critical and pedagogic protocols after it.

Leslie Fiedler was amongst the first to decide that this 'Age of Eliot' had closed with the end of the Second World War.[12] It was in the post-war years after all that the Beat writers met and began writing (if they were not published until the early and mid-fifties) and in this period too that Charles Olson was rector at Black Mountain College, after the years of its direction under the modernist eye of Josef Albers. Olson began to refer to the postmodern age ('post the modern' as he put it) in essays from the early fifties, when students and staff comprised a roll-call of the first post-war American avant-garde (John Cage, Merce Cunningham,

7

Robert Rauschenberg, Robert Creeley, Ed Dorn). Olson's essay, 'Projective verse', was published in 1950 and pioneered a new aesthetic tradition in *American* poetry, set now along the axis of Ezra Pound – William Carlos Williams – Louis Zukofsky, rather than of Eliot – Pound – Allen Tate. In American writing, therefore, 'postmodernism' was first of all a nativist redefinition and re-routing of modernism, one which, as David Antin argues, explored afresh issues and possibilities opened by (some of) the early modernists.[13] Thus poets shifted, he says, from questions of personal expression to matters of construction and composition, reinventing the techniques of collage central to European modernism; returning at the same time, as Olson says, to the example of Pound's incorporation of 'non-poetic' narrative materials in the making of the long poem. All the same, an enduring modernist orthodoxy meant that much of this went unnoticed. In 1958, Delmore Schwartz, once again for example, spoke still of the poetic revolution inspired by the criticism of Eliot as having such authority 'that it is taken for granted not only in poetry and the criticism of poetry, but in the teaching of literature'.[14]

In England meanwhile, in 1952, Donald Davie had published *Purity of Diction in English Verse*, a text he thought of as a common manifesto for the English Movement poets. In this role, leading the post-war English reaction to modernism (a modernism including Yeats and Auden) Davie sought in the late Augustans a model of 'authentic' prose syntax to set against the post-symbolist syntax-as-music of Eliot and company. The Movement poets may not have all recognised this programme as their own, however, and it is of course Philip Larkin who is thought of as the more representative figure, the unofficial laureate indeed of the unpassionate grey tones of a tawdry welfare-state England. To remember that Larkin and Olson, Amis and Kerouac, were contemporaries should put paid to any sense that there was a common Anglo-American response to 'traditionalist modernism' or any single road taken from it. The English reaction entailed a construction of modernism as much as the American did, but in this case it was more commonly, or more 'representatively' a simplification and rejection than either a defence or re-exploration. For Davie, who was certainly aware of 'projective verse', 'modern' had simply 'taken over the functions of the now outmoded adjective "modernist"',[15] whereas for Larkin 'modernist' or 'modern' (he answers a question on the first as if it is about the second) is 'a kind of technique word'. The 'modern' poets Eliot and Pound, he says shamelessly, were like American tourists around 1910 (again 1910) doing Europe, who thought you could 'order culture whole, that it is a separate item on the menu'.[16]

If literary modernism was therefore a particular Anglo-American construction, it was cut to different lengths and widths in these cultures, especially in the period of its simultaneous decline and definition in the post-war years. In England 'modernism' had little more than a walk-on part as a critical term, and could be written into the category 'modern', or dismissed by Larkin's kind of snobbish provincialism. The European alternatives to 'traditionalist modernism' explored in Futurism, Dada, Surrealism, and Cubism had little to no life in English culture, where even Vorticism and Imagism had been short-lived.

As this suggests, the differently inflected tendencies and tones of literary culture participated in the broader making and unmaking of post-war national identities. Where England returned to an insular realism, America awoke in the post-war period to find itself a world power, uncertain of its national and international role. It subsequently swayed, experimentally, through the traumas of the Cold War, listing towards consumerism, conformity, corporate bureaucracy and anti-communist paranoia on one side, to 'un-American' dissent and 'juvenile delinquency' on the other. In the sixties and seventies it lurched on through the contradictions of advanced capitalist societies, giving the lead to the civil rights, gay and feminist protest and liberation movements as well as to the right-wing backlash against these. Criticism (and a new generation of sociologists) recorded as it enacted this epochal loss of consensus, and did so, as English literary and social criticism did not, via deliberations upon modernism. As late as 1976 Alfred Kazin, for example, looked to modernism as 'our only real tradition', conscious that this culture stemmed from a technical, conservative, and 'upper-class revolution', which was now neither popularly believed in nor accessible. He saw its contemporary political realisation in the ordered 'modernist' revolutions of Lenin and Mao's 'totalitarian socialism' at a time elsewhere of technological domination, disruption, and uncontainable mass societies. Neither was desirable and yet the modernist alternative, however ingrained, went unheeded. America was adrift and at risk.[17]

This perplexed and anxious liberal nostalgia had appeared earlier, notably in Harry Levin's much-cited and already retrospective essay 'What Was Modernism?' in 1960. The terms of Levin's own and other arguments anticipated much that was to come and to be thought new later, and while space prevents the inclusion of American critical debate from this period in the contents which follow, these commentaries are worth some attention here. Levin sees 'the modernistic movement', comprising 'one of the most remarkable constellations of genius in the history of the West', receding before a tide of unreason he associates with the postmodern. The invention, 'sweep and richness' of modernism had been both enchained in the academy and compromised in a society of technical reproduction and material consumption. For Levin 'the moderns' emitted a 'glow of ethical insight'; they 'created a conscience for a scientific age'. And as moderns themselves, 'the children of Humanism and Enlightenment', literary critics remained the guardians of that conscience.[18] There is a quite extraordinary contrivance to this ordinary-seeming description. For here an idea of modernism – a European-based movement in the terms in which it is valued, historically opposed in its 'classicist' vein to the progressive Enlightenment tradition and to its own 'modern age' – is mobilised as a stable artistic and intellectual 'modern' tradition to counter a later 'postmodern' phase of American social and cultural development.

These contortions could produce the near-comedy of Ellmann and Feidelson's 'untraditional tradition' of modernists who, however original, were 'classicists, custodians of language, communicators, traditionalists in their fashion',[19] but also the agonies of Irving Howe's commitment to an uncompromising modernism isolated in an uncongenial postmodern world. Howe's 'The Idea of the Modern', which introduced the volume *Literary Modernism* (1967), is itself an uneven, mimetically beleaguered modernist discourse of fragments, in which Howe yokes together nine 'modernist' features (via attributions to the 'modern', the 'modernistic', the 'symbolist', the 'avant-garde'), and closes in notes, as if overcome by the double impossibility of his own position and the task of definition.[20] Howe's difficulty is that he declares himself on the side of social conscience and humanity (later, in 'The New York Intellectuals' he calls for a renewal of 'the values of liberalism, for the politics of a democratic radicalism')[21] when 'commitment' had proved perilous for the artistic integrity of his modernist avant-garde. Rather than a 'tradition', Howe sees a concerted problematising and unchecked dynamism in modernism, and rather than social conscience he sees a disdain for 'the mass, the mire, the street' (p. 15). Modernism exits from history into the self-sufficiency of art, into hermetic silence and nihilism, to be deprived in the present age of even this retreat by the ever-assimilating appetites of an ever-accommodating public. Only Joyce and perhaps Beckett exhibit the necessary heroism of a pure 'literary monasticism' (p. 26), and only Joyce penetrates the depths of the city to emerge in the streets of 'on-going commonplace life' (p. 31). Howe discovers an effective, uncompromised modernism of one; the rest is doomed to live on as 'vulgar re-incarnation and parodic mimesis' (p. 40). The politics of Howe's modernists, whether of the Right or Left, spoiled their art, or so he implies. He therefore responds in a common aestheticising move to repress the ideological entailments of art. For only thus, as a narrowly understood revolution in art (his title 'literary modernism' comes to carry a special cutting edge) could this modernism be esteemed.

Ranged against this combined *angst* and nostalgia, critics and cultural commentators such as William Hamilton, Susan Sontag, Leslie Fiedler, Norman O. Brown, Herbert Marcuse and Marshall McLuhan argued in different ways for a positive acceptance of the energies of mass culture, for an aesthetics of kitsch, happenings, and random composition, for popular American literature to replace the cloistral modernist canon and for the tribal hedonism of the new 'underground'. Leading essays followed through the sixties in rapid succession; Sontag's 'Notes on Camp' (1964), *Against Interpretation* (1967) and *Styles of Radical Will* (1969), Fiedler's 'New Mutants' (1965) and 'Cross the Border, Close the Gap' (1969). For Sontag the period introduced a new pan-cultural sensibility, alive equally to the beauty of a machine or a mathematical solution, to Jasper Johns, Jean-Luc Godard and the Beatles.[22] Hers was a sophisticated cosmopolitanism. Fiedler meanwhile lit out for a gutsy primitivism sheltered by a benign technology and science indebted to McLuhan and Buckminster Fuller. His new age populated by 'imaginary Americans' was to be 'post-humanist, post-male, post-white, post-heroic . . . post-Jewish'.[23] Either way human character seemed changed once more.

If Sontag's was the probe and Fiedler's the scout ship, then Ihab Hassan's was the Star Fleet Postmodernism. In a series of studies through the seventies and eighties Hassan installed postmodernism as a new *episteme* and way of criticism. Amoeba-like, his postmodernism came to absorb Blake and de Sade, late Pound and late Joyce, Dada, Surrealism, the French new novel, Genet, the Beats, popular literature and the New Journalism, as well as a team of proto- and poststructuralist thinkers. Intermittently Hassan has also adopted a method of postmodernist collage (of 'montage and frame', 'perspective and counterpoint', 'scene, text and epitext') crossing borders and closing gaps in a tradition from Wilde to Derrida which makes good the claim in Fiedler's words that 'criticism is literature, or it is nothing'.[24] On a number of occasions Hassan has presented a table of features contrasting modernism and postmodernism. In the article 'The culture of Postmodernism' in 1985, this ran as follows:[25]

Modernism	Postmodernism
Romanticism/Symbolism	Pataphysics/Dadaism
Form (conjunctive, closed)	Antiform (disjunctive, open)
Purpose	Play
Design	Chance
Hierarchy	Anarchy
Mastery/Logos	Exhaustion/Silence
Art Object/Finished Work	Process/Performance/Happening
Distance	Participation
Creation/Totalization/Synthesis	Decreation/Deconstruction/Antithesis
Presence	Absence
Centering	Dispersal
Genre/Boundary	Text/Intertext

11

Semantics	Rhetoric
Paradigm	Syntagm
Hypotaxis	Parataxis
Metaphor	Metonymy
Selection	Combination
Root/Depth	Rhizome/Surface
Interpretation/Reading	Against Interpretation/Misreading
Signified	Signifier
Lisible (Readerly)	*Scriptible* (Writerly)
Narrative/*Grande Histoire*	Anti-narrative/*Petite Histoire*
Master Code	Idiolect
Symptom	Desire
Type	Mutant
Genital/Phallic	Polymorphous/Androgynous
Paranoia	Schizophrenia
Origin/Cause	Difference – Différance/Trace
God the Father	The Holy Ghost
Metaphysics	Irony
Determinacy	Indeterminacy
Transcendence	Immanence

This scheme has been criticised, notably by Christine Brooke-Rose and Susan Rubin Suleiman for its categorial and local inconsistencies (for example the opposition of metaphor and metonymy is not consistent with the opposition of narrative and anti-narrative, nor the same kind of opposition as signifier/signified or *lisible/scriptible*).[26] Hassan remains committed all the same to the view of modernism as 'centred' and of postmodernism as characterised by what he terms 'indeterminacy' and 'immanence'. Both tendencies are comprised of sub-tendencies, evoked in the first, for example, by such terms as 'heterodoxy', 'pluralism', 'eclecticism', 'deformation', 'difference', and so on. These are said to denote a deep and widespread loss of logical and ontological certainty, while the second term 'immanence' Hassan describes as 'the capacity of the mind to generalise itself in the world . . . and so become more and more, im-mediately, its own environment'.[27] Thus a first tendency of unmaking is interfused with a second of symbolic making and remaking.

There are problems typical of postmodernist commentary here. Most obviously, Hassan's scheme is founded on an (if anything structuralist) binary analysis which a poststructuralist postmodernism should have made obsolete. Also, whether this set of contrasts means postmodernism disposes of or radicalises modernism is uncertain. At first sight the 'indeterminacy' of postmodernism sounds close cousin to the endless innovatory drive and problematising which Irving Howe identified as modernist. We might think Howe was talking about the same avant-garde Hassan corrals for postmodernism, but as Hassan points out, periodising these concepts entails 'reinventing' our ancestors,[28] and he and Howe invent (or construct) both the past and present differently. Howe is thrown between a pure and bastardised modernism (his postmodernism), between saintly isolation and degraded diffusion, while Hassan welcomes diffusion as postmodern pluralism. Politically both kinds of critic are in the end also curiously stranded. Whereas those who saw themselves and modernism as the ignored offspring of Enlightenment reason, the conscience of a society which cheapened their values, could only turn to the past or to art's silent integrity, Hassan opposed the Enlightenment heritage in the name of a brave new world free of 'the tyranny of wholes'. Deconstruction's challenge to the 'traditional full subject the *cogito* of Western philosophy' implies a 'corresponding ideological commitment to minorities in politics, sex and language', and this brings Hassan to an aspiration for cultural, and not only epistemological revolution, 'perhaps even to basic political change'.[29] Along these lines, however, postmodernism, the enemy of totalising vision, contradictorally promises a global oneness, the 'one human universe', transcending postmodern heterodoxy.[30] Hassan's cautious micro-politics is teamed with a vision that speeds towards the black hole of an empty humanism. Difference is asserted and then buried in an assumption of universal harmony; a gesture which no more than repeats the central, paradoxical supposition in postmodernism of radically decentred identities in a world of instant and unprecedented technical connection. The challenge facing a progressive postmodernism committed to the possibility and necessity of 'basic political change' is how to articulate this commitment with postmodern dislocation and difference; how to achieve common political aims compatible with diverse social groups and agencies. The mystical humanism which marks Hassan's thinking and which is indeed one postmodern legacy of the counter-cultural movements and utopianism of the sixties and seventies, simply overlooks the new theoretical and material complexities of this situation.

'Have a nice day, M. Derrida, M. Baudrillard'

Hassan's work raises the additional question of the relation of theories of postmodernism to poststructuralism. The latter is said to have arrived in the USA in 1966 at Johns Hopkins University, Baltimore, with the attendance of Lucien Goldmann, Todorov, Barthes, Lacan and Derrida at the conference 'The Languages of Criticism and the Sciences of Man', and in particular with the delivery of Derrida's paper 'Structure, Sign and Play in the Human Sciences'. Derrida's critique of the assumption of a centred system of language in Saussure's structuralism, and thus of a 'metaphysics of presence' (the idea that reality is given immediately to consciousness) and of a 'transcendental signified' (the assumption of a point of origin, first cause of underlying essence) in Western philosophy came thus to inaugurate American deconstruction. The simultaneous appearance of new theory and new movements in art and culture has, not unexpectedly, suggested that poststructuralism and postmodernism are partners in the same paradigm. Together they are seen as exercising a joint critique of ideas of order and unity in language, art and subjectivity, as upending old hierarchies and rattling political convictions. Both are said to share 'a profound sense of *ontological uncertainty*',[31] but to confirm this radical indeterminacy in an attitude of play and reconciliation, outdating the alienated modernist's struggle for wholeness and autonomy. The questing Beat adventurers who slipped between life and art to 'dig it' now, find, we might say, a theoretical home, forever on the road to meaning and the Other, in Derrida's 'différance' and Lacan's 'desire'.

The Beats, of course, were only one manifestation of a new post-war American avant-garde, which the more centrifugal postmodernisms, such as Hassan's, would pull into a common orbit with French theory. In other accounts the relation between poststructuralism and postmodernism is seen differently. Andreas Huyssen, for example, argues that poststructuralism has been 'primarily a discourse of and about modernism' that it can be seen 'to a significant degree, as a theory of modernism'.[32] This relation is evident to begin with in the reference to literary modernism (to Proust, Bataille, Mallarmé, Artaud, Genet, Joyce, Beckett) in poststructuralist writings, including the writings of leading French feminists such as Julia Kristeva and Hélène Cixous. Their common enemies, as Huyssen points out, have not been modernism, but realism and mass culture – as in Roland Barthes's distinctions between the *'lisible'* (readerly, realist text) and the *'scriptible'* (writerly, modernist text), and later between (lowly) *'plaisir'* and (high-class) *'jouissance'*. Alex Callinicos gives further support to this view. The French poststructuralists Deleuze, Derrida and Foucault, he points out, have been consciously indebted to Nietzsche, and Nietzsche himself advanced 'in many respects a philosophical articulation of the main themes of Modernism'.[33]

Callinicos also usefully distinguishes between two trends in poststructuralism. The first he names, after the American philosopher Richard Rorty, 'textualism' and associates especially with Derrida and his North American followers. This seeks to place literature at the centre of culture; or more precisely, to extend the concept of textuality in its critique of theories of representation so as to suggest that all writing and knowledge are figurative and rhetorical. The second strand Callinicos associates particularly with Michel Foucault. This is a 'worldly' poststructuralism which recognises a distinction between textuality or discourse and non-discursive institutional structures of power.

Both these variants are overwhelmingly indebted to Nietzsche and thus in their deep affiliations to modernism, have come, as Callinicos shows, to redeploy the self-reflexive critique of totality and the unified subject *already* present in the earlier movement. He explains this revival in post-war France as a product of the conjuncture, under de Gaulle, of rapid industrialisation and political conservatism with a critical Left intelligentsia and a mass, if Stalinist, Communist Party. This produced in the cinema of Godard, for example, 'one of the few exceptions to (a) general decline of Modernism'[34] and in the internal development of French philosophy a passage from phenomenology and the assumed constitutive role of the individual human subject to its critique in the name of Marx, Nietzsche, Freud and Saussure. In post '68 philosophy the subject was seen instead as constituted by the relations of production, the unconscious, the will to power and language: a series of innovations further radicalised under the poststructuralism of Althusser, Lacan, Foucault and Derrida.

This is to abbreviate an already compressed account. Most importantly Callinicos introduces the kind of conjunctural analysis needed to plot the formations of art and ideas in France, or indeed any other culture. Even so, there are complications to this. To begin with, Callinicos assumes that the artistic *dramatis personae* appearing in poststructuralist writings are all 'modernist' (he names Magritte, Roussel, Lautreamont, Mallarmé, Bataille, Blanchot, Artaud and Godard). This takes no account of the widely accepted distinction between modernism and the avant-garde made by Peter Bürger (see pp. 58–71), or of the disparate projects and different earlier conjunctural placing in France of Symbolism, Dada, Surrealism, or of 'the New Wave', or 'New Novel'. To describe any of these movements at all as 'modernist' is in fact questionable, when, as Susan Rubin Suleiman has commented, 'In France . . . they don't speak much about Modernism in the arts. About modernity or the modern, or the avant-garde, yes; but Modernism, no.'[35] No more, apart from such obvious exceptions as Lyotard, do the French speak of postmodernism or postmodernity (see Cornel West below, p. 214). The more common term and understanding, as Alice Jardine confirms is again of 'modernity'.[36] In French culture and criticism the persistent questions concern the rift between classical realism and the non- or anti-realisms of the period of modernity. Hence Barthes's distinctions noted earlier; hence the general invocation of the avant-garde in critiques of realism; and hence too, one might think, the coinage 'hyper-reality' to describe the postmodern detachment of image from reference.

At the same time, if we are attending to the different vocabularies of particular intellectual and cultural histories, we need to note how modernism has again been differently defined in the further major tradition of Western Marxism (see pp. 37–58). In the German language branch of this tradition, for example, modernism has been diagnosed (following Lukács) as a symptom of alienation under capitalism, or is thought to have retained its adversarial function; whether in an all but hopeless combat, most famously with the mass 'culture industry' (in Adorno and Horkheimer), or in the examples of Benjamin and Brecht as the presage of socialist relations of production and a popular, experimental socialist realism.

The details of even such a cursory sketch warn against generalities. In this comparative perspective, the question of any break or opposition between 'modernism' and 'postmodernism' comes to look like a somewhat parochial topic in Anglo-American culture. For it was here, in this dominant and dominating cultural arena that a 'modernist' tradition stubbornly established itself, in architecture and painting, as well as literary criticism and education. But even then, this process and the initial challenge to it were differently accented, as I have tried to indicate. And it was, to repeat, on the American side of this special relationship, that 'postmodernism' made its first appearance as an index of alternatives to the canon.

Callinicos does not pursue a further distinction he indicates between North American and French variants of 'textualist' poststructuralism, though as Huyssen notes, the 'interweaving and intersecting of poststructuralism with postmodernism (is) a phenomenon that is much more relevant in the US than in France'.[37] Even so, the most publicised form of North American poststructuralist or deconstructionist criticism pays little or no attention to either 'modernist' or 'postmodernist' writing. Those most manifestly influenced by Derrida since the mid-sixties – 'the Yale critics', Paul de Man, Geoffrey Hartman, Harold Bloom and J. Hillis Miller – came to poststructuralism with distinguished reputations as scholars and critics of Romantic and Victorian literature.

An attention to post-war art and culture does not make a postmodernist critic of course. Moreover, the distinguishing feature of deconstruction is not an object of study but a gesture of simultaneous inscription and erasure, the mark of presence and its disruption, the deferral rather than the affirmation or denial of meaning. As Derrida writes 'the passage beyond philosophy does not consist in turning the page of philosophy . . . but in continuing to read philosophers *in a certain way*'.[38] It is this attitude and approach which makes French poststructuralism, at least, a critique, a re-enactment in theory and a never-to-be-realised postponement, rather than a cancellation of (largely French) modernism. And it is this too which allows American deconstructionists to continue to read pre-modernist literature in a certain new way, so as in de Man's work, for example, to demonstrate the self-deconstructive inner workings of that literature. All literature is thereby rendered essentially modernist. Or, one might as well say, essentially Romantic. Yet while such readings apparently lever American deconstruction away from the New Critical paradigm, its inherent formalism, as many have observed, has meant that deconstructive criticism in fact extends and deepens rather than departs from this method. To adopt the terminology of Harold Bloom, the swerve from the authority of the canonic father in acts of misreading and 'misprision' extends rather than shakes the family foundations. American deconstruction therefore enlists the decentring, destabilising effects of the French example, but does this in a way that enlarges the domain of textuality, encountering philosophy and history not as the Other but as the same; translating them, as it translates criticism, into the common tongue of literature. The gesture that enlarges also delimits, however, for the tradition of Romantic and modernist self-reflexivity is shorn of its moments of revolutionary brio and redemptive ideas of beauty and culture. Huyssen concludes that the 'aestheticist trend within poststructuralism itself has facilitated the peculiar American reception'.[39] In so far as poststructuralism, the repeat of a European strand of 'modernism' in theory, is a product of the postmodern moment, then Franco-American postmodernism can be said to follow this same aestheticist trend.

This implication is fully developed in the postmodernism of Jean Baudrillard (see pp. 151–62). Baudrillard's argument is that the nexus of consumption has overtaken the emphasis on production in classical Marxism, that communication technologies have erased all references to the 'real' in any sense of its being anterior to or underlying the image. The signifier swamps the Saussurean signified, difference is everywhere and is all the same: style is all. It might be thought that Marshall McLuhan and the anti-criticism of Fiedler and Sontag had prefigured this trend. 'Camp', for example, most obviously, was as Sontag described it, 'wholly aesthetic'; it was 'Dandyism in the age of mass culture',[40] less disdainful than its nineteenth-century original, but exclusive none the less. This taste for 'bad art', for extravagant stylisation, for the over-ambitious and naive failure, is surely resumed in commentaries on American hyper-reality, the consummate expression of Baudrillard's postmodernism.

One could discover the beginnings, and an instructive contrast with this postmodernism, even earlier, however, in Scott Fitzgerald's *The Great Gatsby*. There is a way too of seeing Jay Gatsby, the gauche overreacher, as 'camp', though it was not Fitzgerald's perspective. For Fitzgerald and his narrator Nick Carraway, the tricks and gestures which compose the self-created individual Gatsby remain meretricious fabrications, however 'gorgeous' or preferable they seem to a cancelled real past. Now in the age of the 'authentic fake' – the goal of Umberto Eco's season in hyper-real America – Gatsby's shirts, purchased at a distance from London, Gatsby's uncut books in a library modelled after Merton College Library, Oxford, Gatsby's house, a 'factual imitation of some *hotel de ville* in Normandy' become the order of the day. It is as if all the tension between art and money, fame and fashion which drove a stylist like Fitzgerald, all the struggle in the modernist narrative of self-formation, had slackened. If one is to believe Baudrillard, the American dream of material advancement and romantic self-fulfilment, of 'starting over', of a public façade built from the best of everything, from everywhere, out of nothing, has been achieved here and now in the sublime banality of a media-directed culture. Its exemplary form is Disneyland, where regular Americans can repeat the past (Gatsby was right) in sanitised ease. Gatsby triumphs over his narrator we might say; but only to be trumped in the postmodern era by the sophisticated, careless survivor Daisy, who drifts beyond his naive quest for a fully unified self. For now, in postmodernism, there can be no unified self, no narrative perspective, and no history. To misread Eliot in a distortion true to this scenario, 'History is now, and in America', at the end of the world.

It would be foolish to suggest that all post-war American literature has joined this trend when in fact it has reworked the problematics of style and society, of autonomy and transformation in art and subjectivity in different and complex ways. We can nevertheless identify two postmodern variants corresponding to the ambiguities of poststructuralism and a Baudrillardian postmodernism. In Black Mountain and Beat poetics, for example, the orthodox unities of self and poem were countered both by a new centring at greater depth, a Romantic reassertion (in Robert Duncan, John Weiners, Allen Ginsberg) of personal style after decades of New Critical 'impersonality', but also, within the tenets of open field poetry (in Olson and Ed Dorn) by a newly mobilised, 'deconstructed' sense of self as defined by the coordinates of language, place, and history. Work in this second vein is 'post' modernist in the sense of being new, or late modernist. In what is then partly a continuation and partly a reaction to this tradition the more recent 'L=A=N=G=U=A=G=E poets' have underscored the arbitrary relation of word and world to produce an aesthetic of the 'new sentence' free of customary reference.[41] For all its appended Marxist class analysis, indeed because of the separated existence of this, L=A=N=G=U=A=G=E poetry comes, in its more extreme forms, to echo Baudrillard's theorisations of the growing autonomy of the signifier.

Tendencies in post-war North American fiction have confirmed this double trajectory. In an early, influential statement, John Barth spoke in 'The literature of exhaustion' (1967) of the 'used-upness' of the conventions of fictional realism. The old forms he said could only be employed ironically, in burlesque or pastiche, an argument openly demonstrated in his own story 'Lost in the Funhouse'. So far this echoes a Janus-faced poststructuralism in which old forms and assumptions are held 'under erasure', simultaneously written in and written through. For many it also describes the dominant tone of parody and pastiche charactersistic of postmodernism, penned between textualism and reference, licensed play and subversion. There may be some reason, again, however, for describing this literary mode (and poststructuralism) as 'late modernist', given their ties with modernism (John Barth's explicit model is Borges), their arguments with realism, and given other developments taking American fiction, like some of the L=A=N=G=U=A=G=E poets, beyond the thrall of mimesis. Jerome Klinkowitz, for example, in one of the earliest studies of this tendency, wrote of the 'post-contemporary' as a newly invigorated fiction 'beyond the death of the death of the novel'. He saw a decisive break, coinciding with the social and cultural disruptions of 1967–68, from the 'exhausted fiction' of Barth and Pynchon into the 'imaginatively transformed' fiction of Robert Coover, Richard Brautigan, Steve Katz and, more decisively, Vonnegut, Barthelme, Kosinski and others. This is the fiction of 'a pluralistic, relativistic, post-modern world, where "Sometimes it's so hard to tell what has really happened."'[42] So this fiction tells 'untellable' stories, stories combining what 'really' happened and all that might possibly happen' (as in Coover's 'The Babysitter'), suggesting (as in Brautigan's *Trout Fishing in America*) 'how language can exist purely as itself, with no reference at all to content'.[43] Raymond Federman, who is one of Klinkowitz's examples, anticipates along similar lines that

> . . . fiction will no longer be regarded as a mirror of life, as a pseudo-realistic document that informs us about life, nor will it be judged on the basis of its social, moral, psychological, metaphysical, commercial value or whatever, but on the basis of what it is and what it does as an autonomous art form in its own right.[44]

A credo of this kind seems once more to follow the logic of a Baudrillardian postmodernism beyond reference, old-fashioned morality and politics.

At the same time there is nothing really new, or inevitable, about this. Protestations of artistic autonomy have been deployed from the turn of the century to offset bourgeois utilitarianism and the exchange values of the market place. Whereas under modernism, however, a retreat, at its extremes, into the sublime indifference of art coexisted with a contrasting avant-garde defiance of the present in the interests of a transformed future, a Baudrillardian postmodernism knows no such contrast. In a world where Surrealist techniques sell cigarettes and consumer durables, where art is fashion, the original political project of the historical avant-garde appears to have lost all credibility. The first option alone remains apparently, a retreat into aestheticism which recycles the last century's decadence, and which can only deny this charge on the grounds that it (or the postmodern world) has done away with old distinctions like 'art and life' (or signifier and signified). As we have seen, however, not all poststructuralism or postmodernism need take the Baudrillardian high road. A second (deconstructive, late modernist) option might still explore the very tensions of text and world in which it is held, opening and reconstructing the past rather than flattening it. If we ask about the politics of this project we are led, in particular, to the debates on postmodernism and Marxism.

Insider Postmodernism: Jameson and Tomorrowland

Baudrillard's reflections, tending more and more to a mandarin avant-gardism of now bold, now vaporous *aperçus*, have comprised a major proposition of what postmodernism means. That this finds its home in the 'achieved utopia' of North America, the cultureless landscape where everything dreamed in Europe 'has a chance of being realised'[45] is not after all surprising. The jaded foreign professor is at once enthralled and appalled by the American Lolita. The appearance of this Franco-American postmodernism (trailing a 'misreading' of poststructuralism) suggests a further adjustment to any conjunctural analysis. For if the features of postmodernism (as of modernism) are historically and culturally specific, they are not culturally hermetic. Indeed one of the most convincing descriptions of postmodernism is of a shift, prompted and enabled by social, economic and technological change, into the heteroglossia of inter-cultural exchange, as idioms, discourse across the arts and academy, and across these and popular or mass forms, are montaged, blended or blurred together. 'Postmodernism' becomes its own best symptom of dissemination and difference.

In what can sound like a confusing Babel of the new, these many voices are joined dialogically, in consensus and disagreement. One such debate, across intellectual cultures, between the 'Western Marxism' of the Frankfurt School, represented by Jürgen Habermas, and French poststructuralist postmodernism, emerged as poststructuralism's debt to Nietzsche (first signalled by Deleuze's *Nietzsche and Philosophy* in 1962) became clearer. Poststructuralism came then to present a challenge not only to the structuralist language paradigm and to a range of loaded hierarchies dependent on a 'metaphysics of presence' (of speech over writing, the author over [his] text, of the phallus over the feminine, of nature over culture, essence over appearance, God over all) but a political challenge to the claims of Reason and enlightened progress. This shift from questions of epistemology (ways of knowing) to questions of ontology (ways of being and acting in the world) becomes then an expression of what some see as fundamental in the very transition to postmodernism. This double articulation and critique was apparent notably in Lyotard's *The Postmodern Condition* (1979).

In this second major thesis of what postmodernism means (see pp. 139–50), Lyotard borrows the concept of the 'language game' from Wittgenstein to argue in poststructuralist and Nietzschean fashion against any unifying language system or underlying truth. He sees scientific knowledge as a model of innovatory language games, a strategy he terms 'paralogism'. Moreover, he extends his critique to propose (in a contradictorily global account) that the characteristically unstable and dispersed social reality of the present cannot be captured in a totalising 'grand narrative' which plots an historical teleology towards equality and justice. His target here is principally Marxism and the Enlightenment heritage – supposedly darkened by the poisoned fruits of Stalinism, the Gulag and Auschwitz credited to it – and in particular Habermas's attempt to reformulate historical materialism as a theory of social progress in his criticism of poststructuralism. Habermas had described the poststructuralists Derrida and Foucault as 'young conservatives' who in enlisting the liberating avantgardist stress on experiment, intensity and desire against the straitjacket of administrative reason, had contradictorally employed 'modernistic attitudes (to) justify an irreconcilable antimodernism' (see p. 137). For Habermas, the project of the Enlightenment is not liquidated but renewable. Human and civil rights, and democratic self-determination remain realisable goals, the struggle for them governed by the conventions of communicative reason and consensus.

Fredric Jameson, in a salutary reminder of historical and political particulars, has pointed out how Habermas's commitment is framed in the historical shadow of fascism.[46] It would be a mistake, however, to see this as restricted to a German national history and character. The stakes in this debate are high, and of vital interest to Marxists, feminists and others in the First, Second and Third Worlds who are committed to a narrative of political and cultural change and betterment, especially now this is said to be redundant. (But see West below, pp. 214–17.)

Jameson's essays and statements on postmodernism have in fact done much to keep this general narrative alive (see pp. 163–79). He describes postmodernism as a 'cultural dominant'; the combined result of a reaction to institutionalised modernism and of a decisive shift from monopoly to multinational capitalism. This faceless expansion of the global market and the accompanying development of electronic media has penetrated all levels of existence, says Jameson, producing a massively coded world of relentless commodification and dramatically altered social and psychic conditions. In this 'depthless' society of the image (an analysis frankly indebted to Baudrillard), old distinctions and orientations are abolished: objects no longer relate at all to their processes of human production, there is a loss of emotional content and of 'objective' or critical distance. The past is recoverable now only as pastiche, in the randomised play by which texts and knowledges are cannibalised and reshuffled to produce *'le style retro'*, evident in fashion, music and the Hollywood nostalgia film. The individual, formerly alienated under monopoly capitalism, now becomes 'schizophrenic', all sense even of a lost authenticity gone. Jameson describes as endemic therefore a condition in which the individual as this newly riven and schizoid personality is cast adrift in the perpetual present of a superficial, centreless world, replete with ever new, recycled images or representations. Deprived thus of historical consciousness the individual cannot hope to gain the interpretative grasp which will yield an explanation of the social and cultural totality.

Jameson's writings are a major focus in the debate on postmodernism and the object of close and sometimes ungenerous scrutiny. His special contribution lies in the connection he presents between culture and capital but his model has been criticised for its vague periodisation, its apparently reductionist view of culture as 'replicating' or simply 'expressing' the logic of capital, for a totalising approach he has argued is impossible, and for allowing no adequate distinction between dominant and oppositional modes or social agencies in present culture.[47] Jameson insists that postmodernism is a historical situation and not merely a cultural style and his defence of his arguments highlights the genuine problems this perspective presents. He defends his totalising approach, for example, as theoretically and politically necessary, while arguing that being *within* postmodernism is precisely what frustrates the drawing of a cognitive map of its totality from a position of critical distance. At the same time he clearly states that he intends his approch to be 'dialectical'; that since it is futile to moralise on a historical situation, we need to understand postmodernism as Marx understood capitalism, in its best and worst, its dominant and resistant aspects. This echoes the idea of 'double coding', of pastiche and parody, of the specialist and popular which others (Charles Jencks, Jim Collins, Linda Hutcheon) also see in postmodernism. The problem for all such analyses, however, lies in distinguishing the critical or subversive from the complicitous, when both are produced by the system it is desired to transform. Hence the questions which have occupied so much radical criticism in the eighties: is Borges, are Calvino, Madonna, 'Eastenders' transgressive? For when there is no 'outside' critical position or social agency this can be more than a 'textual' matter.

Nor do Jameson's own few examples of the subordinate and resistant help here. One literary example he gives is of E.L. Doctorow. Doctorow's fiction adopts the schizoid narrative modes of postmodernism to undo or skirt the system, and especially to investigate the problem of the loss of history this induces. This is akin to Jameson's own insider postmodernism, presenting as he styles it, a 'homeopathic' solution to postmodern ills.[48] He discusses Doctorow's *Ragtime*, especially, in these terms and no more than mentions his other work. Yet *The Book of Daniel*, which combines fact and fiction to examine the trial and execution of the Rosenbergs (the 'Atom Bomb Spies') and its after-effects on their fictionalised children, very directly presents the problem of political analysis and interpretation. Through the figure of the fictional son, Daniel – so named because of the Biblical Daniel who is the interpreter of dreams, visions, apparitions – Doctorow can set the deterministic analysis of the Old Left represented by Julius Isaacson/ Rosenberg (lecturing his son on the lies of capitalism encoded in a cereal ad. or comic book or radio broadcast) against the subversive counter-cultural (early postmodernist) analysis of the New Left. This is represented by Artie Sternlicht, who would use TV to subvert the status quo and would have turned the Rosenberg trial upon the accusers in a piece of political theatre. The message of Artie's wall of collaged cultural images is 'Everything that came before is all the same.' Daniel's own later analysis, however, significantly of the hyperspace of Disneyland, is one which exposes the selective, commercialised cultural memory of middle America, as well as its active principles of exclusion (no unsavoury hippies, few poor blacks or Mexicans in Disneyland). Daniel's 'reading' is a model of a new postmodern ideology-critique, of a kind Jameson appears to say, and others certainly do say, is impossible. Daniel's demythologising interpretation of the American Dream depends, of course, on an assumed distinction between ideological surface and truthful depth (signifier and signified, text and world) we are told has deserted us. But yet Jameson, for one, speaks of the 'deeper level' of the economy and theorises the existence of a 'political unconscious', in a discourse that is full of (for this reader, brilliant) interpretative insight.

A further problem concerns the question of periodisation. As Mike Davis and Callinicos have pointed out, Jameson sees postmodernism as occurring 'in the late fifties and early sixties', whereas Ernest Mandel, whose theory of the development of capital he draws upon, associates late, multinational capitalism with the longer post-war period, and sees a decisive break in 1974–75.[49] Callinicos sees this phase as bringing an intensification in capitalism (as does Jameson) but not a radical break into postmodernism (or the mode of production styled 'post-Fordism'). Along with other commentators (see Harvey, pp. 183–5, and Davis, Sprinker and Pfeil (eds), *The Year Left*, 1985) he views postmodernism as the culture of a new compulsively consumerist middle class (the 'Yuppies' of the eighties), and an expression of the disillusionment of Left intellectuals after the defeats of 1968. This supplies a social anchorage lacking in Jameson, but is not entirely convincing. The social and cultural developments discussed earlier, for example, make postmodernism a broader affair than events of the eighties or the political tone of post-68 can explain, relevant though these are. Also it would be wrong to see Jameson and other 'late' or 'post-Marxists' as having abandoned class politics or Marxist critique in questioning classical Marxism. What is true I think is that Jameson does not at all consider who his postmodernism is a 'cultural dominant' for.

This is brought out in Davis's counter-analysis of the Bonaventure Hotel (see Jameson extract, p. 172–6 and Davis in Kaplan (ed.), 1985). Where Jameson sees a new all-absorbing public hyperspace, Davis shows how the urban renaissance of downtown Los Angeles (as elsewhere) is inspired by a wave of unprecedented financial speculation which has enforced new physical and class polarities. The more general point is that Jameson assumes that his experience and perceptions are emblematic, as in his thoughts on how the escalators and elevators in the hotel replace and self-reflexively designate movement, or the way feeling lost in the lobby encourages him to see disorientation as a general psychic condition of the sublimely unrepresentable postmodern hyperspace. What does it mean, quite simply, if 'we' do not recognise this experience as 'ours'? The problem is that Jameson as a white, male, American (post-) Marxist intellectual (this is not an accusation) presents a highly profiled, perhaps dominant, but primarily West Coast American experience as a cultural universal. Stuart Hall has described postmodernism as the way 'the world has dreamed itself "American"'.[50] To the degree that the world has anticipated or envied the bounty of modernisation, the liberty of the 'little Wests' as Fiedler predicted, even its decadent glamour, North America has indeed been a place, a destiny in the world's unconscious. But yet while the world has been dreaming America, America has in its turn dreamed the world in its own postmodern master image. The old-fashioned political truth to the decentred plentitude and eclecticism of postmodernism is that America holds the centre and most of the options, at the hub of First World Western domination. As an historical condition postmodernism is intimately connected to the blunt facts of economic, political and military power, and has confirmed America and the West's controlling cultural influence – including the magnetism of its mythologies and the control Western intellectuals exercise over communication systems and regimes of truth.

Back to a New Futurism

What is outside or beyond postmodernism? One thing seems clear: radical criticism need not, indeed, cannot return to classical Marxism as if postmodernism were a break for advertisements. The key effect of a politicised, 'worldly', deconstructive postmodernism has been to disarticulate dominant narratives, traditions and ideologies. In this way it has questioned the universalising assumptions of the male self, the super monoagency of the traditional working class, the power of the United States and the ethnocentrism of Western capitalist nations, intellectual debate and media. Postmodern technologies and theory have helped bring the marginal, the repressed and unvoiced into view and into hearing. Thus groups associated with the magazines *Social Text* (including Jameson), *October*, and in England, *Marxism Today*, have worked within and away from classical Marxism, looking to the Gramscian concepts of hegemony and the long-term 'war of position' rather than the all-or-nothing confrontation of the 'war of manoeuvre'. They have attempted to take account of new social movements, mobilising questions of race and gender as well as social class. New political and humanitarian movements, pressure groups, demonstrations, and rock events employing postmodern communication technologies have contributed to this orientation. Whether oppressed and marginalised groups are thereby empowered or lost in a centreless world, or worse, neutralised in the flattery of publicity and imitation, becomes a further theoretical and political question. Chantal Mouffe, arguing for a postmodernist critique of the essentialist assumptions of the Enlightenment project, sets out one strategy:

> Radical democracy demands that we acknowledge difference, the particular, the multiple, the heterogeneous – in effect everything that has been excluded by the concept of Man in the abstract. Universalism is not rejected but particularized: what is needed is a new kind of articulation between the universal and the particular.[51]

To put this from a different angle, in attending to single-issue campaigns and struggles, a critical postmodernism meets the micro-politics of a Foucauldian poststructuralism and joins, indeed learns from, the emphases of feminism. Feminist accounts of postmodernism have made the male domination of the 'tradition' (Habermas, Lyotard, Rorty, Baudrillard, Jameson) obvious. Radical male critics have had the gall, what is more – as Meaghan Morris was among the first to point out – to comment on the apparent failure of women to contribute to the debate.[52] Morris prefers to enlist the postmodernist strategy of 'rereading' and 'rewriting' texts to assist the political goals of feminism rather than contrive a feminist 'contribution' to postmodernism. For others, the association of feminism with French deconstruction has meant that feminism and postmodernism are 'natural allies'. Feminism's allegiance to the Enlightenment goals of equality and justice (if this is not itself rejected as a male tradition) leads still others to reject postmodernism.[53] Feminism therefore very acutely raises the question of the compatibility of these two movements, as well as the political relation between the decentred and local, and the unified and global. As above, one can hazard that effective political action depends on a flexible apprehension of the tension, friction and identity, in short the dialogic relation between these sites, rather than the absorption of one in the other.

In the last decade this cultural dialogics has come more evidently to include relations between the First, Second and Third Worlds, again locally, within national cultures, as well as internationally. The clash between Salman Rushdie's postmodernist satire *The Satanic Verses* and 'premodern' Muslim dogma (the Islamic revolution has also, astonishingly, been described as postmodernist) is a dramatic example of this, as are the world-wide challenge to apartheid, and the fissiparous developments in Eastern Europe and the Soviet Union. Human character seems on the point of changing yet again. Perhaps. For these very real events have forced the ambiguities of the terms 'postmodern' and 'postmodernist' to the surface as features of a general end-of-century uncertainty. I want to offer some final, modest clarification of these terms and some opinion on a future cultural politics.

To begin with, some distinction between 'postmodernism' and 'postmodernity' seems to me necessary. If we reserve the first (as I believe the Rushdie affair confirms we should) for a set of particularised artistic, philosophical and cultural modes, self-consciously but not exclusively adopted in the historical period of postmodernity, and see these as in one way or another defining the lived reality of its structures of thought and feeling, then it is clear (whatever is happening in detail in these first spheres) that the general social, economic and political orders intended by the second term are undergoing momentous, even revolutionary change. Discussion on the direction of this change resembles the arguments referred to earlier on 'postmodernism' ('postmodernity' if you will) as an historical period, as constituting either a radical social and economic break or an intensification of capitalism. On the one hand, as the 'modern(ist)' worlds of the Eastern bloc, and the social, industrial and political model associated with them are brought manifestly to an end, this is proclaimed as the 'end of history' and the unfettered triumph of Western capitalism and liberal democracy (though Francis Fukuyama, the chief author of this thesis, speaks of the shoddiness of consumer culture and of 'an emptiness at the core of liberalism').[54] On the other hand, these events urge the creation of a new pluralist order, a 'democratic radicalism' as above, or a newly grounded concept of rationality which will free the Enlightenment project of its theoretical and historical distortions.[55] For some this means the era of post-anything is over. But yet the projected scenarios for this new phase are tied still to questions of capitalist economic and cultural production, whether of their expansion or transformation, and ideologically to the options of liberal individualism or radical democracy, with Islamic and Communist fundamentalism and neo-facism as outriders. The political questions of postmodernity derive therefore from the project of modernity, brought to a new threshold but not surpassed.

Much the same is true I think of 'postmodernism' (though I do not want to suggest this synchronises with the course of political modernity/ postmodernity). My argument in earlier sections has been that the diverse groupings of 'modernism' were narrowed in Anglo-American criticism to a tradition of predominantly male, predominantly conservative, high modernists, that this 'traditionalist modernism' was valued for its formal innovation and expression of a 'modern' sensibility, and almost simultaneously defined and deployed against the encroachments of modernisation and mass (postmodern) society. In a second, and continuing, simplification this already selective tradition was rejected by critics sympathetic to postmodernism for its supposed vices of artistic autonomy, élitism and denial of the past.[56] It is only too clear, however, that the texts of high modernism employed myth and musical form, for example, in a struggle to incorporate and so order the material of 'chaos', to distance and transcend contemporary history certainly, but also to resuscitate and 'recycle' the past. It has to be said too that though this tradition was likely to reject mass culture it did esteem strands in popular or folk culture. Pound's *Cantos* are a massive example of these features. Like other key modernist texts it is a 'record of struggle', and in the end a self-consciously acknowledged 'failure' as both artistic and ideological unity. To see the *Cantos* as a disengaged, hermetically sealed art object, as some postmodernist critics choose to see the texts of modernism, is, perversely, to endorse the selective reading which canonised 'traditionalist modernism'.

It was the real lack of coherence and unity in modernist works which the new American avant-garde recognised and prised open. With the advent of American mass culture and the first phase of social modernity, postmodernism came to signal a positive revaluation of a reclaimed, diversified modernism. In one direction poetry, the novel and French-imported theory continued this renewal, extending the insights and practices of the historical avant-garde in a series of deconstructive (what I have been inclined to call new or late modernist) gestures. From the sixties and seventies this has meant the publication and critical re-reading of marginalised modernists (W.C. Williams, H.D. Mina Loy). Criticism, literature, and other, newer, art forms have employed mixed modes and media, accentuating while resituating modernist self-reflexiveness in a double-coding which attempted to make good a new cultural politics. In another direction postmodernism has moved towards a resigned, self-parodic or self-deluding aestheticism. While the second abandons mimesis, the first – no longer seriously an avant-garde since no one can be ahead for long – has to do battle in the postmodern arena with the metamorphic giant of the free market, bobbing, weaving, ventriloquising, subdividing, so as to get a grip on 'reality'.

This is the 'homeopathic' postmodernism described by Jameson. There are other tendencies in Anglo-American writing, however, and of course elsewhere, which do not conform to this type. As well as the bulk production of conventionally realist or genre forms in literature, film and television, Afro-American writing, for example, shows a strong attachment to autobiography, to culturally rooted fantasy, and to the historical record, lost or mythologised from cultural memory. Toni Morrison's *Beloved* is a recent striking example of such a fictional re-search. Doctorow, as mentioned, has also wished to restore parts of this memory.

We might think of this work as a 'new realism', having something in common with Latin American 'magic realism' and with East European and African political realism. Realism, however, is a notoriously difficult category. In English criticism Raymond Williams in a late essay 'When was modernism?' called for the restoration of the great nineteenth-century realists.[57] His thinking recalls Lukács's earlier dismissal of 'expressionist modernism', but in this new form voices an impatience with the collocation of structuralist Marxism, Lacanian psychoanalysis and the Brechtian critique of 'classic realism' which shaped the career of British poststructuralism. The 'Brechtian voodoo' is said to have blown itself out; gone the way of the outmoded 'isms' of Marxism, modernism and communism. My own view, as I have argued elsewhere, is that Left postmodernism needs to reclaim the tradition of which Brecht is a leading example rather than surrender or dismiss it.[58] Brecht's description of a popular, flexible and experimental realism was already pluralist and democratic, and remains open to revision, now as in earlier periods (see pp. 37–44).

More generally, the tradition which connects Brecht, Walter Benjamin, the artist and theatre groups of Weimar Germany, and the Revolutionary Soviet avant-garde ran in close counterpoint to Anglo-American traditionalist modernism. And Walter Benjamin, the interpreter of Baudelaire, of Brecht, Proust and Kafka, is a salutary alternative to his sometime contemporary T.S. Eliot. Whereas Eliot wished to absorb the fragmentary and contingent which Baudelaire had identified as the sign of modernity into the unities of a self-correcting tradition and the eternal,

Benjamin situated its shocks and breaks in a history structured by continuous struggle, a series of constellations of the ancient and contemporary. His concept of the *'Jetztzeit'* ('the time of the now'),[59] when a recovered past blasts out of the continuum of history to reshape the present, suggests an alternative to traditionalist modernism's 'make it new', as it does to an avant-garde negation of the past, or to the past's stylisation in a postmodern market-place which makes anything new for now.

If Brecht is thought to be tainted by the record of 'already existing socialism', and Benjamin's thoughts on the democratic potential of the new technologies are seen as at best naive, the 'machine aesthetic' of the revolutionary Soviet avant-garde can expect to lose badly on both counts. What is more, like Brecht, Soviet art is seen as the subject of a political fad, a piece of the mythology of the generation of 1968 who look back simplistically through Godard to Dziga Vertov and Eisenstein.[60] Yet the programme for a popular use of new technologies, for collaborative work and popular control in film, theatre, photography, industrial and domestic design and fashion of the Constructivist groups associated with *Lef* and *Novy Lef* remain, to my mind, an invaluable model. There is every reason in the age of mega-consumption to support the democratic control of newer artistic means of production, and a fuller historical record of Soviet and Weimar art needs to teach us how to seize these examples again for this purpose. We need too a record of the post-war fortunes of independent groups in publishing, theatre, film and video. Have they all been coopted? Is this an inevitable consequence of reaching beyond the local? Increasingly, questions of this kind, about the integrity and connectedness of local and community ventures or struggles have come to command the debates on postmodernism. They are all the more compelling for being questions about the future, as well as about the present and recent past.

Notes

1. FRANK KERMODE, 'Modernisms' in *Continuities* (London: Routledge & Kegan Paul, 1968), p. 27. Subsequent quotations from this essay are accompanied by page numbers in the text.

2. Quoted in Peter Faulkner (ed.), *A Modernist Reader, Modernism in England 1910–1930* (London: Batsford, 1986), p. 13.

3. See Malcolm Bradbury and James McFarlane (eds.), *Modernism* (Harmondsworth: Penguin, 1976), pp. 30–4 for discussion of the variable periodisation of modernism. The examples given here are of STEPHEN SPENDER *The Struggle of the Modern* (London: Hamish Hamilton, 1963); GRAHAM HOUGH,

Image and Experience: Studies in a Literary Revolution (London: Duckworth, 1960); HARRY LEVIN 'What was Modernism?' (1960) in *Refractions: Essays in Comparative Literature* (New York and London: Oxford University Press, 1966); and JULIAN SYMONS, *Makers of the New: the Revolution in Literature 1912–1939* (London: André Deutsch, 1987).

4. See ARNOLD TOYNBEE, *A Study of History*, Vol IX (London: Oxford University Press, 1954); CHARLES OLSON 'The Present is Prologue' (1955) in *Additional Prose* (Bolinas, California: Four Seasons Foundation, 1974), pp. 39–40; IRVING HOWE, 'Mass Society and Postmodern Fiction' (1959), in *The Decline of the New* (London: Victor Gollancz, 1971), pp. 190–297; FREDRIC JAMESON, 'Postmodernism and Consumer Society' in Hal Foster *Postmodern Culture* (London and Sydney, 1985), p. 113 and 'Postmodernism, or the Cultural Logic of Late Capitalism', *New Left Review*, **146** (1984), p. 53; CHARLES JENCKS, *The Language of Post-Modern Architecture* 4th edn. (London: Academy Editions, 1984), p. 9. The time and date given by Jencks were when the Pruitt – Igoe housing scheme in St Louis, Missouri, was dynamited. The use of the terms modernism and postmodernism can have a quite different application in the visual arts and in architecture than in literary debate. See STEVEN CONNOR *Postmodernist Culture* (New York and Oxford: Basil Blackwell, 1989) for an account of these different spheres.

5. VIRGINIA WOOLF, 'Mr Bennett and Mrs Brown' (1924) in *Collected Essays*, Vol. 1 (London: Hogarth Press, 1971), p. 320.

6. ROGER FRY, 'Preface' to 'Catalogue of the Second Post-Impressionist Exhibition' of 1912, *Vision and Design* (London: Chatto and Windus, 1921), pp. 241, 211–12.

7. T.S. ELIOT, *The Criterion* (April 1924), quoted in Julian Symons, op. cit. p. 66.

8. T.S. ELIOT, '*Ulysses*, Order and Myth' in *Selected Prose*, ed. F. Kermode (London: Faber and Faber, 1975), pp. 177–8.

9. ROBERT GRAVES AND LAURA RIDING, *A Survey of Modernist Poetry* (1927, reprinted Michigan: Scholarly Press, 1972), pp. 88, 84. Following quotations from this volume are accompanied by page numbers in the text.

10. DELMORE SCHWARTZ, 'T.S. Eliot as the Internatonal Hero' in *Literary Modernism*, ed. Irving Howe (Greenwich, Connecticut: Fawcett Publications Inc. 1967), pp. 277, 279.

11. F.R. LEAVIS, 'Retrospect 1950' in *New Bearings in English Poetry* (1950), Harmondsworth: Penguin, 1967), p. 177.

12. LESLIE FIEDLER, 'Cross the Border – Close the Gap (1969) in *The Collected Essays of Leslie Fiedler*, vol. 2 (New York: Stein and Day, 1971), pp. 461–85.

13. DAVID ANTIN, 'Modernism and Postmodernism: Approaching the Present in American Poetry', *Boundary,2*. 1 (Fall, 1972): 98–133.

14. DELMORE SCHWARTZ, 'The Present State of Poetry', quoted in Antin, ibid., p. 101.

15. DONALD DAVIE, *Articulate Energy* (London: Routledge & Kegan Paul, 1955), p. 147.

16. IAN HAMILTON, 'Interviews with Philip Larkin and Christopher Middleton' in

Twentieth-Century Poetry, ed. Graham Martin and P. N. Furbank (Milton Keynes: Open University Press, 1975), p. 243.

17. ALFRED KAZIN, 'On Modernism', *The New Republic* (17 January 1976): 29–31.

18. HARRY LEVIN 'What Was Modernism?' in *Refractions*, op. cit., pp. 284, 273, 294–5.

19. RICHARD ELLMANN and CHARLES FEIDELSON Jr (eds), Preface to *The Modern Tradition* (New York and Oxford: Oxford University Press, 1965), p. vii.

20. IRVING HOWE, 'The Idea of the Modern' in *Literary Modernism*, ed. Irving Howe, op. cit., pp. 11–40. Further references to this essay are accompanied by page numbers in the text. A more polished version appeared as 'The Culture of Modernism' reprinted in *Decline of the New* (London: Gollancz, 1971), pp. 3–33.

21. IRVING HOWE, 'New York Intellectuals' in ibid., p. 265.

22. SUSAN SONTAG, *Against Interpretation* (New York: Dell, 1967), p. 297.

23. LESLIE FIEDLER, 'The New Mutants' in *Collected Essays*, op. cit., p. 379.

24. LESLIE FIEDLER, 'Cross the border – Close the Gap' in ibid., p. 464.

25. IHAB HASSAN, 'The Culture of Postmodernism' in *Theory, Culture and Society*, **2**, 3 (1985): 123.

26. CHRISTINE BROOKE-ROSE, *A Rhetoric of the Unreal* (Cambridge: Cambridge University Press, 1981), pp. 346–9; and Susan Rubin Suleiman, 'Naming and Difference, Reflections on "Modernism *versus* Postmodernism" in Literature' in *Approaching Postmodernism*, ed. Douwe Fokkema and Hans Bertens (Amsterdam and Philadelphia: John Benjamins, 1986), especially pp. 259–62. Suleiman's criticisms are directed specifically at the schema as presented in Hassan's 'Postface' to *The Dismemberment of Orpheus: Toward a Postmodern Literature*, 2nd edn. (New York: Oxford University Press, 1982).

27. IHAB HASSAN, 'Ideas of Cultural Change' in *Innovation/Renovation. New Perspectives on the Humanities*, ed. Ihab Hassan and Sally Hassan (Madison: University of Wisconsin Press, 1983), p. 29.

28. IHAB HASSAN, 'The Culture of Postmodernism', op. cit., p. 122.

29. IHAB HASSAN, 'The Critic as Innovator' in *Amerikastudien*, **22**, 1 (Stuttgart: Metzlersche, 1977): 56, 61.

30. IHAB HASSAN, 'Ideas of Cultural Change' in Hassan and Hassan (eds), op. cit., p. 31.

31. RAMAN SELDEN, *A Reader's Guide to Contemporary Literary Theory*, 2nd edn (Brighton: Harvester Press, 1989), p. 72.

32. ANDREAS HUYSSEN, *After the Great Divide, Modernism, Mass Culture, Postmodernism* (Bloomington: Indiana University Press, 1986), p. 207.

33. ALEX CALLINICOS, *Against Postmodernism* (Cambridge: Polity Press/Basil Blackwell, 1989), p. 67.

34. Ibid., p. 71.

35. SUSAN RUBIN SULEIMAN, 'Naming and Difference', op. cit., p. 255.

36. ALICE JARDINE, *Gynesis: Configurations of Women and Modernity* (Ithaca and London: Cornell University Press, 1985), p. 22.

37. HUYSSEN, op. cit., p. 206.

38. JACQUES DERRIDA, *Writing and Difference* (1967) trans. and with introduction by Alan Bass (Chicago: University of Chicago Press, 1978), p. 288.

39. HUYSSEN, op. cit., p. 308.

40. SUSAN SONTAG 'Notes on Camp' (1964) in *A Susan Sontag Reader*, Introduction by Elizabeth Hardwick (Harmondsworth: Penguin, 1983), pp. 115, 116.

41 For an introduction to L=A=N=G=U=A=G=E poetry, see Charles Bernstein and Bruce Andrews (eds), *The L=A=N=G=U=A=G=E Book* (Carbondale: Southern Illinois Press, 1984), and STEVE MCCAFFERY, *North of Intention. Critical Writings 1973–1986* (New York: Roof Books; Toronto: Nightwood Editions, (1986). An excellent discussion of this writing appears in PETER NICHOLLS' 'Difference Spreading. From Getrude Stein to L=A=N=G=U=A=G=E Poetry' in *Contemporary Poetry Meets Modern Theory*, ed. A. Easthope and J. Thompson (Brighton: Harvester Press, 1991).

42. JEROME KLINKOWITZ, *Literary Disruptions: the Making of a Post-Contemporary American Fiction*, 2nd edn. (Urbana: University of Illinois Press, 1980), p. 19.

43. Ibid., p. 20.

44. RAYMOND FEDERMAN (ed.) *Surfiction: Fiction Now . . . And Tomorrow* (Chicago: The Swallow Press, 1975), pp. 8–9.

45. JEAN BAUDRILLARD, *America* (1986) trans. Chris Turner (London and New York: Verso, 1988), p. 84.

46. FREDRIC JAMESON, 'The Politics of Theory: Ideological Positions in the Postmodernism Debate' in *Modern Criticism and Theory. A Reader*, ed. David Lodge (London and New York: Longman, 1988), pp. 377–8.

47. See the discussion in STEVEN CONNOR, *Postmodernist Culture*, op. cit., pp. 43–50; and essays in Douglas Kellner (ed.) *Postmodernism/Jameson/Critique* (Washington: Maisonneuve Press, 1990).

48. ANDERS STEPHANSON, 'Regarding Postmodernism – a Conversation with Fredric Jameson' in *Universal Abandon? The Politics of Postmodernism*, ed. Andrew Ross (Edinburgh: Edinburgh University Press, 1989), p. 17.

49. See MIKE DAVIS 'Urban Renaissance and the Spirit of Postmodernism' in *Postmodernism and its Discontents*, ed. E.A. Kaplan (London and New York: Verso, 1988), especially pp. 80–1; and ALEX CALLINICOS, *Against Postmodernism*, op. cit., pp. 132–44.

50. ELIZABETH BIRD et al., 'On Postmodernism and Articulation: an Interview with Stuart Hall', ed. Lawrence Grossberg, *Journal of Communication Inquiry*, **10** (Summer, 1986): 46.

51. CHANTAL MOUFFE, 'Radical Democracy: Modern or Postmodern?' in *Universal Abandon?* op. cit., p. 36.

52. MEAGHAN MORRIS, Introduction to *The Pirate's Fiancée. Feminism, Reading, Postmodernism* (London and New York: Verso, 1988), pp. 1–16.

53. On these positions see the 'Introduction' and essays in *Feminism/*

Postmodernism, ed. Linda J. Nicholson (New York and London: Routledge, 1990). See especially in this volume IRIS MARION YOUNG 'The Ideal of Community and the Politics of Difference' on the relevance of deconstruction, pp. 300–23, and CHRISTINE DI STEFANO, 'Dilemmas of Difference: Feminism, Modernity, and Postmodernism' on the feminist case against postmodernism, pp. 63–82. A strong statement of the affinities between feminism and Enlightenment ideals is made by SABRINA LOVIBOND, 'Feminism and Postmodernism' in *Postmodernism and Society*, ed. Roy Boyne and Ali Rattansi (Basingstoke: Macmillan, 1990), pp. 154–86.

54. Quoted in the *Guardian*, 4 November 1989, p. 25.

55. In addition to the major example of Jürgen Habermas, see also on this theme ERNESTO LACLAU AND CHANTAL MOUFFE *Hegemony and Socialist Stategy* (London and New York: Verso 1985); ALBRECHT WELLMAR 'On the Dialectic of Modernism and Postmodernism', *Praxis International*, 4, Part 4, (1985): 337–62, and STANLEY ARONOWITZ, 'Postmodernism and Politics' in *Universal Abandon?*, ed. Andrew Ross, op. cit., pp. 46–62.

56. A view taken by LINDA HUTCHEON in *A Poetics of Postmodernism. History, Theory, Fiction* (London and New York: Routledge, 1988). See chapters 1–3 and the categorical statements on pp. 30, 43.

57. RAYMOND WILLIAMS, 'When was Modernism?' in *The Politics of Modernism* (London and New York: Verso, 1989), pp. 31–5. See the introduction to this volume 'Modernism and Cultural Theory' by Tony Pinkney, especially pp. 19–27, and my review in *Textual Practice*, 6:1, 1992.

58. See PETER BROOKER, 'Introduction. Why Should Brecht's Name be Mentioned?' in *Bertolt Brecht. Dialectics, Poetry, Politics* (London and New York: Croom Helm, 1988), and 'Why Brecht, or Is there English after Cultural Studies?' in *Broadening the Context*, ed. Michael Green (London: John Murray, 1989), pp. 20–31.

59. WALTER BENJAMIN, 'Theses on the Philosophy of History' in *Illuminations* (1955), ed. and with introduction by Hannah Arendt, trans. Harry Zohn (London: Fontana, 1973), p. 263.

60. See Introduction to Ian Christie and Richard Taylor (eds), *Film Factory: Russian and Soviet Cinema in Documents* (London and New York: Routledge, 1988).

Part One

Modernist Positions

Until well into the post-war period, studies of modernism followed two main paths, the first in Anglo-American criticism, the second in Western Marxism. The ways in which a modernist orthodoxy was assembled and then defended, rewritten, or discarded in the first tradition are considered in the Introduction (pp. 5–13). The second, beginning in debates in Soviet and European criticism and philosophy in the late nineteenth century, reached its classic formulations in the twenties and thirties. Until the sixties, these traditions showed little cognisance of each other (and are still rarely discussed together), in spite of the fact that the second had already moved its base (albeit forcibly) to the scene of American criticism in the thirties and forties, when the Frankfurt Institute for Social Research, headed by Max Horkheimer and Theodor Adorno, was relocated in New York, and when many artists of the European avant-garde sought work and refuge in the United States. The Institute for Social Research is said to have experienced the constraints of 'the rabidly counter-revolutionary climate of American culture at the time' (*Aesthetics and Politics* (London: New Left Books, 1977),Verso Edition 1980, p. 105) and to have neutralised the politics of its publications accordingly (including alterations to Walter Benjamin's 'Work of Art in the Age of Mechanical Reproduction' in 1936). A figure like Brecht also found life and politics uncongenial in the United States, especially in Hollywood. The times perhaps did not allow for dialogue across the intellectual or artistic traditions of societies at war. Yet the American cinema was much influenced by European Expressionism, and Adorno in particular pursued a subtle and somewhat ascetic defence of modernism close to the hearts of earlier American critics, if unrecognised by them until well into the post-war period. One might think too that the debates in which Adorno, Brecht, Lukács and Benjamin were involved had already given one set of answers to Harry Levin's question 'What Was Modernism?' in 1960.

The topics examined in 'Western Marxism' (on the use and effects of new technologies, on art and mass culture, on avant-garde experiment and realist convention) have also continued to be relevant to discussions of postmodernism. Benjamin and Brecht remain instructive, as suggested in the Introduction, (pp. 28–29) and Brecht's use in his 'epic theatre' of discontinuous narrative, historicised tableau and gesture, contrapuntal music and stage design seems strikingly in tune with the decentred strategies of postmodernism. (See Linda Hutcheon, *Poetics of Postmodernism*, pp. 218–21). Adorno's work, secondly, spans the moments of modernist and postmodern debate as well as raising questions of their continuity and difference – as, for example, in his admiration for Samuel Beckett, a figure claimed otherwise by both camps. Herbert Marcuse, a member of the Frankfurt School who, exceptionally, exerted an influence on the counter-cultural movements of the sixties, identified in the concepts of 'repressive tolerance' and 'desublimation' – the assimilation of dissent and the satisfaction of needs in mass consumer society – what many see as the distinguishing features of cultural postmodernism. Also, even though few would now endorse it in its original terms, Georg Lukács's dismissal of modernism as a nihilistic and subjectivist symptom of alienation under capitalism has returned as a judgement upon the later postmodernism. Many too would draw still on Lukács's arguments in favour of realism. Fredric Jameson, for example, having suggested that the now 'automatised' conventions of modernist disruption and fragmentation have become a cultural habit, argues that they themselves require the corrective jolt of realism – 'a more totalising way of viewing phenomena' (*Aesthetics and Politics*, 1977, p. 211). The intensified reification and opacity of late capitalist society, he argues, if they are to be understood and resisted, stand in need of a new realism, and 'It may be Lukács – wrong as he might have been in the 1930s – who has some provisional last word for us today' (ibid, p. 212; see also Introduction, pp. 21–4).

This is not to suggest that the debates on modernism pre-empt those on postmodernism. It does, however, show, in the invariably conjoined description of these formations, how earlier concepts and perspectives can become redundant or assume a new application.

The work of the figures cited above is readily available and much discussed. The volume *Aesthetics and Politics* is especially useful and contains important work by Adorno, Brecht, Lukács and Benjamin, as well as excellent commentaries. The following extracts have been selected both to introduce this work and because of their interest in relation to later contributions on postmodernism.

1 George Lukács, from *The Meaning of Contemporary Realism*
Bertolt Brecht, from 'The Popular and the Realistic'*

The debate between Lukács and Brecht in the thirties on the forms
and political effect of 'critical' or 'socialist realism' has continued to
rank as a major theme in Marxist criticism. Lukács valued the literary
realism of novelists such as Balzac and Thomas Mann as a correct
reflection of the important determining factors of 'the full process of
life'. In the condensed unity of the individual and universal comprising its 'intensive totality', the realist novel corresponded, Lukács
argued, to the 'extensive totality' of the social whole, faithfully
recording its progressive movement. In the thirties he attacked
modernist Expressionism, particularly, for its failure to meet these
criteria, and returned later to a sustained critique of modernism in his
The Meaning of Contemporary Realism. Here Lukács sees modernism as
a subjectivist and decadent reinforcement of capitalist alienation, a
view opposed in different terms by both Adorno (who viewed
modernism as the negation of that reality) and by Brecht. In *The
Meaning of Contemporary Realism*, Lukács praised the realism of certain
of Brecht's plays (*Galileo, Mother Courage, Caucasian Chalk Circle*), but
his terms were never Brecht's own. Brecht sought to radicalise the
innovatory artistic devices of modernism. In answer to Lukács's
'formalist' model of realism he therefore proposed a flexible popular
realism, open to experiment and the use of new media and to changed
circumstances. The object of this dialectically conceived 'Marxist
modernism' was to provoke a critical knowledge of society's 'laws of
development' and thus make a popular control of present reality and
of the future possible.

---

* Georg Lukács, from *The Meaning of Contemporary Realism*, trans. John and Necke
Mander (London: Merlin Press, 1963), pp. 24–6. Bertolt Brecht from 'The Popular
and the Realistic' (1938, reprinted from *Brecht on Theatre* ed. and trans. John
Willett, New York: Hill and Wang, and London: Eyre Methuen, 1964),
pp. 108–110, 111, 112.

Developments in postmodernist theory, including the influence of psychoanalysis and deconstruction upon Marxist criticism would seem to have left Lukács's reflectionism and his ideas of literary unity and the social totality far behind, making Brecht once more our contemporary. However, the discussions referred to above (see also the Introduction, p. 28) show that there is no simple consensus on these matters.

For further discussion, see Klaus Völker *Brecht: A Biography* (London and Boston: Marion Boyars, 1979); and Lunn *Marxism and Modernism* (1982).

GEORGE LUKÁCS, from *The Meaning of Contemporary Realism*

The literature of realism, aiming at a truthful reflection of reality, must demonstrate both the concrete and abstract potentialities of human beings in extreme situations of this kind. A character's concrete potentiality once revealed, his abstract potentialities will appear essentially inauthentic. Moravia, for instance, in his novel *The Indifferent Ones*, describes the young son of a decadent bourgeois family, Michel, who makes up his mind to kill his sister's seducer. While Michel, having made his decision, is planning the murder, a large number of abstract – but highly suggestive – possiblities are laid before us. Unfortunately for Michel the murder is actually carried out; and, from the sordid details of the action, Michel's character emerges as what it is – representative of that background from which, in subjective fantasy, he had imagined he could escape.

Abstract potentiality belongs wholly to the realm of subjectivity; whereas concrete potentiality is concerned with the dialectic between the individual's subjectivity and objective reality. The literary presentation of the latter thus implies a description of actual persons inhabiting a palpable, identifiable world. Only in the interaction of character and environment can the concrete potentiality of a particular individual be singled out from the 'bad infinity' of purely abstract potentialities, and emerge as the determining potentiality of just this individual at just this phase of his development. This principle alone enables the artist to distinguish concrete potentiality from a myriad abstractions.

But the ontology on which the image of man in modernist literature is based invalidates this principle. If the 'human condition' – man as a solitary being, incapable of meaningful relationships – is identified with reality itself, the distinction between abstract and concrete potentiality becomes null and void. The categories tend to merge. Thus Cesare

Pavese notes with John Dos Passos, and his German contemporary, Alfred Döblin, a sharp oscillation between 'superficial *verisme*' and 'abstract Expressionist schematism'. Criticizing Dos Passos, Pavese writes that fictional characters 'ought to be created by deliberate selection and description of individual features – implying that Dos Passos' characterizations are transferable from one individual to another. He describes the artistic consequences: by exalting man's subjectivity, at the expense of the objective reality of his environment, man's subjectivity itself is impoverished.

The problem, once again, is ideological. This is not to say that the ideology underlying modernist writings is identical in all cases. On the contrary: the ideology exists in extremely various, even contradictory forms. The rejection of narrative objectivity, the surrender to subjectivity, may take the form of Joyce's stream of consciousness, or of Musil's 'active passivity', his 'existence without quality', or of Gide's *'action gratuite'*, where abstract potentiality achieves pseudo-realization. As individual character manifests itself in life's moments of decision, so too in literature. If the distinction between abstract and concrete potentiality vanishes, if man's inwardness is identified with an abstract subjectivity, human personality must necessarily disintegrate.

T.S. Eliot described this phenomenon, this mode of portraying human personality, as

> Shape without form, shade without colour,
> Paralysed force, gesture without motion.

The disintegration of personality is matched by a disintegration of the outer world. In one sense, this is simply a further consequence of our argument. For the identification of abstract and concrete human potentiality rests on the assumption that the objective world is inherently inexplicable. Certain leading modernist writers, attempting a theoretical apology, have admitted this quite frankly. Often this theoretical impossibility of understanding reality is the point of departure, rather than the exaltation of subjectivity. But in any case the connection between the two is plain. The German poet Gottfried Benn, for instance, informs us that 'there is no outer reality, there is only human consciousness, constantly building, modifying, rebuilding new worlds out of its own creativity'. Musil, as always, gives a moral twist to this line of thought. Ulrich, the hero of his *The Man without Qualities*, when asked what he would do if he were in God's place, replies: 'I should be compelled to abolish reality.' Subjective existence 'without qualities' is the complement of the negation of outward reality.

The negation of outward reality is not always demanded with such theoretical rigour. But it is present in almost all modernist literature. In conversation, Musil once gave as the period of his great novel, 'between 1912 and 1914'. But he was quick to modify this statement by adding: 'I have not, I must insist, written a historical novel. I am not concerned with actual events . . . Events, anyhow, are interchangeable. I am interested in what is typical, in what one might call the ghostly aspect of reality.' The word 'ghostly' is interesting. It points to a major tendency in modernist literature: the attenuation of actuality. In Kafka, the descriptive detail is of an extraordinary immediacy and authenticity. But Kafka's ingenuity is really directed towards substituting his *angst*-ridden vision of the world for objective reality. The realistic detail is the expression of a ghostly un-reality, of a nightmare world, whose function is to evoke *angst*. The same phenomenon can be seen in writers who attempt to combine Kafka's techniques with a critique of society – like the German writers, Wolfgang Koeppen, in his satirical novel about Bonn, *Das Treibhaus*. A similar attenuation of reality underlies Joyce's stream of consciousness. It is, of course, intensified where the stream of consciousness is itself the medium through which reality is presented. And it is carried *ad absurdum* where the stream of consciousness is that of an abnormal subject or of an idiot – consider the first part of Faulkner's *Sound and Fury* or, a still more extreme case, Beckett's *Molloy*.

Attenuation of reality and dissolution of personality are thus interdependent: the stronger the one, the stronger the other. Underlying both is the lack of a consistent view of human nature. Man is reduced to a sequence of unrelated experiential fragments.

Bertolt Brecht, from 'The Popular and the Realistic'

We now come to the concept of 'Realism'. It is an old concept which has been much used by many men and for many purposes, and before it can be applied we must spring-clean it too. This is necessary because when the people takes over its inheritance there has to be a process of expropriation. Literary works cannot be taken over like factories, or literary forms of expression like industrial methods. Realist writing, of which history offers many widely varying examples, is likewise conditioned by the question of how, when and for what class it is made use of: conditioned down to the last small detail. As we have in mind a fighting people that is changing the real world we must not cling to 'well-tried' rules for telling a story, worthy models set up by literary history, eternal aesthetic laws. We must not abstract the one and only realism from certain given works, but shall make a lively use of all means, old and new, tried and untried, deriving from art and deriving from other sources, in order to put living reality in the hands of living people in such a way that it can be mastered. We shall take care not to ascribe realism to a particular historical form of novel belonging to a particular period, Balzac's or Tolstoy's, for instance, so as to set up purely formal and literary criteria of realism. We shall not restrict ourselves to speaking of realism in cases where one can (e.g.) smell, look, feel whatever is depicted, where 'atmosphere' is created and stories develop in such a way that the characters are psychologically stripped down. Our conception of *realism* needs to be broad and political, free from aesthetic restrictions and independent of convention. *Realist* means: laying bare society's causal network/showing up the dominant view-point as the viewpoint of the dominators/writing from the standpoint of the class which has prepared the broadest solutions for the most pressing problems afflicting human society/emphasizing the dynamics of development/concrete and so as to encourage abstraction.

It is a tall order, and it can be made taller. And we shall let the artist apply all his imagination, all his originality, his sense of humour and power of invention to its fulfilment. We will not stick to unduly detailed literary models or force the artist to follow over-precise rules for telling a story.

We shall establish that so-called sensuous writing (in which everything can be smelt, tasted, felt) is not to be identified automatically with realist writing, for we shall see that there are sensuously written works which are not realist, and realist works which are not sensuously written. We shall have to go carefully into the question whether the story is best developed by aiming at an eventual psychological stripping-down of the characters. Our readers may quite well feel that they have not been given the key to what is happening if they are simply induced by a combination of arts to take part in the inner emotions of our books' heroes. By taking over the forms of Balzac and Tolstoy without a thorough inspection we might perhaps exhaust our readers, the people, just as these writers often do. Realism is not a pure question of form. Copying the methods of these realists, we should cease to be realists ourselves.

For time flows on, and if it did not it would be a poor look-out for those who have no golden tables to sit at. Methods wear out, stimuli fail. New problems loom up and demand new techniques. Reality alters; to represent it the means of representation must alter too. Nothing arises from nothing; the new springs from the old, but that is just what makes it new.

The oppressors do not always appear in the same mask. The masks cannot always be stripped off in the same way. There are so many tricks for dodging the mirror that is held out. Their military roads are termed motor roads. Their tanks are painted to look like Macduff's bushes. Their agents can show horny hands as if they are workers. Yes: it takes

43

ingenuity to change the hunter into the quarry. What was popular yesterday is no longer so today, for the people of yesterday were not the people as it is today.

Anybody who is not bound by formal prejudices knows that there are many ways of suppressing truth and many ways of stating it: that indignation at inhuman conditions can be stimulated in many ways, by direct description of a pathetic or matter-of-fact kind, by narrating stories and parables, by jokes, by over- and understatement. In the theatre reality can be represented in a factual or a fantastic form. The actors can do without (or with the minimum of) makeup, appearing 'natural', and the whole thing can be a fake; they can wear grotesque masks and represent the truth. There is not much to argue about here: the means must be asked what the end is. The people knows how to ask this. Piscator's great experiments in the theatre (and my own), which repeatedly involved the exploding of conventional forms, found their chief support in the most progressive cadres of the working class. The workers judged everything by the amount of truth contained in it; they welcomed any innovation which helped the representation of truth, of the real mechanism of society; they rejected whatever seemed like playing, like machinery working for its own sake, i.e. no longer, or not yet, fulfilling a purpose. The workers' arguments were never literary or purely theatrical. 'You can't mix theatre and film': that sort of thing was never said. If the film was not properly used the most one heard was: 'that bit of film is unnecessary, it's distracting'. . . .

So the criteria for the popular and the realistic need to be chosen not only with great care but also with an open mind. They must not be deduced from existing realist works and existing popular works, as is often the case. Such an approach would lead to purely formalistic criteria, and questions of popularity and realism would be decided by form.

One cannot decide if a work is realist or not by finding out whether it resembles existing, reputedly realist works which must be counted realist for their time. In each individual case the picture given of life must be compared, not with another picture, but with the actual life portrayed. And likewise where popularity is concerned there is a wholly formalistic procedure that has to be guarded against. The intelligibility of a work of literature is not ensured exclusively by its being written in exactly the same way as other works which people have understood. These other works too were not invariably written just like the works before them. Something was done towards their understanding. In the same way we must do something for the understanding of the new works. Besides *being popular* there is such a thing as *becoming popular*.

2 Walter Benjamin, from 'The Work of Art in the Age of Mechanical Reproduction'*

Benjamin's accomplishment was to link the advent of modernism with the altered conditions of modernity. Thus the new milieu introduced by the boulevards and arcades of late-nineteenth-century Paris produced a new urban type, the anonymous *flâneur* (the stroller or window-shopper); a type registered in the persona and poetry of Charles Baudelaire. Benjamin's study of Baudelaire argued that under capitalism art itself is induced to become a commodity. Yet to preserve its autonomy and wholeness in the doctrine of art for arts sake was only to divorce it from new technologies and social being. In the celebrated essay 'The Work of Art in the Age of Mechanical Reproduction', Benjamin presents the reverse case. His argument is that the autonomous work of art loses its traditional status (its 'aura') as an effect of mechanical reproduction. Art is thereby removed from the realm of ritual to that of politics, and a new, distracted but critical audience, is mobilised in the direction of greater democracy by the new mass arts. Both here and in the related essay 'The Author as Producer', where he argues that the author must revolutionise artistic technique to give it a political function within contemporary production relations, Benjamin therefore confirmed the project of a politicised modernism suggested by Brecht.

The present essay was first published in 1936 (substituting certain phrases: 'totalitarian democracy' for 'fascism'; 'modern warfare' for 'imperialist warfare', and without Benjamin's preface) in the *Zeitschrift für Sozialforschung*, the journal of the Institute for Social Research then established in New York. Theodor Adorno was critical of Benjamin's arguments and of Brecht's influence (see below), and in the later 'Some Motifs in Baudelaire' (in *Illuminations*, 1973), and *Charles*

---

* Reprinted from *Illuminations*, ed. Hannah Arendt (London: Collins/Fontana, 1973), sections IV, XII, XIV.

45

Baudelaire: A Lyric Poet in the Era of High Capitalism, 1973) Benjamin responded by revising his views on the work of art's loss of 'aura'.

For further discussion see Lunn, *Marxism and Modernism* (1982) and Eagleton, *Walter Benjamin* (1981). *New German Critique*, **34** (1985) and **39** (1986) are special issues on Benjamin. The magazine Block, **14** (Autumn 1989) examines the relevance of his views for an age of 'electronic reproduction'. See also Chamber's essay in the present volume (p. 81).

The uniqueness of a work of art is inseparable from its being imbedded in the fabric of tradition. This tradition itself is thoroughly alive and extemely changeable. An ancient statue of Venus, for example, stood in a different traditional context with the Greeks, who made it an object of veneration, than with the clerics of the Middle Ages, who viewed it as an ominous idol. Both of them, however were equally confronted with its uniqueness, that is, its aura. Originally the contextual integration of art in tradition found its expression in the cult. We know that the earliest art works originated in the service of a ritual – first the magical, then the religious kind. It is significant that the existence of the work of art with reference to its aura is never entirely separated from its ritual function. In other words, the unique value of the 'authentic' work of art has its basis in ritual, the location of its original use value. This ritualistic basis, however remote, is still recognizable as secularized ritual even in the most profane forms of the cult of beauty. The secular cult of beauty, developed during the Renaissance and prevailing for three centuries, clearly showed that ritualistic basis in its decline and the first deep crisis which befell it. With the advent of the first truly revolutionary means of reproduction, photography, simultaneously with the rise of socialism, art sensed the approaching crisis which has become evident a century later. At the time, art reacted with the doctrine of *l'art pour l'art*, that is, with a theology of art. This gave rise to what might be called a negative theology in the form of the idea of 'pure' art, which not only denied any social function of art but also any categorizing by subject matter. (In poetry, Mallarmé was the first to take this position).

An analysis of art in the age of mechanical reproduction must do justice to these relationships, for they lead us to an all-important insight: for the first time in world history, mechanical reproduction emancipates the work of art from its parasitical dependence on ritual. To an ever greater degree the work of art reproduced becomes the work of art designed for reproducibility. From a photographic negative, for example, one can make any number of prints; to ask for the 'authentic' print makes no sense. But the instant the criterion of authenticity ceases to be applicable to artistic production, the total function of art is reversed. Instead of being based on ritual, it begins to be based on another practice – politics.

Mechanical reproduction of art changes the reaction of the masses toward art. The reactionary attitude toward a Picasso painting changes into the progressive reaction toward a Chaplin movie. The progressive reaction is characterized by the direct, intimate fusion of visual and emotional enjoyment with the orientation of the expert. Such fusion is of great social significance. The greater the decrease in the social significance of an art form, the sharper the distinction between criticism and enjoyment by the public. The conventional is uncritically enjoyed, and the truly new is criticized with aversion. With regard to the screen, the critical and the receptive attitudes of the public coincide. The decisive reason for this is that individual reactions are predetermined by the mass audience response they are about to produce, and this is nowhere more pronounced than in the film. The moment these responses become manifest they control each other. Again, the comparison with painting is fruitful. A painting has always had an excellent chance to be viewed by one person or by a few. The simultaneous contemplation of paintings by a large public, such as developed in the nineteenth century, is an early symptom of the crisis of painting, a crisis which was by no means occasioned exclusively by photography but rather in a relatively independent manner by the appeal of art works to the masses.

Painting simply is in no position to present an object for simultaneous collective experience, as it was possible for architecture at all times, for the epic poem in the past, and for the movie today. Although this circumstance in itself should not lead one to conclusions about the social role of painting, it does constitute a serious threat as soon as painting, under special conditions and, as it were, against its nature, is confronted directly by the masses. In the churches and monasteries of the Middle Ages and at the princely courts up to the end of the eighteenth century, a collective reception of paintings did not occur simultaneously, but by graduated and hierarchized mediation. The change that has come about is an expression of the particular conflict in which painting was implicated by the mechanical reproducibility of paintings. Although paintings began to be publicly exhibited in galleries and salons, there was no way for the masses to organize and control themselves in their reception. Thus the same public which responds in a progressive manner toward a grotesque film is bound to respond in a reactionary manner to Surrealism.

One of the foremost tasks of art has always been the creation of a demand which could be fully satisfied only later. The history of every art form shows critical epochs in which a certain art form aspires to effects which could be fully obtained only with a changed technical standard, that is to say, in a new art form. The extravagances and crudities of art which thus appear, particularly in the so-called decadent epochs, actually arise from the nucleus of its richest historical energies. In recent years, such barbarisms were abundant in Dadaism. It is only now that its impulse becomes discernible: Dadaism attempted to create by pictorial – and literary – means the effects which the public today seeks in the film.

Every fundamentally new, pioneering creation of demands will carry beyond its goal. Dadaism did so to the extent that it sacrificed the market values which are so characteristic of the film in favor of higher ambitions – though of course it was not conscious of such intentions as here described. The Dadaists attached much less importance to the sales value of their work than to its uselessness for contemplative immersion. The studied degradation of their material was not the least of their means to achieve this uselessness. Their poems are 'word salad' containing obscenities and every imaginable waste produce of language. The same is true of their paintings, on which they mounted buttons and tickets. What they intended and achieved was a relentless destruction of the aura of their creations, which they branded as reproductions with the very means of production. Before a painting of Arp's or a poem by August Stramm it is impossible to take time for contemplation and evaluation as one would before a canvas of Derain's or a poem by Rilke. In the decline of middle-class society, contemplation became a school for asocial behavior; it was countered by distraction as a variant of social conduct. Dadaistic activities actually assured a rather vehement distraction by making works of art the center of scandal. One requirement was foremost: to outrage the public.

From an alluring appearance or persuasive structure of sound the work of art of the Dadaists became an instrument of ballistics. It hit the spectator like a bullet, it happened to him, thus acquiring a tactile quality. It promoted a demand for the film, the distracting element of which is also primarily tactile, being based on changes of place and focus which periodically assail the spectator. Let us compare the screen on which a film unfolds with the canvas of a painting. The painting invites the spectator to contemplation; before it the spectator can abandon himself to his associations. Before the movie frame he cannot do so. No sooner has his eye grasped a scene that it is already changed. It cannot be arrested. Duhamel, who detests the film and knows nothing of its significance, though something of its structure, notes this circumstance as follows: 'I can no longer think what I want to think. My thoughts have been replaced by moving images'.[1] The spectator's process of association in view of these images is indeed interrupted by their constant, sudden change. This constitutes the shock effect of the film, which, like all shocks, should be cushioned by heightened presence of mind. By means of its technical structure, the film has taken the physical shock effect out of the wrappers in which Dadaism had, as it were, kept it inside the moral shock effect.

Note

1 . Georges Duhamel, *Scènes de la vie future* (Paris, 1930), p. 52.

3 Theodor Adorno, 'Letter to Walter Benjamin'*

For Adorno the defining aspect of modern art was its autonomy and hence its capacity to operate at a critical remove from both totalitarian and 'authoritarian' advanced capitalist societies; a view influenced by Hegelian Marxism and the combined experience of Nazism and the USA in the 1930s and 1940s. In the following response to Benjamin's 'The Work of Art in the Age of Mechanical Reproduction' he disputes Benjamin's assessment of the loss of this autonomy and of the progressive effects of technology and of cinema. Both autonomous and 'utilitarian' or 'dependent art', Adorno says, are dialectical. Both 'bear the stigmata of capitalism, both contain elements of change . . . Both are torn halves of a integral freedom, to which however they do not add up.' Under Brecht's influence Benjamin had simplified this relationship.

Unfortunately, Adorno did not at all times observe his own postulate for 'more dialectics'. His key essay on the culture industry, for example, coauthored with Max Horkheimer (in *The Dialectic of Enlightenment*, 1972), draws an unrelenting line between the disruptive formal obscurity of an avant-garde modernism and commercially produced and manipulative mass art. Elsewhere, however, and particularly in the volume *Aesthetic Theory*, Adorno argues with great dialectical finesse how art both takes the imprint of and resists the reifications of modern capitalist society. Art, he replied to Georg Lukács, does not reflect; it reveals, producing 'a negative knowledge of the actual world' (*Aesthetics and Politics*, p. 160). While this 'negative dialectics' might easily prove pessimistic (Samuel Beckett was an exemplary modernist for Adorno) it also confers a critical and utopian aspect upon art: 'It is to works of art', said Adorno, 'that has fallen

---

* Trans. Harry Zohn, reprinted from Ernst Bloch et. al., *Aesthetics and Politics* (London and New York: Verso), pp. 120–6.

Theodor Adorno

the burden of wordlessly asserting what is barred to politics' (ibid., p. 194).

The 'critical theory' of the Frankfurt School (associated principally with Adorno, Horkheimer and Marcuse), and its account of a 'totally administered' managerial capitalism (see Marcuse's *One-Dimensional Man*, 1964), has influenced a second generation of German philosophers, including Jürgen Habermas (see below, pp. 125–38) and continues to influence debates on postmodernism. Habermas would reject the association of rationality with totalitarianism which informs Frankfurt school theory, while others find its austere condemnation of mass art over-simple. For many, however, the apparently unrelieved hegemony of capitalism and its neutralisation of criticism has served to confirm Adorno's analysis, and his emphasis on art's resistant autonomy.

For further discussion, see Enzensberger, *The Consciousness Industry* (1974); Andrew Benjamin (ed.), *The Problems of Modernity. Adorno and Benjamin* (1989); and also Jameson, *Marxism and Form* (1971) and *Late Marxism: Adorno or the Persistence of the Dialectic* (1990). On the Frankfurt School, see most recently, Steven Bronner and Douglas Kellner (eds), *Critical Theory and Society: A Reader* (1989).

London, 18 March 1936

Dear Herr Benjamin,

If today I prepare to convey to you some notes on your extraordinary study ('The Work of Art in the Age of Mechanical Reproduction'), I certainly have no intention of offering you criticism or even an adequate response. The terrible pressure of work on me – the big book on logic,[1] the completion of my contribution to the monograph on Berg,[2] which is ready except for two analyses, and the study on jazz[3] – makes any such endeavour hopeless. This is especially true of a work in the face of which I am very seriously aware of the inadequacy of written communication, for there is not a sentence which I would not wish to discuss with you in detail. I cling to the hope that this will be possible very soon, but on the other hand I do not want to wait so long before giving you some kind of response, however insufficient it may be.

Let me therefore confine myself to one main theme. My ardent interest and my complete approval attach to that aspect of your study which appears to me to carry out your original intention – the dialectical construction of the relationship between myth and history – within the intellectual field of the materialistic dialectic: namely, the dialectical self-dissolution of myth, which is here viewed as the disenchantment of art.

51

You know that the subject of the 'liquidation of art' has for many years underlain my aesthetic studies and that my emphatic espousal of the primacy of technology, especially in music, must be understood strictly in this sense and in that of your second technique. It does not surprise me if we find common ground here; it does not surprise me, because in your book on the Baroque you accomplished the differentiation of the allegory from the symbol (in the new terminology, the 'aural' symbol) and in your *Einbahnstrasse*[4] you differentiated the work of art from magical documentation. It is a splendid confirmation – I hope it does not sound immodest if I say: for both of us – that in an essay on Schönberg which appeared in a *Festschrift* two years ago[5] and with which you are not familiar, I proposed formulations about technology and dialectics as well as the alteration of relationships to technology, which are in perfect accord with your own.

It is this accord which for me constitutes the criterion for the differences that I must now state, with no other aim than to serve our 'general line', which is now so clearly discernible. In doing so, perhaps I can start out by following our old method of immanent criticism. In your earlier writings, of which your present essay is a continuation, you differentiated the idea of the work of art as a structure from the symbol of theology and from the taboo of magic. I now find it disquieting – and here I see a sublimated remnant of certain Brechtian motifs – that you now casually transfer the concept of magical aura to the 'autonomous work of art' and flatly assign to the latter a counter-revolutionary function. I need not assure you that I am fully aware of the magical element in the bourgeois work of art (particularly since I constantly attempt to expose the bourgeois philosophy of idealism, which is associated with the concept of aesthetic autonomy, as mythical in the fullest sense). However, it seems to me that the centre of the autonomous work of art does not itself belong on the side of myth – excuse my topic parlance – but is inherently dialectical; within itself it juxtaposes the magical and the mark of freedom. If I remember correctly, you once said something similar in connection with Mallarmé, and I cannot express to you my feeling about your entire essay more clearly than by telling you that I constantly found myself wishing for a study of Mallarmé as a counterpoint to your essay, a study which, in my estimation, you owe us as an important contribution to our knowledge. Dialectical though your essay may be, it is not so in the case of the autonomous work of art itself; it disregards an elementary experience which becomes more evident to me every day in my own musical experience – that precisely the uttermost consistency in the pursuit of the technical laws of autonomous art changes this art and instead of rendering it into a taboo or fetish, brings it close to the state of freedom, of something that can be consciously produced and made. I know of no better materialistic programme than that statement by Mallarmé in which he defines works of literature as something not inspired but made out of words; and the greatest figures of reaction, such as Valéry and Borchardt (the latter with his essay about villas[6] which, despite an unspeakable comment about workers, could be taken over in a materialistic sense in its entirety), have this explosive power in their innermost cells. If you defend the *kitsch* film against the 'quality' film, no one can be more in agreement with you than I am; but *l'art pour l'art* is just as much in need of a defence, and the united front which exists against it and which to my knowledge extends from Brecht to the Youth Movement, would be encouragement enough to undertake a rescue.

[In your essay on *The Elective Affinities*][7] you speak of play and appearance as the elements of art; but I do not see why play should be dialectical, and appearance – the appearance which you have managed to preserve in Ottilie who, together with Mignon and Helena,[8] now does not come off so well – should not. And at this point, to be sure, the debate turns political quickly enough. For if you render rightly technicization and alienation dialectical, but not in equal measure the world of objectified subjectivity, the political effect is to credit the proletariat (as the cinema's subject) directly with an achievement which, according to Lenin, it can realize only through a theory introduced by intellectuals as dialectical subjects, who themselves belong to the sphere of works of art which you have consigned to Hell.

Understand me correctly. I would not want to claim the autonomy of the work of art as a prerogative, and I agree with you that the aural element of the work of art is declining – not only because of its technical reproducibility, incidentally, but above all because of the fulfilment of its own 'autonomous' formal laws (this is the subject of the theory of musical reproduction which Kolisch and I have been planning for years). But the autonomy of the work of art, and therefore its material form, is not identical with the magical element in it. The reification of a great work of art is not just loss, any more than the reification of the cinema is all loss. It would be bourgeois reaction to negate the reification of the cinema in the name of the ego, and it would border on anarchism to revoke the reification of a great work of art in the spirit of immediate use-values. '*Les extrèmes me touchent*' [Gide], just as they touch you – but only if the dialectic of the lowest has the same value as the dialectic of the highest, rather than the latter simply decaying. Both bear the stigma of capitalism, both contain elements of change (but never, of course, the middle-term between Schönberg and the American film). Both are torn halves of an integral freedom, to which however they do not add up. It would be romantic to sacrifice one to the other, either as the bourgeois romanticism of the conservation of personality and all that stuff, or as the anarchistic romanticism of blind confidence in the spontaneous power of the proletariat in the historical process – a proletariat which is itself a product of bourgeois society.

To a certain extent I must accuse your essay of this second romanticism. You have swept art out of the corners of its taboos – but it is as though you feared a consequent inrush of barbarism (who could share your fear more than I?) and protected yourself by raising what you fear to a kind of inverse taboo. The laughter of the audience at a cinema – I discussed this with Max, and he has probably told you about it already – is anything but good and revolutionary; instead, it is full of the worst bourgeois sadism. I very much doubt the expertise of the newspaper boys who discuss sports; and despite its shock-like seduction, I do not find your theory of distraction convincing – if only for the simple reason that in a communist society work will be organized in such a way that people will no longer be so tired and so stultified that they need distraction. On the other hand, certain concepts of capitalist practice, like that of the test, seem to me almost ontologically congealed and taboo-like in function – whereas if anything does have an aural character, it is surely the film which possesses it to an extreme and highly suspect degree. To select only one more small item: the idea that a reactionary is turned into a member of the avant-garde by expert knowlege of Chaplin's films strikes me as out-and-out romanticization. For I cannot count Kracaeur's[9] favourite director, even after *Modern Times*, as an avant-garde artist (the reason will be perfectly clear from my article on jazz), nor do I believe that any of the decent elements in this work will attract attention. One need only have heard the laughter of the audience at the film to know what is actually happening.

Your dig at Werfel gave me great pleasure. But if you take Mickey Mouse instead, things are far more complicated, and the serious question arises as to whether the reproduction of every person really constitutes that *a priori* of the film which you claim it to be, or whether instead this reproduction belongs precisely to that 'naïve realism' whose bourgeois nature we so thoroughly agreed upon in Paris. After all, it is hardly an accident if that modern art which you counterpose to technical art as aural, is of such inherently dubious quality as Vlaminck[10] and Rilke. The lower sphere, to be sure, can score an easy victory over this sort of art; but if instead there were the names of, let us say, Kafka and Schönberg, the problem would be posed very differently. Certainly Schönberg's music is *not* aural.

Accordingly, what I would postulate is *more* dialectics. On the one hand, dialectical penetration of the 'autonomous' work of art which is transcended by its own technology into a planned work; on the other, an even stronger dialecticization of utilitarian art in its negativity, which you certainly do not fail to note but which you designate by relatively abstract categories like 'film capital', without tracking it down to its ultimate lair

as immanent irrationality. When I spent a day in the studios of
Neubabelsberg two years ago, what impressed me most was how *little*
montage and all the advanced techniques that you emphasize are
actually used; rather, reality is everywhere *constructed* with an infantile
mimetism and then 'photographed'. You underestimate the technicality
of autonomous art and overestimate that of dependent art; this, in plain
terms, would be my main objection. But this objection could only be
given effect as a dialectic between extremes which you tear apart. In my
estimation, this would involve nothing else than the complete liquidation
of the Brechtian motifs which have already undergone an extensive
transformation in your study – above all, the liquidation of any appeal to
the immediacy of interconnected aesthetic effects, however fashioned,
and to the actual consciousness of actual workers who have absolutely no
advantage over the bourgeois except their interest in the revolution, but
otherwise bear all the marks of mutilation of the typical bouregois
character. This prescribes our function for us clearly enough – which I
certainly do not mean in the sense of an activist conception of
'intellectuals'. But it cannot mean either that we may only escape the old
taboos by entering into new ones – 'tests', so to speak. The goal of the
revolution is the abolition of fear. Therefore we need have no fear of it,
nor need we ontologize our fear. It is not bourgeois idealism if, in full
knowledge and without mental prohibitions, we maintain our solidarity
with the proletariat instead of making of our own necessity a virtue of
the proletariat, as we are always tempted to do – the proletariat which
itself experiences the same necessity and needs us for knowledge as
much as we need the proletariat to make the revolution. I am convinced
that the further development of the aesthetic debate which you have so
magnificently inaugurated, depends essentially on a true accounting of
the relationship of the intellectuals to the working-class.

Excuse the haste of these notes. All this could be seriously settled only
on the basis of the details in which the Good Lord – possibly not magical
after all – dwells.[11] Only the shortage of time leads me to use the large
categories which you have taught me strictly to avoid. In order at least to
indicate to you the concrete passages to which I refer, I have left my
spontaneous pencilled annotations on the manuscript, though some of
them may be too spontaneous to be communicated. I beg your
indulgence for this as well as for the sketchy nature of my letter.

I am going to Germany on Sunday. It is possible that I shall be able to
complete my jazz study there, something that I unfortunately did not
have time to do in London. In that case I would send it to you without a
covering letter and ask you to send it on to Max immediately after reading
it (it probably will amount to more than twenty-five printed pages). This
is not certain, because I do not know whether I shall find the time or,
especially, whether the nature of this study will permit me to send it

from Germany without considerable danger. Max has probably told you that the idea of the clown is its focal point. I would be very pleased if it appeared together with your study. Its subject is a very modest one, but it probably converges with yours in its decisive points, and will attempt to express positively some of the things that I have formulated negatively today. It arrives at a complete verdict on jazz, in particular by revealing its 'progressive' elements (semblance of montage, collective work, primacy of reproduction over production) as façades of something that is in truth quite reactionary. I believe that I have succeeded in really decoding jazz and defining its social function. Max was quite taken with my study, and I could well imagine that you will be, too. Indeed I feel that our theoretical disagreement is not really a discord between us but rather, that it is my task to hold your arm steady until the sun of Brecht has once more sunk into exotic waters. Please understand my criticisms only in this spirit.

I cannot conclude, however, without telling you that your few sentences about the disintegration of the proletariat as 'masses' through revolution[12] are among the profoundest and most powerful statements of political theory that I have encountered since I read *State and Revolution*.

Your old friend,

Teddie Wiesengrund[13]

I should also like to express my special agreement with your theory of Dadaism. It fits into the essay as nicely as the 'bombast' and the 'horrors' fit into your Baroque book.

Notes

1. This was the philosophical work, a critique of phenomenology, on which Adorno was engaged while at Oxford. It was eventually published in Stuttgart in 1956 as *Zur Metakritik der Erkenntnistheorie. Studien über Husserl and die phänomenologischen Antinomien*.

2. Included in Willi Reich (ed.), *Alban Berg*, (Vienna, 1937).

3. Published as 'Über Jazz' in the *Zeitschrift für Sozialforschung*, 5 (1936), and later included in Adorno's volume *Moments Musicaux*, (Frankfurt, 1964). For Adorno's views on Jazz, see also his essay 'Perennial Fashion – Jazz, *Prisms* (London 1967).

4. Benjamin's volume of aphorisms *Einbahnstrasse* was published in Berlin in 1928 and then later included in Adorno's collection *Impromptus* (Frankfurt, 1968).

5. This essay, 'Der dialektische Komponist', was originally published in Vienna in 1934.

6. RUDOLF BORCHARDT (1877–1945) was a prominent litterateur in Germany,

whose essay on Tuscan villas is included in the edited volume of his writings, *Prosa III*, (Stuttgart, 1960), pp. 38–70.

7. Benjamin's essay, *Goethes Wahlverwandtschaften* was published in Hofmannsthal's journal *Neue Deutsche Beiträge* in 1924–5.

8. Characters in Goethe's *Elective Affinities*, *Wilhelm Meister's Apprenticeship*, and *Faust II*, respectively.

9. SIEGFRIED KRACAUER, long a friend of Adorno, was the author of *From Caligari to Hitler*, (Princeton, 1947), an attack on German expressionist cinema.

10. Changed to Derain in the published version of Benjamin's essay.

11. A reference to the programmatic dictum of the art historian Aby Warburg: *Der liebe Gott steckt im Detail* (The Good Lord dwells in detail).

12. This passage does not appear in any of the published versions of Benjamin's essay.

13. Wiesengrund was Adorno's paternal name.

4 Peter Bürger, 'Avant-Garde' and Engagement'*

Adorno's writings made no distinction between modern art and modernism and little between kinds of modernism in different art forms. Essentially he had generalised a theory of the avant-garde to all art from the mid-nineteenth century. (In the earlier major study of the avant-garde, Renato Pogglioli (1962) similarly ascribes a 'culture of negation' to a broad sweep of literature from romanticism to the present day.) Bürger's work has brought a more historically precise distinction between modernism and the 'avant-garde' to this debate. In this model the avant-garde is distinguished not merely by signs of technical or stylistic rebellion, but by its rejection of the institution of art as such. Its project (in which it failed, says Bürger) was to remove art from its official discourses and venues and integrate it in to a reformed social praxis. Bürger's discussion suggests that the negation of bourgeois rationality which Adorno had attributed to modern or modernist art is a particular feature of aestheticism, subsequently radicalised by the historical avant-gardes of the early twentieth century. In the following selection Bürger examines Adorno's claims for the authenticity of a 'non-organic' avant-gardist art and Lukács's dismissal of the avant-garde in favour of an 'organic' realism. Neither position, he says, is true or false, so much as unwittingly historical. Both critics accordingly misjudged Brecht, a writer who conformed neither to the model of an organic realism nor to the avant-garde rejection of art. Brecht created an effective political art, with a new relation to reality and to the institution of art, but he too, warns Bürger, mindful of a new post avant-garde pluralism, must be understood historically and not as a norm.

For further discussion see Jochen Schulte-Sasse's foreword to

---

* Reprinted from the *Theory of the Avant-Garde*, trans. by Michael Shaw, foreword by Jochen Schulte-Sasse (Manchester: Manchester University Press; Minneapolis: University of Minnesota, 1984), pp. 83–94.

Bürger's volume, especially section IV; also Eagleton 'Capitalism, Modernism and Postmodernism' in Eagleton, *Against the Grain* (1986). On the avant-garde, see Russell, *Poets, Prophets and Revolutionaries* (1985); Krauss, *The Originality of the Avant-Garde and Other Modernist Myths* (1985); Perloff, *The Futurist Moment* (1986); Calinescu, *Five Faces of Modernity* (1987); and essays in Raymond Williams, *The Politics of Modernism* (1989).

The Debate between Adorno and Lukács

In a theory of the avant-garde, a section on engagement is justified only if it can be shown that the avant-garde has radically changed the place value of political engagement in art, that the concept of engagement prior and subsequent to the avant-garde movements is not the same. It is our intent, in what follows, to show that this is the case. This means that the discussion of the question whether it is necessary to deal with engagement within the framework of a theory of the avant-garde cannot be separated from a discussion of the problem itself.

So far, the theory of the avant-garde has been treated at two levels: the level of the intention of the historical avant-garde movements, and that of the description of the avant-gardiste work. The intention of the historical avant-garde work movements was defined as the destruction of art as an institution set off from the praxis of life. The significance of this intention is not that art as an institution in bourgeois society was in fact destroyed and art thereby made a direct element in the praxis of life, but that the weight that art as an institution has in determining the real social effect of individual works became recognizable. The avant-gardiste work is defined as nonorganic. Whereas in the organic work of art, the structural principle governs the parts and joins them in a unified whole, in the avant-gardiste work, the parts have a significantly larger autonomy vis-à-vis the whole. They become less important as constituent elements of a totality of meaning and simultaneously more important as relatively autonomous signs.

The contrast between organic and avant-gardiste work underlies both Lukács's and Adorno's theories of the avant-garde. They differ in their evaluation. Whereas Lukács holds onto the organic work of art ('realistic' in his terminology) as an aesthetic norm and from that perspective rejects avant-gardiste works as decadent,[1] Adorno elevates the avant-gardiste, nonorganic work to an – albeit merely historical – norm and condemns as aesthetic regression all efforts to create a realistic art in Lukács's sense in our time.[2] In both cases, we are dealing with a theory of art that already advances decisive definitions at the theoretical level. This does not mean, of course, that Lukács and Adorno, like the authors of Renaissance and Baroque poetics, construct general, metahistorical laws by which to measure individual works. Their theories are normative only in the sense in which Hegel's aesthetics, to which both theoreticians owe a diverse debt, contains a normative element. Hegel historicizes aesthetics. The form–content dialectic realizes itself in different ways in symbolic (Oriental), classical (Greek), and romantic (Christian) art. But for Hegel, this historicizing does not mean that the romantic art form is also the most perfect. On the contrary, he considers the interpenetration of form and matter in classical Greek art a peak that is tied to a particular stage in the development of the world spirit and will necessarily pass away with it. Classical perfection whose essence it is that 'the spiritual was completely drawn through its external appearance'[3] (Hegel, vol. I, p.517) can no longer be attained by the romantic work of art, because 'the elevation of the spirit to itself' is the fundamental principle of romantic art. As spirit withdraws 'from the external into its own intimacy with itself and posits external reality as an existence inadequate to itself' (p.518), the interpenetration of the spiritual and material that classical art attained disintegrates. Hegel even goes one step further and anticipates a 'culmination of the romantic in general' which he characterizes as follows: 'the contingency of both outer and inner, and the separation of these two sides, whereby art annuls [sublates (*aufhebt*)] itself' (p.529). With romantic art, art comes to its end and makes way for higher forms of consciousness, i.e., philosophy.[4]

Lukács adopts essential elements of the Hegelian conception. Hegel's confrontation of classical and romantic returns in his work as the opposition between realistic and avant-gardiste art. And like Hegel, Lukács also develops this opposition within the framework of a philosophy of history. In Lukács, of course, that philosophy is no longer the movement of the world spirit, who withdraws to itself from the external world and thus destroys the possibility of a classical harmony between intellect and sensuousness. It is materialistic, the history of bourgeois society. With the end of the bourgeois emancipation movement, the 1848 June revolution, the bourgeois intellectual also loses the ability to portray bourgeois society as a changing society in the totality of a realistic work of art. In the naturalistic absorption in detail and the associated loss of an encompassing perspective, we have the intimation of the dissolution of bourgeois realism, which reaches its climax in the avant-garde. This development is the development of a historically necessary decline.[5] Lukács thus transfers Hegel's critique of romantic art, as a historically necessary symptom of decay, to the art of the avant-garde. On the other hand, he largely adopts Hegel's view that the organic work of art constitutes a type of absolute perfection, except that he sees the realization of this type in the great realistic novels of

Goethe, Balzac, and Stendhal rather than in Greek art. This suggests that for Lukács also, the culmination of art lies in the past, though it is true that he differs from Hegel in not feeling that perfection is necessarily unattainable in the present. Not only do the great realistic writers of the ascent of the bourgeoisie become models of socialist realism, according to Lukács, but he goes further and tries to attenuate the radical consequences of his historical–philosophical construct (the impossibility of a bourgeois realism after 1848 or 1871) by also allowing for a bourgeois realism in the twentieth century.[6]

Adorno is more radical on this point: for him, the avant-gardiste work is the only possible authentic expression of the contemporary state of the world. Adorno's theory is also based on Hegel but does not adopt its evaluations (negative view of romantic art versus high estimation of classical art), which Lukács transferred to the present. Adorno attempts to think radically and to take to its conclusion the historicizing of the art forms that Hegel had undertaken. This means that no historical type of the form–content dialectic will be given a higher rank than any other. In this perspective, the avant-gardiste work of art presents itself as the historically necessary expression of alienation in late-capitalist society. To propose measuring it against the organic coherence of the classical or realistic work would be improper. It seems at first as if Adorno had definitively broken with any normative theory. But it is not difficult to see how, by way of a radical historicizing, the normative again enters into theory and stamps it no less markedly than in Lukács's case.

For Lukács also, the avant-garde is the expression of alienation in late-capitalist society, but for the socialist it is also the expression of the blindness of bourgeois intellectuals vis-à-vis the real historical counterforces working toward a socialist transformation of this society. It is on this political perspective that Lukács bases the possibility of a realistic art in the present. Adorno does not have this political perspective; therefore, avant-garde art becomes for him the only authentic art in late capitalist society. Every attempt to create organic, coherent works (which Lukács calls 'realist') is not merely a regression beyond an already attained level of artistic techniques,[7] it is ideologically suspect. Instead of baring the contradictions of society in our time, the organic work promotes, by its very form, the illusion of a world that is whole, even though the explicit contents may show a wholly different intent.

This is not the place to decide which of the two approaches is 'correct'; rather, the intention of the theory sketched here is to demonstrate that the debate itself is historical. To do so, it must be shown that the premises of the two authors are already historical today and that it is therefore impossible to simply adopt them. One may formulate the following thesis: the dispute between Lukács and Adorno concerning the

61

legitimacy of avant-gardiste art as outlined above is confined to the sphere of artistic means and the change in the kind of work this involves (organic versus avant-gardiste). Yet the two authors do not thematize the attack that the historical avant-garde movements launched against art as an institution. According to the theory here set forth, it is this attack, however, that is the decisive event in the development of art in bourgeois society, because that attack first made recognizable the institution that is art, as it made recognizable that institution's determining influence on the effect individual works will have. Where the significance of the break in the development of art as caused by the historical avant-garde movements is not seen in the attack on art as an institution, the formal problem (organic versus nonorganic work) necessarily comes to occupy the center of reflection. But once the historical avant-garde movements revealed art as an institution as the solution to the mystery of the effectiveness or ineffectiveness of art, no form could any longer claim that it alone had either eternal or temporally limited validity. The historical avant-garde movements liquidated such a claim. Because Lukács and Adorno make it once more, they show that their thought is still dominated by a pre-avant-gardiste period that knew historically conditioned stylistic change.

It is certainly true that Adorno brought out the significance of the avant-garde for aesthetic theory in our time. But in so doing, he insisted exclusively on the new type of work, not on the intent of the avant-garde movements to reintegrate art in the praxis of life. In that way, the avant-garde becomes the only type of art that is appropriate to our time.[8] This view is true in the sense that today, the farther-reaching intentions of the avant-garde movements can in fact be judged to have failed. Its untruth lies in the fact that it is precisely this failure that had certain consequences. The historical avant-garde movements were unable to destroy art as an institution; but they did destroy the possibility that a given school can present itself with the claim to universal validity. That 'realistic' and 'avant-gardiste' art exist side by side today is a fact that can no longer be objected to legitimately. The meaning of the break in the history of art that the historical avant-garde movements provoked does not consist in the destruction of art as an institution, but in the destruction of the possibility of positing aesthetic norms as valid ones. This has consequences for scholarly dealings with works of art: the normative examination is replaced by a functional analysis, the object of whose investigation would be the social effect (function) of a work, which is the result of the coming together of stimuli inside the work and a sociologically definable public within an already existing institutional frame.[9]

Lukács's and Adorno's failure to deal with art as an institution will have to be seen in connection with something else the two theoreticians share, and that is their critical attitude toward the work of Brecht. In Lukács's case the rejection of Brecht is a direct result of his theoretical approach: Brecht's work falls under the same verdict as all nonorganic work. In Adorno's case, the rejection is not a direct outflow of a central theoretical position but of a subsidiary theorem, according to which works of art are 'the unconscious historiography of what is norm and what is monstrous in history' (*des geschichtlichen Wesens und Unwesens*).[10] Where the nexus between the work and the society that conditions it is posited as necessarily unconscious, Brecht, who endeavored to give shape to this nexus with the highest possible degree of consciousness, can hardly be adequately received.[11]

To summarize: the Lukács–Adorno debate, which in many respects resumes the expressionism debate of the mid-thirties, ends with an aporia: two theories of culture that understand themselves as materialist confront each other antagonistically, and both are tied to specific political positions. Adorno not only sees late capitalism as definitively stabilized but also feels that historical experience has shown the hopes placed in socialism to be ill-founded. For him, avant-gardiste art is a radical protest that rejects all false reconciliation with what exists and thus the only art form that has historical legitimacy. Lukács, on the other hand, acknowledges its character as protest but condemns avant-gardiste art because that protest remains abstract, without historical perspective, blind to the real counter forces that are seeking to overcome capitalism. A common element in both approaches in which the aporia is not abolished but intensified is that for reasons relevant to their theories, both authors are incapable of understanding the most important materialist writer of our time (Brecht).

In this situation, a way out seems to offer itself, and that would be to make the theory of this materialist writer the yardstick of judgment. But this solution has a considerable drawback: it does not permit an *understanding* of Brecht's work. For Brecht cannot become the horizon of judgment and simultaneously be understood in his distinctiveness. If one makes Brecht the yardstick for what literature can accomplish today, Brecht himself can no longer be judged and the question whether the solution he found for certain problems is tied to the period of its creation or not can no longer be asked. In other words: it is precisely when one attempts to grasp Brecht's epochal significance that his theory must not be made the framework of the investigation. To resolve this aporia, I would propose that the historical avant-garde movements be seen as a break in the development of art in bourgeois society, and that literary theory be conceived on the basis of this break. Brecht's work and theory also would have to be defined with reference to this historical discontinuity. The question then would be: what is Brecht's relation to the historical avant-garde movements? So far, this question has not been asked, because Brecht was taken for an avant-gardiste and a precise concept of historical avant-garde movements did not exist. This complex question cannot be examined here, of course, and we will have to content ourselves with a few suggestions.

Brecht never shared the intention of the representatives of the historical avant-garde movements to destroy art as an institution. Even the young Brecht who despised the theater of the educated bourgeoisie (*Bildungsbürgertum*) did not conclude that the theater should be abolished altogether; instead, he proposed to radically change it. In sport, he found the model for a new theater whose central category is fun.[12]

Not only does the young Brecht define art as its own end and thus retain a central category of classical aesthetics: he intends to change rather than destroy the theater as an institution, and thus makes clear the distance that separates him from the representatives of the historical avant-garde movements. What they and Brecht share is, first, a conception of the work in which the individual elements attain autonomy (this being the condition that must be met if alienation is to become effective) and, second, the attention he devotes to art as an institution. But whereas the avant-gardistes believe they can directly attack and destroy that institution, Brecht develops a concept that entails a change of function and sticks to what is concretely achievable. These few comments may have shown that a theory of the avant-garde permits one to situate Brecht within the context of modern art and thereby to define his distinctiveness. There is thus reason to assume that a theory of the avant-garde can contribute to a resolution of the aporia of materialist literary scholarship (between Lukács and Adorno) as sketched above, and that this can be done without canonizing Brecht's theory and artistic practice.

It goes without saying that the thesis being advanced here refers not only to Brecht's work but to the place of political engagement in art generally. It is this: through the historical avant-garde movements, the place of political engagement in art was fundamentally changed. In consonance with the twofold definition of the avant-garde as given above (attack on art as institution and the coming into existence of a nonorganic work of art), the question will have to be discussed at both levels. That there existed political and moral engagement in the art preceding the historical avant-garde movements is beyond doubt. But the relationship between this engagement and the work in which it articulated itself is strained. In the organic work of art, the political and moral contents the author wishes to express are necessarily subordinated to the organicity of the whole. This means that whether the author wants to or not, they become parts of the whole, to whose constitution they contribute. The engaged work can be successful only if the engagement itself is the unifying principle that articulates itself throughout the work (and this includes its form). But this is rarely the case. The degree to which already existing traditions in a genre can resist being used for purposes of moral or political engagement can be observed in Voltaire's tragedies and the freedom lyric of the Restoration. In the organic work of art, the danger is always present that engagement remains external to the form–content totality and destroys its substance. It is at this level of argument that most criticism of engaged art moves. But two presuppositions must be met if this argument is to claim validity: it applies only to organic works of art, and only when engagement has not been made the unifying principle of the work. Where the author is successful in organizing the work around the engagement, another danger threatens the political tendency: neutralization through the institution that is art. Received in the context of artifacts whose shared characteristic is their apartness from the praxis of life, the work that shapes engagement according to the aesthetic law of organicity tends to be perceived as a 'mere' art product. Art as an institution neutralizes the political content of the individual work.

The historical avant-garde movements made clear the significance art as an institution has for the effect of individual works, and thereby brought about a shift in the problem. It became apparent that the social effect of a work of art cannot simply be gauged by considering the work itself but that its effect is decisively determined by the institution within which the work 'functions'.

Had there never been any avant-garde movements, Brecht's and Benjamin's reflections from the twenties and thirties regarding a restructuring of the production apparatus[13] would not have been possible. Here also, however, one will have to take care not to adopt Brecht's and Benjamin's *solutions* along with their recognition of the problem and to transfer them ahistorically to the present.[14]

For the shift in the problem of engagement, the development of a type of nonorganic work is as important as the attack on art as an institution. If, in the avant-gardiste work, the individual element is no longer necessarily subordinate to an organizing principle, the question concerning the place value of the political contents of the work also changes. In the avant-gardiste work, they are aesthetically legitimate even as individual elements. Their effect is not necessarily mediated through the whole of the work but to be thought of as standing on its own.[15] In the avant-gardiste work, the individual sign does not refer primarily to the work as a whole but to reality. The recipient is free to respond to the individual sign as an important statement concerning the praxis of life, or as political instruction. This has momentous consequences for the place of engagement within the work. Where the work is no longer conceived as organic totality, the individual political motif also is no longer subordinate to the work as a whole but can be effective in isolation. On the basis of the avant-gardiste type of work, a

new type of engaged art becomes possible. One may even go a step
further and say that the avant-gardiste work does away with the old
dichotomy between 'pure' and 'political' art, although it will have to be
made clear what the sentence means. Following Adorno, it may mean
that the structural principle of the nonorganic is emancipatory in itself,
because it permits the breakup of an ideology that is increasingly
congealing into a system. In such a view, avant-garde and engagement
ultimately coincide. But since the identity rests wholly in the structural
principle, it follows that engaged art is defined only formally, not in its
substance. The tabooing of political art in the avant-gardiste work is just
one step away from this. But the abolition of the dichotomy between
'pure' and 'political' art can take a different form. Instead of declaring the
avant-gardiste structural principle of the nonorganic itself to be a political
statement, it should be remembered that it enables political and
nonpolitical motifs to exist side by side in a single work. On the basis of
the nonorganic work, a new type of engaged art thus becomes possible.[16]

To the extent that individual motifs in the avant-gardiste work are
largely autonomous, the political motif also can have a direct effect: the
spectator can confront it with life as he experiences it. Brecht recognized
and made use of this possibility. In his *Arbeitsjournal,* he writes: 'in the
Aristotelian composition of plays and the acting that goes along with it
. . . the delusion of the spectator concerning the way events on the stage
take place in real life and come about there is furthered by the fact that
the presentation of the fable constitutes an absolute whole. The details
cannot be individually compared with those parts which correspond to
them in real life. Nothing must be "taken out of context" to set it into the
context of reality. This is changed by a performance that produces
estrangement. Here, the progress of the fable is discontinuous, the
unified whole consists of independent parts each of which can and
indeed must be directly confronted with the corresponding partial events
in reality.'[17] Brecht is avant-gardiste to the extent that the avant-garde
work of art makes possible a new kind of political art because it frees the
parts from their subordination to the whole. Brecht's comments make
clear that although the avant-garde work of art necessarily falls short of
attaining the goal of the historical avant-garde movements, which is the
revolutionizing of the praxis of life, it yet preserves their intent.
Although the total return of art to the praxis of life may have failed, the
work of art entered into a new relationship to reality. Not only does
reality in its concrete variety penetrate the work of art but the work no
longer seals itself off from it. It must be remembered, however, that it is
art as an institution that determines the measure of political effect avant-
garde works can have, and that art in bourgeois society continues to be a
realm that is distinct from the praxis of life.

Concluding Remark and a Comment on Hegel

We have seen that Hegel historicizes art but not the *concept* of art. Although it has its origins in Greek art, he accords metahistorical validity to it. Szondi is correct in this observation: 'While in Hegel everything starts to move and everything has its specific place value in historical development . . . the concept of art can hardly develop for it bears the unique stamp of Greek art.'[18] Yet Hegel was perfectly aware that this concept of art was inappropriate to the works of his time: 'If in considering them [works of art] we keep before our eyes the essential nature of works of art proper (i.e., the Ideal) where the important thing is both a subject matter not inherently arbitrary and transient and also a mode of portrayal fully in correspondence with such a subject-matter, then in the face of works of that kind the art products of the stage we are now considering must undoubtedly fall far short.'[19]

We recall that for Hegel, romantic art (which takes in the period from the Middle Ages to Hegel's time) is already the dissolution of the interpenetration of form and content which was the characteristic of classical (Greek) art. This dissolution is caused by the discovery of autonomous subjectivity.[20] The principle of romantic art is the 'elevation of the spirit to itself' (*Esthetics*, vol.I, p.518), which is the result of Christianity. Spirit no longer immerses itself in the sensuous as in classical art but returns to itself and thus posits 'external reality as an existence inadequate to it' (ibid.). Hegel sees a connection between the development of the autonomous subjectivity and the contingency of external existence. For that reason, romantic art is both an art of subjective inwardness and one that portrays the world of phenomena in their contingency:

> External appearance cannot any longer express the inner life, and if it is still called to do so, it merely has the task of proving that the external is an unsatisfying existence and must point back to the inner, to the mind and feeling as the essential element. But just for this reason romantic art leaves externality to go its own way again for its part freely and independently, and in this respect allows any and every material down to flowers, trees, and the commonest household gear, to enter the representation without hindrance even in its contingent natural condition (vol.I, p.527).

For Hegel, romantic art is the product of the dissolution of the interpenetration of spirit and sensuousness (external appearance) characteristic of classical art. But beyond that, he conceives of a further stage where romantic art also dissolves. This is brought about by the radicalization of the opposites of inwardness and external reality that define romantic art. Art disintegrates into 'the subjective imitation of the given' (realism of detail) and 'subjective humor'. Hegel's aesthetic theory thus leads logically to the idea of the end of art where art is understood to be what Hegel meant by classicism, the perfect interpenetration of form and content.

But outside his system, Hegel at least sketched the concept of a post-romantic art.[21] Using Dutch genre painting as his example, he writes that here the interest in the object turns into interest in the skill of presentation: 'What should enchant us is not the subject of the painting and its lifelikeness, but the pure appearance (*interesseloses Scheinen*) which is wholly without the sort of interest that the subject has. The one thing certain about beauty is, as it were, appearance [semblance (*Scheinen*)] for its own sake, and art is mastery in the portrayal of all the secrets of this ever profounder pure appearance (*Scheinen*) of external realities' (vol.I, p.598). What Hegel alludes to here is nothing other than what we called the developing autonomy of the aesthetic. He says expressly 'that the artist's subjective skill and his application of the means of artistic production are raised to the status of an objective matter in works of art' (vol.I, p.599). This announces the shift of the form–content dialectic in favor of form, a development that characterizes the further course of art.

What we deduced for post avant-gardiste art from the failure of avant-gardiste intentions, the legitimate side-by-side existence of styles and forms of which none can any longer claim to be the most advanced, is already observed by Hegel with reference to the art of his time. 'Herewith we have arrived at the end of romantic art, at the standpoint of most recent times, the peculiarity of which we may find in the fact that the artist's subjective skill surmounts his material and its production because he is no longer dominated by the given conditions of a range of content and form already inherently determined in advance, but retains entirely within his own power and choice both the subject-matter and the way of presenting it' (vol.I, p.602). Hegel grasps the development of art with the pair of concepts 'subjectivity:external world' (or spirit:sensuousness). The analysis here presented, on the other hand, is based on the crystallization of social subsystems and thus arrives at the antithesis between art and the praxis of life. That as early as the 1820s Hegel should have been able to foresee what did not definitively occur until after the failure of the historical avant-garde movements demonstrates that speculation is a mode of cognition.

The standard for any contemporary theory of aesthetics is Adorno's, whose historicalness has become recognizable. Now that the development of art has passed beyond the historical avant-garde movements, an aesthetic theory based on them (such as Adorno's) is as historical as Lukacs's, which recognizes only organic works as works of art. The total availability of material and forms characteristic of the post avant-gardiste art of bourgeois society will have to be investigated both for its inherent possibilities and the difficulties it creates, and this concretely, by the analysis of individual works.

Whether this condition of the availability of all traditions still permits an aesthetic theory at all, in the sense in which aesthetic theory existed from Kant to Adorno, is questionable, because a field must have a structure if it is to be the subject of scholarly or scientific understanding. Where the formal possibilities have become infinite, not only authentic creation but also its scholarly analysis become correspondingly difficult. Adorno's notion that late-capitalist society has become so irrational[22] that it may well be that no theory can any longer plumb it applies perhaps with even greater force to post avant-gardiste art.

Notes

1. See GEORG LUKÁCS, *The meaning of Contemporary Realism* (London: Merlin Press, 1962).

2. See TH. W. ADORNO, 'Erpresste Versöhnung, Zu Georg Lukács: "Wider den missverstandenen Realismus"', in Adorno, *Noten zur Literatur II* (Frankfurt: Suhrkamp, 1963), pp. 152–87.

3. G. W. F. HEGEL, *Esthetics*, trans. T. M. Knox (Oxford: Clarendon Press, 1975), vol. I, p. 517.

4. See also the 'concluding comment' in this book.

5. The two elements of Lukács's theory of the avant-garde, i.e., historical necessity of the genesis of avant-gardiste art and its rejection on aesthetic grounds, are also recognizable in the essay, 'Narrate or Describe', in Arthur D. Kahn, ed., trans., *Writer and Critic and other Essays* (New York: Grosset and Dunlap, 1970), pp. 110–48. Lukács contrasts the description, which is functionally subordinate to the whole in Balzac, and its treatment in Flaubert and Zola, where it exists for its own sake. He refers to this as 'the product of a social development', but also criticizes it: 'necessity can also be the necessity for the artistically false, distorted, and corrupt'.

6. See G. LUKÁCS, *The Meaning of Contemporary Realism* (London, 1962).

7. It may seem surprising that Adorno should endorse the concept of technical progress in art, considering that together with Horkheimer (in *Dialectic of Enlightenment* [Herder & Herder, 1972]), he showed the radical difficulties in technical progress: although technical progress opens up the possibility of an existence more worthy of man, that is by no means its inevitable result. The diverse attitude toward industrial technique on the one hand, and artistic technique on the other is owing to Adorno's separation of the two. See B. LINDNER, 'Brecht/Benjamin/Adorno. Über Veränderungen der Kunstproduktion im wissenschaftlichtechnischen Zeitalter', in H. L. Arnold, ed., *Bertold Brecht I*, (München: Sonderband der Reihe *Text + Kritik*, 1972), pp. 14–36. But one certainly cannot reproach Critical Theory with identifying 'the economic production relations with the technical structure of the productive

forces' (Lindner, p. 27). Critical Theory reflects the historical experience that the unfolding of the productive forces does not necessarily break up the production relations, that, on the contrary, it may perfectly well make available the means for the control of man. 'The signature of the age is the preponderance of production relations over the forces of production which have long since made a mockery of them.' (TH. W. ADORNO, 'Einleitungsvortrag zum 16. deutschen Soziologentag', in Th. W. Adorno, ed., *Verhandlungen des 16. deutschen Soziologentages vom 8. bis 11. April 1968 in Frankfurt. Spätkapitalismus oder Industriegesellschaft?*, (Stuttgart, 1969), p. 20.

8. 'Art finds itself within reality, has its functions in reality, and entertains a relationship of manifold mediation to it. That does not change the fact that as art, in its very concept, it is the antithesis of what is the case' (TH. W. ADORNO, "Erpresste Versöhnung," in *Noten II*, p. 163.) This sentence defines with precision the distance separating Adorno from the most radical aims of the European avant-garde movements: the clinging to the autonomy of art.

9. On functional analysis, see chapter one of this volume.

10. TH. W. ADORNO, 'Selbstanzeige' for *Versuch über Wagner* (1952), reprinted in *Die Zeit*, 9 (Oct. 1964), p. 23.

11. In the *Ästhetische Theorie*, Adorno attempted an appropriate judgment on and evaluation of Brecht. But that does not change the fact that Adorno's theory leaves no room for a writer such as Brecht.

12. See B. BRECHT, 'Emphasis on Sport', in John Willett, ed., trans., *Brecht on Theatre. The development of an aesthetic* (New York: Hill and Wang, 1966), p. 48.

13. See B. BRECHT, 'Radiotheorie', in Brecht, *Schriften zur Literatur und Kunst*, vol. I (Berlin/Weimar, 1966), pp. 125–47; W. BENJAMIN, 'The Author as Producer', in *Walter Benjamin, Reflections*, trans. Edmund Jephcott (New York: Harcourt Brace Jovanovich, 1978), and W. BENJAMIN, 'The Work of Art in the Age of Mechanical Reproduction', in *Illuminations* (New York: Schocken, 1969).

14. This occurs in H. M. ENZENSBERGER, 'Baukasten zu einer Theorie der Medien', in *Kursbuch*, no. 20 (1970), pp. 159–86. Reprinted in Enzensberger, *Palaver* (Frankfurt/Main, 1974).

15. Seen from this perspective, it would seem that my interpretation of the opening pages of Aragon's *Paysan de Paris* should be reconsidered. The comment early in the analysis that description in the *Paysan* 'is no longer functionally related to something else . . . but the subject of the story' (P. Bürger, *Der französische Surrealismus*, p. 104) is not adequately taken into account when the documentation relating to the misery of the expropriated merchants is evaluated (p. 109). The avant-gardiste work is no longer centered on a principle but can bring divergent approaches at one and the same time. Social condemnation and a sense of the end of things are found side by side without its being admissible to maintain that a given element is the dominant one, as is the case in the organic work.

16. The nonorganic work makes it possible to rephrase the question concerning the possibility of engagement. The criticism that has often been leveled against engaged art did not recognize this. It still treats the problem as if it were a question of determining the place of political contents in the organic work. In other words: Criticism has ignored the change in the problem due to the historical avant-garde movements.

17. B. BRECHT, *Arbeitsjournal*, ed. W. Hecht (Frankfurt, 1973), p. 140; entry of August 3, 1940.

18. P. SZONDI, 'Hegels Lehre von der Dichtung', in Szondi, *Poetik und Geschichtsphilosophie* (Frankfurt: Suhrkamp, 1974), p. 305.

19. G. W. HEGEL, *Esthetics*, vol. I, p. 596.

20. If, for Greece, 'the immediate coalescence of the individual with the universality of politics' (*Esthetics*, vol. I, p. 510) is characteristic, 'the need for a higher freedom of the subject in himself' (*Esthetics*, vol. I, p. 510) awakens for the first time with Socrates, a need that subsequently became dominant in Christianity. Compare the section devoted to Socrates in Hegel's *Lectures on the Philosophy of History*.

21. See W. OELMÜLLER, *Die unbefriedigte Aufklärung. Beiträge zu einer Theorie der Moderne von Lessing, Kant und Hegel* (Frankfurt: Suhrkamp, 1969), pp. 240–64.

22. See TH. W. ADORNO, Einleitungsvortrag zum 16. Deutschen Soziologentag, p. 17.

Repositioning Modernism

In a late essay Raymond Williams confirmed that the theoretical contours and associated authors of 'modernism' promoted 'a highly selected version of the modern which then offers to appropriate the whole of modernity'. 'We have only to review the names in the real history', he adds, 'to see the open ideologizing which permits the selection.' (*The Politics of Modernism* (1989), p. 33.) The following essays represent the active attempt to counter this orthodoxy and recover the 'real history'; even to show that this reality is comprised not of a single history but of the non-synchronous movement of different histories with different uses for 'modernism'.

Marshall Berman's *All that is Solid Melts into Air* appeared, appropriately enough, to have dissolved all the settled categories of a canonic modernism. His modernists include not only Baudelaire and Joyce but Goethe and Marx, and his modernist epoch stretches from 1600, or in its period of greatest intensity, from the eighteenth century to the present. This is a full and progressive modernism, embracing philosophy, architecture and urban planning as well as literature, all of them powered by the vision of a transformed human society.

In an important response to Berman's study, Perry Anderson returned modernism to its familiar period home in the early twentieth century ('Modernity and Revolution' in Nelson and Grossberg (eds), *Marxism and the Interpretation of Culture* (1988), pp. 317–33). To replace Berman's epochal or 'planar' narrative Anderson urged a 'conjunctural analysis' which set modernism in a triangulated intersection of the changing economic, political and class factors arising before 1914. These coordinates – summarised as 'a semi-aristocratic ruling order, a semi-industrialised capitalist economy, and a semi-emergent, or insurgent labour movement' (ibid., p. 326) – comprised modernism's conditions of possibility. Raymond Williams's essay makes a special contribution to this debate, turning our attention to the processes of modernism's formation, and to the artist's changed position in the metropolitan milieu.

These perspectives have brought a new vigour and specificity, and, in Williams's word, a necessary 'strangeness', to the study of modernism. Yet certain additional factors, though brought into view, remain on the periphery: the questions of female suffrage and national identity in the early modern period, for example, and the general importance of gender and race. As Jean Radford's essay and the following selections here show, questions of gender, or race and cultural identity do not simply add to, but alter our sense of modernist coordinates, affecting the formation and, importantly, the reformations of modernism. The implication is that 'modernism' emerged and has mutated, under definite conditions, through a series of conjunctures. If it seems now, therefore, in its 'ideologised' or most orthodox forms, to be a finished and empty category, it can, in new readings and settings, present a still radical example and resource.

5 Marshall Berman, 'The Twentieth Century: the Halo and the Highway'*

In an unconventionally broad picture of modernism, Marshall Berman views cultural modernism as mediating between the social and political experience of modernity and its corresponding processes of scientific and technical modernisation. True aesthetic modernity comes fully to register the many-sidedness – the expansions as well as the constrictions – of economic and self-development in modern urban life. What follows, however, perhaps inevitably, is a narrative of loss, as the tradition (in Marx, Goethe and Baudelaire) of transformative analysis, self-discovery and creation, forged in the midst of earlier complexities, is seen to recede before a tide of greater complexity and dissolution. The advantage of Berman's perspective is that it frees modernism from a narrowly defined literary enclave and inspires a dynamic and original reading of authors, texts and environments. The evangelical Marxist humanism, moreover, which leads him to urge a contemporary collective renewal of modernism's submerged creative energies, stands in sharp contrast to the pessimism of other positions, notably of Frankfurt School 'critical theory'.

The reference to 'the halo' in the extract which follows alludes simultaneously to Marx's belief in *The Communist Manifesto* that bourgeois society has stripped formerly honoured professions (the doctor, lawyer, priest, poet) of their halo in making them wage-labourers and to Charles Baudelaire's prose poem 'Loss of a halo', which depicts the 'primal modern scene' of the poet's loss of his halo. Berman discusses both image and poem elsewhere in his study (pp. 115–20, 155–64). This central common theme of 'desanctification' also clearly relates to Walter Benjamin's argument on the autonomous work of art's loss of its 'aura' (see above, pp. 45–9).

See Perry Anderson's 'Modernity and Revolution' and Berman's

---

* Reprinted from *All that is Solid Melts into Air. The Experience of Modernity* (London: Verso, 1983), pp. 164–171.

response in *New Left Review*, **144** (March–April 1984); also Janet Wolff's 'The Invisible *Flâneuse'* on the exclusion of women in the literature and criticism of modernity (in A. Benjamin (ed.) *The Problems of Modernity* (1989), pp. 141–52). Of related interest is Angela Carter's story 'Black Venus' (1985) which subverts Baudelaire's male eroticism with a discourse representing his mulatto mistress, Jeanne Duval.

In many ways, the modernism of Baudelaire's primal modern scenes is remarkably fresh and contemporary. In other ways, his street and his spirit seem almost exotically archaic. This is not because our epoch has resolved the conflicts that give *Paris Spleen* its life and energy – class and ideological conflicts, emotional conflicts between intimates, conflicts between the individual and social forces, spiritual conflicts within the self – but rather because our epoch has found new ways to mask and mystify conflict. One of the great differences between the nineteenth and twentieth centuries is that our century has created a network of new haloes to replace the ones that Baudelaire's and Marx's century stripped away.

Nowhere is this development clearer than in the realm of urban space. If we picture the newest urban spatial complexes we can think of – all those that have been developed, say, since the end of the Second World War, including all our newer urban neighborhoods and new towns – we should find it hard to imagine Baudelaire's primal encounters happening here. This is no accident: in fact, for most of our century, urban spaces have been systematically designed and organized to ensure that collisions and confrontations will not take place here. The distinctive sign of nineteenth-century urbanism was the boulevard, a medium for bringing explosive material and human forces together; the hallmark of twentieth-century urbanism has been the highway, a means for putting them asunder. We see a strange dialectic here, in which one mode of modernism both energizes and exhausts itself trying to annihilate another, all in modernism's name.

What makes twentieth-century modernist architecture especially intriguing to us here is the very precisely Baudelairean point from which it starts out – a point that it soon does its best to blot out. Here is Le Corbusier, possibly the greatest twentieth-century architect and certainly the most influential, in *L'Urbanisme* (translated as *The City of Tomorrow*), his great modernist manifesto of 1924. His Preface evoked a concrete experience from which, so he tells us, his great vision arose. We shouldn't take him literally, but rather understand his narrative as a modernist parable, formally similar to Baudelaire's. It began on a boulevard – specifically, on the Champs Elysées – on an Indian summer evening in 1924. He had gone for a peaceful walk in the evening twilight, only to find himself driven off the street by traffic. This is half a century after Baudelaire, and the automobile has arrived on the boulevards full force: 'it was as if the world had suddenly gone mad'. From moment to moment, he felt, 'the fury of the traffic grew. Every day increased its agitation'. (Here the time frame and the dramatic intensity are somewhat broken.) Le Corbusier felt himself threatened and vulnerable in the most direct way: 'To leave our house meant that, once we had crossed our threshold, we were in danger of being killed by the passing cars.' Shocked and disoriented, he contrasts the street (and the city) of his middle age with that of his youth before the Great War: 'I think back twenty years, to my youth as a student: *the road belonged to us then*; we sang in it, we argued in it, while the horse-bus flowed softly by.' (Emphasis mine.) He is expressing a plaintive sadness and bitterness as old as culture itself, and one of poetry's perennial themes; *Où sont les neiges d'antan*? Whither hath fled the visionary gleam? But his feeling for the textures of urban space and historical time making his nostalgic vision free and new. 'The road belonged to us then.' The young students' relation to the street was their relation to the world: it was – at least it seemed to be – open to them, theirs to move through, at a pace that could accommodate both argument and song; men, animals and vehicles could coexist peaceably in a kind of urban Eden; Haussmann's enormous vistas spread out before them all, leading to the Arc de Triomphe. But now the idyll is over, the streets belong to the traffic, and the vision must flee fcr its life.

How can the spirit survive this change? Baudelaire showed us one way: transform the *mouvements brusques* and *soubresauts* of modern city life into the paradigmatic gestures of a new art that can bring modern men together. At the ragged edge of Baudelaire's imagination we glimpsed another potential modernism: revolutionary protest that transforms a multitude of urban solitudes into a people, and reclaims the city street for human life. Le Corbusier will present a third strategy that will lead to a third, extremely powerful mode of modernism. After fighting his way through the traffic, and just barely surviving, he makes a sudden daring leap: he identifies himself totally with the forces that have been bearing down on him:

On that 1st of October, 1924, I was assisting in the titanic rebirth [*renaissance*] of a new phenomenon . . . traffic. Cars, cars, fast, fast! One is seized, filled with enthusiasm, with joy . . . the joy of power. The simple and naïve pleasure of being in the midst of power, of strength. One participates in it. One takes part in this society that is just dawning. One has confidence in this new society: it will find a magnificent expression of its power. One believes in it.

This Orwellian leap of faith is so fast and so dazzling (just like that traffic) that Le Corbusier hardly seems to notice that he has made it. One moment he is the familiar Baudelairean man in the street, dodging and fighting the traffic; a moment later his point of view has shifted radically, so that now he lives and moves and speaks from *inside* the traffic. One moment he is speaking about himself, about his own life and experience – 'I think back twenty years . . . the road belonged to us then'; the next moment the personal voice utterly disappears, dissolved in a flood of world-historical processes; the new subject is the abstract and impersonal *on*, 'one', who is filled with life by the new world power. Now, instead of being menaced by it, he can be in the midst of it, a believer in it, a part of it. Instead of the *mouvements brusques* and *soubresauts* that Baudelaire saw as the essence of everyday modern life, Le Corbusier's modern man will make one big move that will make further moves unnecessary, one great leap that will be the last. The man in the street will incorporate himself into the new power by becoming the man in the car.

The perspective of the new man in the car will generate the paradigms of twentieth-century modernist urban planning and design. The new man, Le Corbusier says, needs 'a new type of street' that will be 'a machine for traffic', or, to vary the basic metaphor, 'a factory for producing traffic'. A truly modern street must be 'as well equipped as a factory'. In this street, as in the modern factory, the best-equipped model is the most thoroughly automated: no people, except for people operating machines; no unarmoured and unmechanized pedestrians to slow the flow. 'Cafés and places of recreation will no longer be the fungus that eats up the pavements of Paris.' In the city of the future, the macadam will belong to the traffic alone.

From Le Corbusier's magic moment on the Champs Elysées, a vision of a new world is born: a fully integrated world of high-rise towers surrounded by vast expanses of grass and open space – 'The tower in the park' – linked by aerial superhighways, serviced by subterranean garages and shopping arcades. This vision had a clear political point, stated as the last words of *Towards a New Architecture*: 'Architecture or Revolution. Revolution can be avoided.'

The political connections were not fully grasped at the time – it is not clear whether Le Corbusier entirely grasped them himself – but we should be able to understand them now. *Thesis*, a thesis asserted by urban people starting in 1789, all through the nineteenth century, and in the great revolutionary uprisings at the end of World War One: the streets belong to the people. *Antithesis*, and here is Le Corbusier's great contribution: no streets, no People. In the post-Haussmann city street, the fundamental social and psychic contradictions of modern life converged and perpetually threatened to erupt. But if this street could only be wiped off the map – Le Corbusier said it very clearly in 1929: 'We must kill the street!' – then maybe these contradictions need never come to a head. Thus modernist architecture and planning created a modernized version of pastoral: a spatially and socially segmented world – people here, traffic there; work here, homes there; rich here, poor there; barriers of grass and concrete in between, where haloes could begin to grow around people's heads once again.[1]

This form of modernism has left deep marks on all our lives. The city development of the last forty years, in capitalist and socialist countries alike, has systematically attacked, and often successfully obliterated, the 'moving chaos' of nineteenth-century urban life. In the new urban environment – from Lefrak City to Century City, from Atlanta's Peachtree Plaza to Detroit's Renaissance Center – the old modern street, with its volatile mixture of people and traffic, businesses and homes, rich and poor, is sorted out and split up into separate compartments, with entrances and exits strictly monitored and controlled, loading and unloading behind the scenes, parking lots and underground garages the only mediation.

All these spaces, and all the people who fill them, are far more ordered and protected than any place or anybody in Baudelaire's city could be. The anarchic, explosive forces that urban modernization once brought together, a new wave of modernization, backed by an ideology of developing modernism, has pulled apart. New York is now one of the very few American cities in which Baudelaire's primal scenes can still take place. And these old cities or segments of cities are under pressures far more threatening than the ones that gripped them in Baudelaire's day. They are economically and politically condemned as obsolete, beset by chronic blight, sapped by disinvestment, cut off from opportunities for growth, constantly losing ground in completion with areas that are considered more 'modern'. The tragic irony of modernist urbanism is that its triumph has helped to destroy the very urban life it hoped to set free.[2]

Corresponding in a most curious way to this flattening out of the urban landscape, the twentieth century has also produced a dismal flattening out of social thought. Serious thinking about modern life has polarized itself into two sterile antitheses, which may be called, as I suggested earlier, 'modernolatry' and 'cultural despair'. For modernolators, from Marinetti and Mayakovsky and Le Corbusier to Buckminster Fuller and the later Marshall McLuhan and Herman Kahn, all the personal and social dissonances of modern life can be resolved by technological and administrative means; the means are all at hand, and the only thing needful is leaders with the will to use them. For the visionaries of cultural despair, from T.E. Hulme, and Ezra Pound and Eliot and Ortega, onward to Ellul and Foucault, Arendt and Marcuse, all of modern life seems uniformly hollow, sterile, flat, 'one-dimensional', empty of human possibilities: anything that looks or feels like freedom or beauty is really only a screen for more profound enslavement and horror. We should note, first of all, that both these modes of thought cut across the political divisions of left and right; second, that many people have clung to both these poles at different points in their lives, and some have even tried to cling to both at once. We can find both polarities in Baudelaire, who, indeed might lay claim to having invented both. But we can also find in Baudelaire something that is missing in most of his successors: a will to wrestle to the end of his energy with modern life's complexities and contradictions, to find and create himself in the midst of the anguish and beauty of its moving chaos.

It is ironic that both in theory and in practice the mystification of modern life and the destruction of some of its most exciting possibilities have gone on in the name of progressive modernism itself. And yet in spite of everything, that old moving chaos has kept – or perhaps has renewed – its hold on a great many of us. The urbanism of the past two decades has conceptualized and consolidated this hold. Jane Jacobs wrote the prophetic book of this new urbanism: *The Death and Life of Great American Cities*, published in 1961. Jacobs argued brilliantly, first, that the urban spaces created by modernism were physically clean and orderly, but socially and spiritually dead; second, that it was only the vestiges of nineteenth century congestion, noise and general dissonance that kept contemporary urban life alive, third, that the old urban 'moving chaos' was in fact a marvelously rich and complex human order, unnoticed by modernism only because its paradigms of order were mechanical, reductive and shallow; and finally, that what still passed for modernism in 1960 might turn out to be evanescent and already obsolete.[3] In the last two decades, this perspective has gathered widespread and enthusiastic assent, and masses of Americans have worked steadfastly to save their neighborhoods and cities from the ravages of motorized modernization. Every movement to stop the construction of a highway is a movement to give the old moving chaos a new lease on life. Despite sporadic local successes, no one has had the power to break the accumulated power of the halo and the highway. But there have been enough people with enough passion and dedication to create a strong undertow, to give city life a new tension and excitement and poignancy while it lasts. And there are signs that it may last longer than anyone – even those who loved it most – would have thought. Amid the fears and anxieties of the contemporary energy crisis, the motorized pastoral appears to be breaking down. As it does, the moving chaos of our nineteenth-century modern cities looks more orderly and more up-to-date every day. Thus Baudelaire's modernism, as I have portrayed it here, may turn out to be even more relevant in our time than it was in his own; the urban men and women of today may be the ones to whom he was truly, in his image, *épousé*.

All this suggests that modernism contains its own inner contradictions and dialects; that forms of modernist thought and vision may congeal into dogmatic orthodoxies and become archaic; that other modes of modernism may be submerged for generations, without ever being superseded; and that the deepest social and psychic wounds of modernity may be repeatedly sealed, without ever being really healed. The contemporary desire for a city that is openly troubled but intensely alive is a desire to open up old but distinctively modern wounds once more. It is a desire to live openly with the split and unreconciled character of our lives, and to draw energy from our inner struggles, wherever they may lead us in the end. If we learned through one modernism to construct haloes around our spaces and ourselves, we can learn from another modernism – one of the oldest but also, we can see now, one of the newest – to lose our haloes and find ourselves anew.

Notes

1. Le Corbusier was never able to make much headway in his undefatigable schemes for destroying Paris. But many of his most grotesque visions were realized in the Pompidou era, when elevated highways cleft the Right Bank, the great markets of Les Halles were demolished, dozens of thriving streets were razed and substantial and venerable neighborhoods were turned over to 'les promoteurs' and obliterated without a trace. See Norma Evenson, *Paris: A Century of Change, 1878–1978* (Yale, 1979); Jane Kramer, 'A Reporter In Europe: Paris'. *The New Yorker* (19 June 1978); Richard Cobb, 'The Assassination of Paris', *New York Review of Books* (7 February 1980); and several of Godard's later films, particularly *Two or Three Things I know About Her* (1973).

2. This needs to be qualified. Le Corbusier dreamt of an ultramodernity that could heal the city's wounds. More typical of the modernist movement in architecture was an intense and unqualified hatred for the city, and a fervent hope that modern design and planning could wipe it out. One of the primary modernist clichés was the comparison of the metropolis to the stagecoach or (after World War One) to the horse and buggy. A typical modernist orientation toward the city can be found in *Space, Time and Architecture*, a monumental work by Le Corbusier's most articulate disciple, and the book that, more than any other, was used for two generations to define the modernist canon. The book's original edition, composed in 1938–39, concludes with a celebration of Robert Moses' new network of urban highways, which Giedion sees as the ideal model for the planning and construction of the future. The highway demonstrates that 'there is no longer any place for the city street, with heavy traffic running between rows of houses; it cannot possibly be permitted to persist' (p. 832). This idea comes directly out of *The City of Tomorrow*; what is different, and disturbing, is the tone. Le Corbusier's lyrical, visionary enthusiasm has been replaced by the truculent and threatening impatience of the commissar. 'Cannot possibly be permitted to persist': can the police be far behind? Even more ominous is what comes next: the urban

highway complex looks forward to the time when, after the necessary surgery has been performed, the artificial city will be reduced to its natural size'. This passage, which has the chilling effect of a marginal note by Mr Kurtz, suggests how, for two generations of planners, the campaign against the street was only one phase of a wider war against the modern city itself.

The antagonism between modern architecture and the city is explored sensitively by Robert Fishman, *Urban Utopias in the Twentieth Century* (Basic Books, 1977).

3. 'It is disturbing to think that men who are young today, men who are being trained now for their careers, should accept, *on the grounds that they should be modern in their thinking*, conceptions about cities and traffic which are not only unworkable, but also to which nothing new of any significance has been added since their fathers were children.' *Death and Life of Great American Cities* (Random House and Vintage, 1961), p. 371; Jacob's emphasis. The Jacobs perspective is developed interestingly in Richard Sennett, *The Uses of Disorder: Personal Identity and City Life* (Knopf, 1970), and in Robert Caro, *The Power Broker: Robert Moses and the Fall of New York* (Knopf, 1974). There is also a rich European literature in this vein. See, for instance, Felizitas Lenz-Romeiss, *The City: New Town or Home Town* (1970), translated from the German by Edith Kuestner and Jim Underwood (Praeger, 1973).

    Within the architectural profession, the critique of Le Corbusier's mode of modernism, and of the sterilities of the International Style as a whole, begins with Robert Venturi, *Complexity and Contradiction in Architecture*, with an Introduction by Vincent Scully (Museum of Modern Art, 1966). In the past decade it has come not only to be generally accepted but to generate an orthodoxy of its own. This is codified most clearly in Charles Jencks, *The Language of Post-Modern Architecture* (Rizzoli, 1977).

6 Raymond Williams, 'The Metropolis and the Emergence of Modernism'*

Raymond Williams suggests that the key social basis of modernism lies in the experience of immigration from the provinces to the metropolis. This central and startling insight means that he can both point to continuities with an earlier experience of urban industrial culture and situate what was distinctive, socially and artistically, in the early twentieth-century metropolis. For immigration, Williams argues, intensified and shifted the themes of the crowd and alienation, of unity and diversity characterising perceptions of the urban or industrial centre during the nineteenth century. In lieu of an inherited sense of community, this experience produced the modernist attention to the artistic medium itself. The much observed 'autonomy' and 'self-consciousness' of modernist art is therefore freshly historicised. Any universalising claim for modernism becomes untenable, since its particular conditions and forms are seen now to belong in the early twentieth century, to 'the imperial and capitalist metropolis'.

Modernism's historical parameters lead Williams briefly to consider the 'deprived hinterlands' and 'poor world' outside the metropolis. We might reflect too on those who experienced the modern city differently, though on the inside: women modernists, for example, or American modernists committed in their own terms to a strong sense of urban idiom and locale. And we might ask how this account would alter in relation to the experience of enforced exile in the thirties, sometimes for the same generation of deracinated, but more freely mobile, artists of the 1910s and twenties.

A further question inevitably arises. Williams writes from a literally postmodernist position, beyond modernism's historical moment and

---

* Reprinted from *Unreal City. Urban Experience in Modern European Literature and Art*, ed. Edward Timms and David Kelley (Manchester: Manchester University Press and New York: St Martin's Press (1985), pp. 13–24.

its canonisation, yet is disdainful of postmodernism's glossy consumerism. What then, of value, can supersede modernism? If Williams's writing seems to suggest a return to realism, his lasting interest in Ibsen's 'modernist naturalism' and in the mixed modes of film and television suggest what a complex alternative this would be.

See Williams, *The Politics of Modernism* (1989); Bradbury and McFarlane (eds), *Modernism*, Part One: **3** (1976), and further essays in Timms and Kelley (eds), *Unreal City* (1985).

Modernism as a critical concept

It is now clear that there are decisive links between the practices and ideas of the avant-garde movements of the twentieth century and the specific conditions and relationships of the twentieth-century metropolis. The evidence has been there all along, and is indeed in many cases obvious. Yet until recently it has been difficult to disengage this specific historical and cultural relationship from a less specific but widely celebrated (and execrated) sense of 'the modern'.

In the late twentieth century it has become increasingly necessary to notice how relatively far back the most important period of 'modern art' now appears to be. The conditions and relationships of the early twentieth-century metropolis have in many respects both intensified and been widely extended. In the simplest sense, great metropolitan aggregations, continuing the development of cities into vast conurbations, are still historically increasing (at an even more explosive rate in the Third World). In the old industrial countries, a new kind of division between the crowded and often derelict 'inner city' and the expanding suburbs and commuter developments has been marked. Moreover, within the older kinds of metropolis, and for many of the same reasons, various kinds of avant-garde movement still persist and even flourish. Yet at a deeper level the cultural conditions of the metropolis have decisively changed.

The most influential technologies and institutions of art, though they are still centred in this or that metropolis, extend and indeed are directed beyond it, to whole diverse cultural areas, not by slow influence but by immediate transmission. There could hardly be a greater cultural contrast than that between the technologies and institutions of what is still mainly called 'modern art' – writing, painting, sculpture, drama, in minority presses and magazines, small galleries and exhibitions, city-centre theatres – and the effective output of the late twentieth-century metropolis, in film, television, radio and recorded music. Conservative analysts still reserve the categories 'art' or 'the arts' to the earlier technologies and institutions, with continued attachment to the metropolis as the centre in which an enclave can be found for them or in which they can, often as a 'national' achievement, be displayed. But this is hardly compatible with a continued intellectual emphasis on their 'modernity', when the actual modern media are of so different a kind. Secondly, the metropolis has taken on a much wider meaning, in the extension of an organised global market in the new cultural technologies. It is not every vast urban aggregation, or even great capital city, which has this cultural metropolitan character. The effective metropolis – as is shown in the borrowing of the word to indicate relations between nations, in the neo-colonial world – is now the modern transmitting metropolis of the technically advanced and dominant economies.

Thus the retention of such categories as 'modern' and 'modernism' to describe aspects of the art and thought of an undifferentiated twentieth-century world is now at best anachronistic, at worst archaic. What accounts for the persistence is a matter for complex analysis, but three elements can be emphasised. First, there is a factual persistence, in the old technologies and forms but with selected extensions to some of the new, of the specific relations between minority arts and metropolitan privileges and opportunities. Secondly, there is a persistent intellectual hegemony of the metropolis, in its command of the most serious publishing houses, newspapers and magazines, and intellectual institutions, formal and especially informal. Ironically, in a majority of cases, these formations are in some important respects residual: the intellectual and artistic forms in which they have their main roots are for social reasons – especially in their supporting formulations of 'minority' and 'mass', 'quality' and 'popular' – of that older, early twentieth-century period, which for them is the perennially 'modern'. Thirdly, and most fundamentally, the central product of that earlier period, for reasons which must be explored, was a new set of 'universals', aesthetic, intellectuals and psychological, which can be sharply contrasted with the older 'universals' or specific cultures, periods and faiths, but which in just that quality resist all further specificities, of historical change or of cultural and social diversity: in the conviction of what is beyond question and for all effective time the 'modern absolute', the defined universality of a human condition which is effectively permanent.

There are several possible ways out of this intellectual deadlock, which now has so much power over a whole range of philosophical, aesthetic and political thinking. The most effective involve contemporary analysis in a still rapidly changing world. But it is also useful, when faced by this curious condition of cultural stasis – curious because it is a stasis which is continually defined in dynamic and experientially precarious terms – to identify some of the processes of its formation: seeing a present beyond 'the modern' by seeing how, in the past, that specifically absolute 'modern' was formed. For this indentification, the facts of the development of the city into the metropolis are basic. We can see how certain themes in art and thought developed as specific responses to the new and expanding kinds of nineteenth-century city and then, as the central point of analysis, see how these went through a variety of actual artistic transformations, supported by newly offered (and competitive) aesthetic universals, in certain metropolitan conditions of the early twentieth century: the moment of 'modern art'.

Nineteenth-century antecedents to the theme of urban alienation

It is important to emphasise how relatively old some of these apparently modern themes are. For that is the inherent history of themes at first contained within 'pre-modern' forms of art which then in certain conditions led to actual and radical changes of form. It is the largely hidden history of the conditions of these profound internal changes which we have to explore, often against the clamour of the 'universals' themselves.

For convenience I will take examples of the themes from English literature, which is particularly rich in them. Britain went through the first stages of industrial and metropolitan development very early, and almost at once certain persistent themes were arrived at. Thus the effect of the modern city as a crowd of strangers was identified, in a way that was to last, by Wordsworth:

> O Friend! one feeling was there which belonged
> to this great city, by exclusive right;
> How often, in the overflowing streets,
> Have I gone forward with the crowd and said
> Unto myself, 'The face of every one
> That passes by me is a mystery!'
>
> Thus have I looked, nor ceased to look, oppressed
> By thoughts of what and whither, when and how,
> Until the shapes before my eyes became
> A second-sight procession, such as glides
> Over still mountains, or appears in dreams.
> And all the ballast of familiar life,
> The present, and the past; hope and fear; all stays
> All laws of acting, thinking, speaking man
> Went from me, neither knowing me, nor known.[1]

What is evident here is the rapid transition from the mundane fact that the people in the crowded street are unknown to the observer – though we now forget what a novel experience that must in any case have been to people used to customary small settlements – to the now characteristic interpretation of strangeness as 'mystery'. Ordinary modes of perceiving others are seen as overborne by the collapse of normal relationships and their laws: a loss of 'the ballast of familiar life'. Other people are then seen as if in 'second sight' or, crucially, as in dreams: a major point of reference for many subsequent modern artistic techniques.

Closely related to this first theme of the crowd of strangers is a second major theme, of an individual lonely and isolated within the crowd. We can note some continuity in each theme from more general Romantic motifs: the general apprehension of mystery and of extreme and precarious forms of consciousness; the intensity of a paradoxical self-realisation in isolation. But what has happened, in each case, is that an apparently objective milieu, for each of these conditions, has been identified in the newly expanding and overcrowded modern city. There are a hundred cases, from James Thomson to George Gissing and beyond, of the relatively simple transition from earlier forms of isolation and alienation to their specific location in the city. Thomson's poem, 'The Doom of a City' (1857), addresses the theme explicitly, as 'Solitude in the midst of a great City':

> The cords of sympathy which should have bound me
> In sweet communication with earth's brotherhood
> I drew in tight and tighter still around me,
> Strangling my lost existence for a mood.[2]

Again, in the better-known 'City of Dreadful Night' (1870), a direct relationship is proposed between the city and a form of agonised consciousness:

> The City of Night, but not of Sleep;
> There sweet sleep is not for the weary brain;
> The pitiless hours like years and ages creep,
> A night seems termless hell. This dreadful strain
> Of thought and consciousness which never ceases,
> Of which some moment's stupor but increases,
> This, worse than woe, makes wretches there insane.[3]

There is direct influence from Thomson in Eliot's early city poems. But more generally important is the extension of the association between isolation and the city to alienation in its most subjective sense: a range from dream or nightmare (the formal vector of 'Doom of a City'), through the distortions of opium or alcohol, to actual insanity. These states are being given a persuasive and ultimately conventional social location.

On the other hand, alienation in the city could be given a social rather than a psychological emphasis. This is evident in Elizabeth Gaskell's interpretation of the streets of Manchester in *Mary Barton*, in much of Dickens, especially in *Dombey and Son*, and (though here with more emphasis on the isolated and crushed observer) in Gissing's *Demos* and *The Nether World*. It is an emphasis drawn out and formally argued by Engels:

> They crowd by one another as though they had nothing in common, nothing to do with one another . . . The brutal indifference, the unfeeling isolation of each in his private interest becomes the more repellent and offensive, the more these individuals are crowded together, within a limited space. And, however much one may be aware that this isolation of the individual, this narrow self-seeking is the fundamental principle of our society everywhere, it is nowhere so shamelessly barefaced, so self-conscious as just here in the crowding of the great city. The dissolution of mankind into monads . . . is here carried out to its utmost extremes.[4]

These alternative emphases of alienation, primarily subjective or social, are often fused or confused within the general development of the theme. In a way their double location within the modern city has helped to override what is otherwise a sharp difference of emphasis. Yet both the alternatives and their fusion or confusion point ahead to observable tendencies in twentieth-century avant-garde art, with its at times fused, at times dividing, orientations towards extreme subjectivity (including subjectivity as redemption or survival) and social or social/cultural revolution.

There is also a third theme, offering a very different interpretation of the strangeness and crowding and thus the 'impenetrability' of the city. Already in 1751 Fielding had observed:

> Whoever considers the Cities of London and Westminster, with the late vast increases of their suburbs, the great irregularity of their buildings, the immense numbers of lanes, alleys, courts and bye-places, must think that had they been intended for the very purpose of concealment they could not have been better contrived.[5]

This was a direct concern with the facts of urban crime, and the emphasis persisted. The 'dark London' of the late nineteenth century, and particularly the East End, were often seen as warrens of crime, and one important literary response to this was the new figure of the urban detective. In Conan Doyle's *Sherlock Holmes* stories there is a recurrent image of the penetration by an isolated rational intelligence of a dark area of crime which is to be found in the otherwise (for specific physical reasons, as in the London fogs, but also for social reasons, in that teeming, maze-like, often alien area) impenetrable city. This figure has persisted in the urban 'private eye' (as it happens, an exact idiom for the basic position in consciousness) in cities without the fogs.

On the other hand, the idea of 'darkest London' could be given a social emphasis. It is already significant that the use of statistics to understand an otherwise too complex and too numerous society had been pioneered in Manchester from the 1830s. Booth in the 1880s applied statistical survey techniques to London's East End. There is some relation between these forms of exploration and the generalising panoramic perspectives of some twentieth-century novels (Dos Passos, Tressell). There were naturalistic accounts from within the urban environment, again with an emphasis on crime, in several novels of the 1890s, for example, Morrison's *Tale of Mean Streets* (1894). But in general it was as late as the 1930s, and then in majority in realist modes, before any of the actual inhabitants of these dark areas wrote their own perspectives, which included the poverty and the squalor but also, in sharp contradiction to the earlier accounts, the neighbourliness and community which were actual working-class responses.

A fourth general theme can, however, be connected with this explicit late response. Wordsworth, interestingly, saw not only the alienated city but new possibilities of unity:

> Among the multitudes
> Of that huge city, oftentimes was seen
> Affectingly set forth, more than elsewhere
> Is possible, the unity of men.[6]

What could be seen, as often in Dickens, as a deadening uniformity, could be seen also, as again in Dickens and indeed, crucially, in Engels, as the site of new kinds of human solidarity. The ambiguity had been there from the beginning, in the interpretation of the urban crowd as 'mass' or 'masses', a significant change from the earlier 'mob'. The masses could indeed be seen, as in one of Wordsworth's emphases, as:

> slaves unrespited of low pursuits,
> Living amid the same perpetual flow
> Of trivial objects, melted and reduced
> To one identity . . .[7]

But 'mass' and 'masses' were also to become the heroic, organising words of working-class and revolutionary solidarity. The factual development of new kinds of radical organisation within both capital and industrial cities sustained this positive urban emphasis.

A fifth theme goes beyond this, but in the same positive direction. Dickens's London can be dark, and his Coketown darker. But although, as also later in H.G. Wells, there is a conventional theme of escape to a more peaceful and innocent rural spot, there is a specific and unmistakable emphasis of the vitality, the variety, the liberating diversity and mobility of the city. As the physical conditions of the cities were improved, this sense came through more and more strongly. The idea of the pre-Industrial and pre-metropolitan city as a place of light and learning, as well as of power and magnificence, was resumed with a special emphasis on physical light: the new illuminations of the city. This is evident in very simple form in Le Gallienne in the 1890s:

> London, London, our delight,
> Great flower that opens but at night,
> Great city of the midnight sun,
> Whose day begins when day is done.
>
> Lamp after lamp against the sky
> Opens a sudden beaming eye,
> Leaping a light on either hand
> The iron lilies of the Strand.[8]

The metropolis as a melting-pot: new attitudes to the medium of art

It is not only the community, it is also the diversity of these themes, composing as they do so much of the repertory of modern art, which should now be emphasised. Although modernism can be clearly identified as a distinctive movement, in its deliberate distance from and challenge to more traditional forms of art and thought, it is also strongly characterised by its internal diversity of methods and emphases: a restless and often directly competitive sequence of innovations and experiments, always more immediately recognised by what they are breaking from than by what, in any simple way, they are breaking towards. Even the range of basic cultural positions, within modernism, sketches from an eager embrace of modernity, either in its new technical and mechanical forms or in the equally significant attachments to ideas of social and political revolution, to conscious options for past or exotic cultures, as sources or at least as fragments *against* the modern world.

Many elements of this diversity have to be related to the specific cultures and situations within which different kinds of work and position were to be developed, though within the simpler ideology of modernism this is often resisted: the innovations being directly related only to themselves (as the related critical procedures of formalism and structuralism came to insist). But the diversity of position and method has another kind of significance. The themes, in their variety, including as we have seen diametrically opposite as well as diverse attitudes to the city and its modernity, had formerly been included within relatively traditional forms of art. What then stands out as new, and is in this defining sense 'modern', is the series (including the competitive sequence) of breaks in form. Yet if we say only this we are carried back inside the ideology, ignoring the continuity of themes from the nineteenth century and isolating the breaks of form, or worse, as often in subsequent pseudo-histories, relating the formal breaks to the themes as if both were comparably innovative. For it is not the general themes of response to the city and its modernity which compose anything that can be properly called modernism. It is rather the new and specific location of the artists and intellectuals of this movement within the changing cultural milieu of the metropolis.

For a number of social and historical reasons the metropolis of the second half of the nineteenth century and of the first half of the twentieth century moved into a quiet new cultural dimension. It was now much more than the very large city, or even the capital city of an important nation. It was the place where new social and economic and cultural relations, beyond both city and nation in their older senses, were beginning to be formed: a distinct historical phase which was in fact to be extended, in the second half of the twentieth century, at least potentially, to the whole world.

In the earliest phases this development had much to do with imperialism: with the magnetic concentration of wealth and power in imperial capitals and the simultaneous cosmopolitan access to a wide variety of subordinate cultures. But it was always more than the orthodox colonial system. Within Europe itself there was a very marked unevenness of development, both within particular countries, where the distances between capitals and provinces widened, socially and culturally, in the uneven developments of industry and agriculture, and of a monetary economy and simple subsistence of market forms. Even more crucial differences emerged between individual countries, which came to compose a new kind of hierarchy not simply, as in the old terms, of military power, but in terms of development and thence of perceived enlightenment and modernity.

Moreover, both within many capital cities, and especially within the major metropolises, there was at once a complexity and a sophistication of social relations, supplemented in the most important cases – Paris, above all – by exceptional liberties of expression. This complex and open milieu contrasted very sharply with the persistence of traditional social, cultural and intellectual forms in the provinces and in the less developed countries. Again, in what was not only the complexity but the miscellaneity of the metropolis, so different in these respects from traditional cultures and societies beyond it, the whole range of cultural activity could be accommodated.

The metropolis housed the great traditional academies and museums and their orthodoxies; their very proximity and powers of control were both a standard and a challenge. But also, within the new kind of open, complex and mobile society, small groups in any form of divergence or dissent could find some kind of foothold, in ways that would not have been possible if the artists and thinkers composing them had been scattered in more traditional, closed societies. Moreover, within both the miscellaneity of the metropolis – which in the course of capitalist and imperialist development had characteristically attracted a very mixed population, from a variety of social and cultural origins – and its concentration of wealth and thus opportunities of patronage, such groups could hope to attract, indeed to form, new kinds of audience. In the early stages the foothold was usually precarious. There is a radical contrast between these often struggling (and quarrelling and competitive) groups, who between them made what is now generally referred to as 'modern art', and the funded and trading institutions, academic and commercial, which were eventually to generalise and deal in them. The continuity is one of underlying ideology, but there is still a radical difference between the two generations: the struggling innovators and the modernist establishment which consolidated their achievement.

Thus the key cultural factor of the modernist shift is the character of the metropolis: in these general conditions but then, even more decisively, in its direct effects on form. The most important general element of the innovations in form is the fact of immigration to the metropolis, and it cannot too often be emphasised how many of the major innovators were, in this precise sense, immigrants. At the level of theme, this underlies, in an obvious way, the elements of strangeness and distance, indeed of alienation, which so regularly form part of the repertory. But the decisive aesthetic effect is at a deeper level. Liberated or breaking from their national or provincial cultures, placed in quite new relations to those other native languages or native visual traditions, encountering meanwhile a novel and dynamic common enviroment from which many of the older forms were obviously distant, the artists and

91

writers and thinkers of this phase found the only community available to them: a community of the medium; of their own practices.

Thus language was perceived quite differently. It was no longer, in the old sense, customary and naturalised, but in many ways arbitrary and conventional. To the immigrants especially, with their new second common language, language was more evident as a medium – a medium that could be shaped and reshaped – than as a social custom. Even within a native language, the new relationships of the metropolis, and the inescapable new uses in newspapers and advertising attuned to it, forced certain productive kinds of strangeness and distance: a new consciousness of conventions and thus of changeable, because now open, conventions. There had long been pressures towards the work of art as artefact and commodity, but these now greatly intensified, and their combined pressures were very complex indeed. The preoccupying visual images and styles of particular cultures did not disappear, any more than the native languages, native tales, the native styles of music and dance, but all were now passed through this crucible of the metropolis, which was in the important cases no mere melting-pot but an intense and visually and linguistically exciting process in its own right, from which remarkable new forms emerged.

At the same time, within the very openness and complexity of the metropolis, there was no formed and settled society to which the new kinds of work could be related. The relationships were to the open and complex and dynamic social process itself, and the only accessible form of this practice was an emphasis on the medium: the medium as that which, in an unprecedented way, defined art. Over a wide and diverse range of practice this emphasis on the medium, and on what can be done in the medium, became dominant. Moreover, alongside the practice, theoretical positions of the same kind, most notably the new linguistics, but also the new aesthetics of significant form and structure, rose to direct, to support, to reinforce and to recommend. So nearly complete was this vast cultural reformation that, at the levels directly concerned – the succeeding metropolitan formations of learning and practice – what had once been defiantly marginal and oppositional became, in its turn, orthodox, although the distance of both from other cultures and peoples remained wide. The key to this persistence is again the social form of the metropolis, for the facts of increasing mobility and social diversity, passing through a continuing dominance of certain metropolitan centres and a related unevenness of all other social and cultural development, led to a major expansion of metropolitan forms of perception, both internal and imposed. Many of the direct forms and media-processes of the minority phase of modern art thus became what could be seen as the common currency of majority communication, especially in films (an art form created, in all important respects, by these perceptions) and in advertising.

It is then necessary to explore, in all its complexity of detail, the many variations in this decisive phase of modern practice and theory. But it is also time to explore it with something of its own sense of strangeness and distance, rather than with the comfortable and now internally accommodated forms of its incorporation and naturalism. This means, above all, seeing the imperial and capitalist metropolis as a specific historical form, at different stages: Paris, London, Berlin, New York. It involves looking, from time to time, from outside the metropolis: from the deprived hinterlands, where different forces are moving, and from the poor world which has always been peripheral to the metropolitan systems. This need involve no reduction of the importance of the major artistic and literary works which were shaped within metropolitan perceptions. But one level has certainly to be challenged: the metropolitan interpretation of its own processes as universals.

The power of metropolitan development is not to be denied. The excitements and challenges of its intricate processes of liberation and alienation, contact and strangeness, stimulation and standardisation, are still powerfully available. But it should no longer be possible to present these specific and traceable processes as if they were universals, not only in history but as it were above and beyond it. The formulation of the modernist universals is in every case a productive but imperfect and in the end fallacious response to particular conditions of closure, breakdown, failure and frustration. From the necessary negations of these conditions, and from the stimulating strangeness of a new and (as it seemed) unbonded social form, the creative leap to the only available universality – of raw material, of medium, of process – was impressively and influentially made.

At this level as at others – 'modernisation' for example – the supposed universals belong to a phase of history which was both creatively preceded and creatively succeeded. While the universals are still accepted as standard intellectual procedures, the answers come out as impressively as the questions determine. But then it is characteristic of any major culture phase that it takes its local and traceable positions as universal. This, which modernism saw so clearly in the past which it was rejecting, remains true for itself. What is succeeding it is still uncertain and precarious, as in its own initial phases. But it can be foreseen that the period in which social strangeness and exposure isolated art as only a medium is due to end, even within the metropolis, leaving from its most active phases the new cultural monuments and their academies which in their turn are being challenged.

Notes

1. *Prelude, VII; Wordsworth: Poetical Works,* ed. de Selincourt and Darbishire (London, 1949), p. 261.

2. Ridler (ed.) *Poems and Some Letters of James Thomson,* (London, 1963), p. 25.

3. Ibid., p. 180.

4. Friedrich Engels, *The Condition of the Working Class in England in 1844,* trans. F.K. Wischnewetzky (London, 1934), p. 24.

5. Henry Fielding, *Inquiry into the Cause of the Late Increase of Robbers* (1751), p. 76.

6. Wordsworth, op. cit., p. 286.

7. Ibid., p. 292.

8. C. Trent, *Greater London,* London (1965), p. 200.

7 Jean Radford, from 'Coming to terms: Dorothy Richardson, Modernism and Women'*

Book-length feminist studies of modernism only began to appear from the late eighties (Benstock, *Women of the Left Bank*, 1987; Hanscombe and Smyers, *Writing for their Lives*, 1987; Gilbert and Gubar, *No Man's Land*, vols 1 and 2; 1989; 1990). In her essay Jean Radford traces the approaches taken in French and Anglo-American feminism, including some of the above. Both, she suggests, have ironically reinforced the cultural and aesthetic authority of the canonic model of modernism. Her own argument is that 'the feminist project, at its most radical, affects *what* is read, *how* it is read, and perhaps even *who* reads' and that therefore rethinking modernism entails a broader, more fundamental reconstruction of 'English' in education. These considerations determine her discussion of the search for 'a new more feminine form' and ways of reading this in Dorothy Richardson's *Pilgrimage* (as well as explaining why this novel remains so unread). The general procedures and priorities of her essay, especially the intertextual conjunctural analysis which Radford recommends, suggest a comparison with Anderson's 'Modernity and Revolution' (1984) referred to above (p. 66). The narrative of Richardson's novel also, of a woman's being forced out of her class and into the metropolitan job market, suggest a comparison with the poet and male professional's 'loss of a halo' discussed by Marshall Berman and Williams's account of the immigrant situation of the modernist artist in the previous essay.

See the later contributions by Kristeva and Kipnis and the headnotes to these (pp. 197–212). As well as the book-length studies mentioned above, see Bonnie Kime Scott (ed.), *The Gender of Modernism* (1990) and Huyssen, 'Mass culture as Woman: Modernism's Other' in *After the Great Divide* (1986), pp. 44–62. Two articles which

---

* Reprinted from *News from Nowhere*, 7 (Winter, 1989), pp. 25–36.

consider gender and modernism are Naomi Segal, 'Sexual Politics and The Avant-Garde' in Timms and Collier, *Visions and Blueprints* (1988), pp. 235–49 and Peter Nicholls 'Futurism, Gender and Theories of Postmodernity', *Textual Practice*, **3**: 2 (Summer 1989), pp. 202–21.

One of the effects of the postmodernism debate has been to reopen the case of 'modernism', that umbrella term under which early twentieth-century cultural objects were assembled and settled into syllabuses by various academics in the fifties. Despite some efforts, by Marxist critics and cultural historians, to dispense with the term, Eng. Lit. continued to refine and redefine both 'modernism' and its membership. Joyce, Pound and Eliot – with Woolf as the token woman – were its senior members, but was Henry James a closet realist? Did Yeats finally make it? Etc. etc. . . .

Over the last ten years, the development of critical theory has had the paradoxical effect of revalorising or reinvigorating certain flagging courses like modernism, because literature of this type brings into the foreground questions of language and representation. The 'Great Authors' of the modernist canon provide a convenient stamping ground for theoretical debates. One strand of feminist criticism has noticeably contributed here, by posing women's writing (or rather *écriture féminine*) as a prime example of anti-realist conventions. Realism, in this kind of argument, is identified as 'masculine', and disruptions or departures from it are, in terms of this binary logic, equated with the feminine – the feminine is taken as an instance of the subversive or dissident, the return of what is repressed from the dominant culture. Cixous and Kristeva theorise such elements in male-authored texts by Joyce and others, in different ways; but in practice – I've found in my own teaching – the result has often been disappointing. Although the theories have changed, the material theorised (the canon) remains in place. It has proved easier to look for the seminotic chora in *Ulysses* than in, say, suffragette autobiographies of the period.

Feminist criticism started of course from a critique of male writing, if we take Kate Millett's *Sexual Politics* as one such starting point. Her polemical reading of D.H. Lawrence, for example, opened up the whole question of 'value'. It offered me, as a student in the early seventies, a model of the resisting reader, of how one might read canonical texts against the grain. It put questions of gender and reader activity on the agenda, and the re-reading of the great tradition and the modernist canon as it stood in the early seventies was launched.

In the so-called second-wave of feminist criticism, the emphasis shifted from men's to women's writing, to the re-reading of women-authored texts and the rediscovery of what Elaine Showalter called 'the lost continent' of women's writing. The positive effects of this project, supported by feminist publishing houses and the work of social and cultural historians, have been enormous and ongoing. It has helped to undermine the Art/popular divide and to expose the links between criticism and pedagogy by treating the literary texts as 'fields of exploration and critique rather than materials for transmission'.[1] The insistence that women's writings be read in terms of the social and political conditions in which they are produced and reproduced, recharged the old debates about 'literature and history' by offering concrete instances of what in much Marxist criticism had become a rather abstract 'call to history'. Generating new questions at each step, the feminist project, at its most radical, affects *what* is read, *how* it is read, and perhaps even *who* reads. For the women's movement has produced a new readership outside or across traditional disciplinary boundaries, a non-professional 'amateur' reader to whose interests feminist criticism also speaks. And, as Jonathan Culler, that most highly referenced professional reader, says: 'The rights of amateurs should be asserted, for the amateur's perspective has special value.'[2]

Back in the institutional frame, the feminist intervention has had two main effects on the teaching of 'modernism' within English studies:

(1) The unequal representation of women writers on modernist courses led into 'representivity' arguments, to the demand for fair shares of the canonical cake – a redivision of spoils so that writers like Katherine Mansfield, Dorothy Richardson, H. D., Gertrude Stein, etc., could be given equal speaking time on the same platform. This seems to me positive insofar as it works against the 'token' woman writer and the reading practices that go with that position. For the token woman writer, like Virginia Woolf, is always read as 'Woman', 'different from Man in some absolute sense',[3] but with half a dozen women writers, sexual difference has to be related to other kinds of difference: class, ethnicity, sexual orientation. Thus the differences between or within women writers come into view.

However, the struggle to get these figures onto the syllabus has too often been argued on the grounds of their being 'good enough' to join the Great Authors, thus capitulating to the terms of the great tradition. In this case, affirmation as a political project slips into an aesthetics of affirmation as a method of reading the literary text, as Jacqueline Rose says: 'In this context the affirmation of the woman writer – her retrieval from one history of inequality and subordination – can paradoxically produce a complicity with another [system of inequality and subordination].'[4] Thus the attack on the privileged group is transmuted into a demand to join that group and the feminist critic becomes, in Gramsci's terms, just another 'expert in legitimation'.

(2) The alternative strategy was to focus on women writers as a counter-history to the dominant literary paradigms. This proved useful in posing new material as the object of study or by reading the same material in different contexts with different questions. In some cases, however, this has led to the construction of rival canons, to great traditions of *The Madwomen of the Attic* type, or to *Women of the Left Bank* or *Modernist Women* being posed as alternatives to *The Men of 1914*.

Both these developments stem from the proposition 'that feminist critics do not accept the view that the canon reflects the objective value judgements of history and posterity, but see it instead as a culture-bound political construct';[5] but neither of these feminist initiatives managed to shift the problem of the canon from its central position within literary studies. Different but convergent attempts by black critics and left cultural historians at 'firing the canon' have met with similar difficulties. As Pierre Macherey noted some years ago, talking about the inclusion of comic strips into cultural analysis:

Far from changing the initial context by studying different material, these different materials have in fact completely reinforced the traditional categories and systems of thinking. (In that sense nothing has changed – on the contrary a supplementary system of camouflage has been produced.) It is not simply a question of the mechanical introduction and consideration of new material in literary studies; we must also completely change the system in which the categories of literary studies are thought out.[6]

Since then, it has become even clearer that although the material (the reading lists for Modernism courses, for example) has changed, the categories remain largely in place. New theories and new material will not *in themselves* enable us to change the categories of literary studies. Rethinking 'Modernism' involves rethinking 'English' as a subject, rethinking the Humanities and what, in the midst of arguments about market forces and centres of excellence, their role in the Education of the nineties might become.

Moving back from these thoughts to 'Dorothy Richardson', I want then *not* to make a case for her on the Modernism ticket, but to ask why at present *Pilgrimage* is not widely read and in what ways it might be.

For at present, it seems to me, *Pilgrimage* is not read; the first of its four volumes reprinted by Virago in 1979 is now out of print,[7] but the subsequent volumes remain on the shelves. It remains one of those books 'that culturally literate people have read about but haven't read'.[8] The problem, it is said, is its length: the thirteen serial novels ('chapters' as Richardson called them) number over two thousand pages. The body of this text is too big, too bulky to be good canon fodder; a loose baggy monster, it exasperates its readers and critics by its excessive length, its shapelessness, its naricissism. 'Feminine without the charm', as Lionel Trilling called it. It goes on and on, pleonastic, plotless, like some interminable analysis which refuses to come to an end. The thirteenth novel, *March Moonlight*, is indeed an unfinished, unrevised draft, which Dent included in the posthumous 1967 edition. Only Richardson's death (and her publishers) brought it to a close.

Richardson's rejection of linear story-based narratives and her dissatisfaction with current forms is of course common to the period. As she stated in the Preface to the 1939 edition of *Pilgrimage*: 'The material that moved me to write would not fit the framework of any novel I had experienced . . . I believed myself intolerant of the romantic and the realist novel alike. Each . . . left out certain essentials.' The same point, the same phrase, is used within the novel by the heroine, when discussing contemporary novelists: 'The torment of all novels is what is left out . . . Bang, bang, bang, on they go, these men's books, like an LCC tram, yet unable to make you forget them, the authors, for a moment.'[9] The anxiety about what is 'left out' of male fiction may be one reason for the inclusion of enormous amounts of description, for the repetition of narrative movements which might have been condensed or composited. So the 'excessive' length, as I read it, is a symptom of the search for a new, more feminine, form and is crucial to Richardson's poetics of the novel. This search is motivated within the text by the heroine's growing sense that narrative conventions are simply an organisation of the fantasies of the dominant culture and are dependent, as Richardson wrote elsewhere, 'on a whole set of questionable agreements and assumptions between reader and writer'.[10] Where Joyce *uses* these dominant fantasies, playfully, parodically, Richardson attempts to evade them, to write round them, continually dispersing any 'story interest' into descriptions of her heroine's thought processes and surroundings. The six-page description of Miriam's room at the beginning of *The Tunnel* (II, pp. 11–17) is one example of this method in practice.

Given the fact, as Rachel Blau du Plessis argues in *Writing Beyond the Ending*, 'that "story" for women typically meant plots of seduction, courtship, [where] the energies of quest are deflected into . . . the choice of a marriage partner',[11] the enormous lack of 'story' in this novel may be read as a defensive structure, a form of resistance which itself testifies to the power of the dominant narrative forms. In a similar way, the deferral of the ending (Richardson's publishers constantly pressured her to provide one as the novels continued to appear through the twenties and thirties), may be read as a refusal of the still hegemonic closure devices of marriage and death, as an attempt to keep her narrative options open. Just as, somewhat differently, the enormous and protracted close-up of Miriam Henderson's 'consciousness' constitutes a resistance to 'character' – to 'character' as the set of possible representations of women available in previous narrative discourses. There is much more that could be said about gender and the ideological significance of form in *Pilgrimage* but which I don't have time to go into here.

Let me return for a moment to the problem of reading *Pilgrimage*. If not based on 'story' interest, what inducement does it offer the reader to read on – and on? As Jonathan Culler points out, one of 'the basic conventions governing the novel is the expectation that readers will be able to recognise a world which it produces and to which it refers'.[12] The 'recognition effect' is maintained by the inclusion of descriptive detail (trivial gestures, insignificant objects, superfluous dialogue). 'In a description of a room, for example, items which are not picked up and integrated by symbolic or thematic codes . . . and which do not have a function in the plot produce what Barthes calls a "reality effect".' Their function, Culler goes on to argue, is to confirm the mimetic contract and assure the reader that he or she can interpret the text as about a real world, and after a process of recognition and identification the reader can move on or back 'to compose and give meaning to what has been identified'. The interpretive activity – the second move in this cycle of reading – can then take place.

But 'if the text undertakes an excessive proliferation of elements whose function seems purely referential' – as I would argue is the case with *Pilgrimage* – the interpretive activity (meaning-construction) is problematised. For example, it is difficult, though not impossible, to construct the thematic purpose of the description of Miriam's room at the beginning of *The Tunnel*. Descriptions like these 'seem determined only by a desire for objectivity', and thus the reader can construct the world (or room) but finds it difficult to construct a meaning for it. 'A mania of precision produces *une thématique vide*.'

Pilgrimage thus breaks with the nineteenth-century contract as described by Barthes and Culler. It uses physical description, the descriptive residue, repeatedly and at great length – not to ensure the 'reality effect', but as a means to impel the reader onward toward the ever-deferred point where its significance will become recognisable. It is a double-edged strategy in that it risks losing the reader unwilling to defer his or her interpretive pleasures. With this type of writing (Joyce is a key example), criticism is used to point to the interpretive options, and the interpretive problem is shifted from reader to critic. The two moves in Culler's cycle of reading are thus split between the amateur reader and the professional critic. *Pilgrimage*, lacking the kind of interpretive apparatus which surrounds *Ulysses* or *Finnegans Wake* is left to the transferences of its amateur readers.[13]

One way it might become an interpretable text, I want to argue next, is to read it as a dialogue with other discourses of the period. What those discourses are is very clearly signalled in *Pilgrimage* via references to the heroine's own reading: of Villette in *Pointed Roofs*, of Ouida in *Backwater*, of Darwin, Geddes, Schenk in *The Tunnel*, of the Fabian pamphlets and the titles from science, religion and philosophy which feature in the subsequent volumes; of Goethe and Schiller and the German romantics, and the fiction of Wells and Bennett, Conrad and James. These names and the italicised titles operate as signposts, not only for Miriam Henderson's discursive journey, but for a reading of *Pilgrimage* as a polemic set within and against the late Victorian/Edwardian discourses about class, gender and being English in a specific period. I want therefore, briefly, to outline some of the ways in which Richardson stages her dialogue and her differences with the discourses of her time. Not to give the *vide* a content, but to suggest ways in which it might be structured.

'Difference' and 'being different' are key terms within the novel sequence, both in the gender-based sense that Virginia Woolf refers to in 'Women and Fiction', but also in the sense that Raymond Williams refers to when he characterises the 'modernist project' as 'taking nothing as it appeared but looking for deep forms, deep structures with the eyes of a stranger'.[14] Richardson was not an exile or an emigré in the literal sense that Pound, Eliot, Joyce and Conrad were, but because she looks 'with the eyes of a stranger' at the life of a middle-class English woman. It is her own life in the period 1891–1912, read from another period, 1912–46. A past recreated as an enormous present, the minutiae of daily life operate as a 'making strange', a defamiliarised image of the writer's own class and the values and conditions it created for women during a period of transition. The 'blow-up' of surface appearances, can be read then, not as the naturalism deplored by Lukács, but as a way of looking for the 'deep forms and shaping forces' which produce those appearances.

So, for example, *Pilgrimage* could be said to reflect upon what Eric Hobsbawm in *Age of Empire* describes as 'the uncertainties of the bourgeoisie',[15] through the consciousness of a character forced out of her class (by the father's bankruptcy) and into the job-market – untrained, unskilled, without capital or income. After a brief anachronistic 'impersonation' of the governess role, she becomes a clerical worker – part of the growing tertiary sector staffed mainly by the lower middle-class and the upwardly mobile working class; an employee of the type of professional men she once met socially at tennis parties and musical evenings. The precision of detail about accent, voice and manner registers this class-displacement as both individual trauma and a presentation of the anxieties over demarcation lines within the bourgeoisie at the turn of the century. Poised below the 'secure' rentier class of her childhood, and above the 'abyss' of the working-classes, Miriam Henderson looks 'with the eyes of a stranger': with hatred and longing at the forms of class life she has left, with shame and anxiety at the shifts and deprivations of the lower middle-class world she has joined.

Existing in genteel poverty on her £1 a week, eating frugally in the new ABC restaurants serving the clerical world of London, her intellectual development is a conscious project to realise her condition and, the text suggests, less consciously a desire to redeem it. Unlike Forster's caricature of the bourgeois writer of the period – 'In came the dividends, up went the lofty thoughts' – Dorothy Richardson locates her heroine's 'lofty thoughts' as both an attempt to understand and disguise the struggle for survival. Attempts to get back to the safety of bourgeois life, through marriage for example, confirm Miriam's growing estrangement: 'There were other eyes looking at it. Those eyes were inside her: not caring for the things she had cared for, dragging her away from them' (II, p. 109). The syntactic oddity/irregularity here is, by the way, typical of *Pilgrimage*. It marks the dissolution of the unitary 'she' (who 'had cared for' certain things), and the presence of a new vision or viewpoint ('eyes inside her'); but these 'other eyes' are not integrated into being *her* eyes, they remain 'Those eyes': other. Miriam, one might say, is like a Monica Madden with the eyes of a Rhoda Nunn, but unlike Gissing's odd women, in Richardson's rewriting, her character does not die in childbirth (nor succumb to drink), she lives to tell the tale of these internal differences.

Entering a *déclassé* circle of writers and intellectuals, centred around Hypo Wilson (a fictionalised H. G. Wells), she glimpses the possibility of a new community which would accept her with all her differences: 'They knew one was "different" and liked it. . . . It made them a home and a refuge' (II, p. 131). But once again this is followed by a separating-out, a definition of her incompatibility with other members of the group, the male Fabians and the bohemian women. This movement of identification, of 'belonging', followed by rejection or self-imposed exile, is repeated in each of the thirteen novels. The major 'events' of *Pilgrimage* are a series of attractions and withdrawals, from social groups, from sexual relationships, from new definitions of self. The text charts this compulsive repetition, in which the drive toward an Imaginary unity is cancelled by Miriam's fear of engulfment, her need to mark her 'difference'. *Pilgrimage* thus textualises both the desire to be relieved of this difference and the fear of losing it. In traditional 'modernist' criticism, this sense of difference or estrangement would be taken as one more example of 'alienation' – a specific instance of the *Zeitgeist* – but this simplifies and de-historicises a very powerful and complex articulation of class and gender differences staged in this *Bildungsroman*.

Questions of sexual difference, for instance, are presented in terms of psychic positions as well as social roles. The theme of 'being different' is first introduced in the family context, where her identification with the father marks her distance from her mother and sisters. At seventeen, her sense of being different is described as a paranoid resistance, a fear of being engulfed in the hellish world of women: 'And it would really be those women, expecting things of her. They would be so affable at first. She had been through it a million times – all her life – all eternity. They would smile those hateful women's smiles – smirks – self-satisfied smiles as if everybody were agreed about everything' (I, p. 21). Her male identification is, necessarily, a precarious one which, in the novel, does not survive her mother's suicide. Guilt and reparation to the mother lead her to project 'the masculine within' into a series of men in the external world who are then energetically denounced. Cannoning violently between masculine and feminine identifications, from 'I am like a man' (II, p. 261) to 'I wouldn't have a man's – *consciousness*, for anything' (II, p. 149), she enters a long struggle to construct a gender position which will include her sense of being different from either 'Man' or 'Woman'; to squeeze the myr-iad 'I ams' that her name suggests into a stable position represented by a single 'I'. She never succeeds. Even the temporary resolutions – 'I am something between a man and a woman, looking both ways . . .' (II, p. 187) – are constantly breaking down.

Richardson pins the psychic to the social by mapping these psychic movements over a grid of discourses about gender and sexual difference. She stages her heroine's search for a gender position through visits to libraries, as Woolf did later in *A Room of One's Own*, and her heroine's reading becomes a quest: not a quest to find 'Woman' and what she 'really wants', but a journey through the discursive constructions of women as they stood in the 1890s. Working through these, she works through the contradictions of her own 'nature', which, she discovers, cannot be known except as a form of culture: '*All* that has been said and known in the world is in *language*, in words . . . Then no-one *knows* anything for certain. Everything depends upon the way a thing is put, and that is a question of some particular civilisation . . . So the Bible is not true; it is a culture' (II, p. 990). In the later novel-chapters, to cut a long story short, Miriam arrives at a new identification with the feminine, despite some faintly persisting Schopenhauerian views. Women are no longer seen as an enclosed, monolithic group 'agreed about everything', but like herself as diverse, heterogeneous, polymorphous.[16] Their newly recognised capacity for tolerating contradiction, accepting multiple and divergent viewpoints is what enables the myriad-minded heroine to accept the feminine in herself and others. This may be read, as Rachel Blau du Plessis implicitly does, as a return to some kind of essentialist view of woman as *das Ewig Weibliche*. But the text offers other possibilities. Miriam has moved from one historically specific construction of women – as wives and mothers within the bourgeois family – to a point at which she can identify many other constructions of women, a point where she sees them as a collection of possibilities. Their infinite variety ('a million sides to every question') represents both what has been made of them and what might be. In this way they are linked with the celestial city 'hidden beyond the hard visible horizon' (III, p.198) to which she has been journeying all her life. This image also relates to the London that Miriam elects to return to, at the end of the novel, after a stay with a Quaker community in the country; and I want to end by briefly mentioning the role of the city in *Pilgrimage* and Richardson's different views of it.

Pilgrimages in search of the past became a feature of literary culture in the late Victorian/Edwardian period, in William Morris' late writings, in Gissing, Forster, Masterman, Belloc and others. Critiques of industrial capitalism and its effects and values – from right, left and centre – took the city as its symbolic target. As Williams and others have argued, idealisation of the countryside has a long history, but at the turn of the century this anti-urbanism played a key role in the construction of the idea of 'Englishness', the English way of life, the English character. In brief, the best of English traditions was deemed to be in the past and the past was to be found in the countryside. The city stood for change, the country for continuity, stability and permanence. As Masterman put it in *The Condition of England* (1904): 'The life of old England is the life of the village', or as the journalist Philip Gibbs later claimed: 'England is not to be judged only by the monstrous ant heap called London. . . . There is still the English countryside where life goes on traditionally in old farmsteads.' This construction had, of course, crucial effects which are well charted elsewhere on architecture, on demographic movements, and on the formation of the national cultural identity.

In canonical English modernism, with the notable exception of Joyce, this construction of the city is dominant. The city as a wasteland, the site of usury (as in the City of London), a place of debilitating decadence. Raymond Williams, in his discussion of these issues in *The Country and the City*, singles out Wells as the writer of the period who most forcefully challenges this construction, moving on to discuss London as the city of light, in the physical sense of its new street lighting. In *Pilgrimage*, however, London is a city of light in another sense, a place of work and freedom, of experience and education for the pilgrim who wanders its carnival streets. Miriam moves from suburban home to central London, where seven of the novels are set, and significantly it is to London that she returns at the end of the last novel, *March Moonlight*, to continue her journey in writing. London for her becomes 'this mighty lover' (III, p. 272),figuring not as a 'wasteland' but as a 'prairie' (II, p. 156).

What motivates *this* difference of view? Both class and gender – but gender specifically. If there is very little sense generated in the novel-sequence of a past spoilt or compromised by urbanism, it may be for the very basic reason that the 'English way of life' was already spoilt for the woman the heroine has become. The conservatism of the English past, the text indicates, meant only restriction, dependence, imprisonment. In contrast, London is imaged as positive, enabling – 'always receiving her back, engulfing and leaving her untouched, liberated and expanding to the whole range of her being' (III, p. 272). As a *'batteur de pavé'* (II, p. 392), London is the only community open to her and she plants her bean-rows on its grey pavements with neo-romantic effusions of gratitude. So in this respect too, *Pilgrimage* looks at the dominant construction of the city, and the ideology of 'Englishness' forged from it, with 'the eyes of a stranger'.

By way of conclusion, I see that I too have slipped into the affirmative reading warned against earlier. But as I hope I've made clear, I want to see *Pilgrimage* read not just alongside *Ulysses*, *Mrs Dalloway* and *The Waste Land*, but with Schreiner's *Woman and Labour*, suffragette autobiographies, romance fiction by Ouida, the Co-op Guild writings, Freud's 'A Case of Homosexuality in a Woman', and G. R. Sims' *Living London*, and so on. And, not to become too historicist, in relation to Barthes and Jameson, Kristeva and Cixous, Lacan and Derrida. For me, *Pilgrimage* needs to be read as Jameson argues Conrad should be read, as 'a projected solution, on the aesthetic or imaginary level, to a genuinely contradictory situation in the concrete world of everyday social life.'[17] In this respect, *Pilgrimage* may be more useful on the margins of the syllabus than in the canon precisely because, there, it continues to generate critical questions about the terms of its exclusion. For the term 'modernism' may only matter in conjunction with questions like 'and women?'

Notes

1. JONATHAN CULLER, *Framing the Sign: Criticism and Its Institutions* (Oxford: Basil Blackwell, 1988), p. 55.

2. Ibid, p. 54. Culler continues: 'Encouraging the application of one discourse to another, it [the amateur perspective] provides critical corrections of the

assumptions of disciplines and generates new insights, as well as errors that can lead specialists to rethink what needs to be said to prevent them.'

3. RACHEL BOWLBY, *Virginia Woolf* (Oxford: Basil Blackwell, 1988), p. 11.

4. JACQUELINE ROSE. 'The State of the Subject (ii) The Institutions of Feminism', *Critical Quarterly*, **29**, 4, p. 11.

5. ELAINE SHOWALTER (ed.), *The New Feminist Criticism Essays on Women, Literature and Theory* (New York: Pantheon Books, 1985; London: Virago, 1986), p. 11.

6. P. MACHEREY, Interview in *Red Letters*, 5 (trans. Jean Radford and Colin Mercer).

7. Reprinted in June 1989.

8. E.D. HIRSCH, *Cultural Literacy*, p. xiv; cited in Culler *Framing the Sign*, (1988), p. 47.

9. *Pilgrimage* IV, p. 239. All subsequent references will be cited in text as volume number followed by page number.

10. D. RICHARDSON, *Literary Essays, Memory of 1909*, cited in Blau du Plessis, p. 151.

11. RACHEL BLAU DU PLESSIS, *Writing Beyond the Ending: Narrative Strategies of Twentieth Century Women Writers* (Bloomington, Indiana: Indiana University Press, 1985), p. 151.

12. JONATHAN CULLER, *Structuralist Poetics: Structuralism, Linguistics and the Study of Literature* (London: Routledge, 1990), p. 193. In the following paragraphs I quote freely from Culler's discussion of 'Narrative Contracts' (pp. 192–6).

13. For a discussion of transference and interpretation see Jane Gallop's *Reading Lacan* (Cornell: Cornell University Press, 1985) and Jean Radford, *Dorothy Richardson* (forthcoming).

14. R. WILLIAMS, *Writing in Society* (London: Verso, 1983), p. 223.

15. ERIC HOBSBAWM *Age of Empire, 1875–1914* (London: Weidenfeld and Nicolson, 1987), p. 165. Chapter 7 is actually entitled 'Who's Who, or the Uncertainties of the Bourgeois'.

16. See Richardson's own statement in 'Leadership in Marriage', *New Adelphi*, 1929: 'The characteristic . . . of being all over the place and in all camps at once, accounts for her famous inability "to make up her mind" and her unashamed inconsistency. . . . It explains her capacity for "living in the present".'

17. FREDRIC JAMESON, *The Political Unconscious: Narrative as a Socially Symbolic Act* (London: Methuen, 1983 and Routledge, 1990), p. 225.

8 Houston A. Baker Jnr, from *Modernism and the Harlem Renaissance**

Criticism has been slow to recognise the integrity of an American modernism and slower still to consider the relation between modernism and Black writers and artists in the 'Harlem Renaissance' of the twenties. This movement included the writers Langston Hughes, Claude Mckay, Jean Toomer, Countee Cullen and, more distantly, Zorah Neale Hurston. It was welcomed in Alain Locke's anthology *The New Negro* (1925) as the sign of 'spiritual emancipation', representing the Negro's passage 'from medieval American to modern'. Harlem, said Locke, was a new 'race capital', 'the progressive Negro community of the American metropolis': the augury of 'a new democracy in American culture' – a description worth comparing with accounts of the cities of European modernism (see Bradbury and McFarlance (eds), *Modernism* (1976); Timms and Kelley (eds), *Unreal City* (1985); and Raymond Williams, Chapter 6, above.

Yet as Houston Baker's book points out, the writers of the 'Harlem Renaissance' have been consistently faulted in comparison with Anglo-American modernists. This, he says, assumes an irrelevant standard; arguing that the histories given to Anglo-American and European modernism 'are radically opposed to any adequate and accurate account of the history of Afro-American modernism, especially the *discursive* history of such modernism' (p. xvi). Baker identifies two vital discursive strategies in this history: a 'mastery of form' and a 'deformation of mastery'. The first describes the new, ironic use, or 'blackening' of standard or stereotypical (Anglo-American) social and literary forms, the second a strategy of aggressive self-advertisement and proprietorial display using 'alien' (Afro-American) folk forms. Rather than a periodisation restricted to the 'Harlem Renaissance' of the twenties or the confinements of a literary modern-

---

* (Chicago and London: University of Chicago Press, 1987), Chapter 10, pp. 91–8.

ism, Baker seeks a history of 'renaissancism' in Afro-American culture as a whole, following the constellations of literature, music, art, design, political speeches and writing. This brings him to the example of the thirties poet, Sterling A. Brown and to a consummately 'modern' blend of intellectual mastery and deformative folk sound; of 'class and mass', poetry and blues.

For further reading, see James de Jongh, *Vicious Modernism: Black Harlem and the Literary Imagination* (1990), and also Cornel West, below, chapter 18, and Chambers, chapter 15.

The ready acknowledgment that *The New Negro*[1] is the first fully modern figuration of a nation predicated upon mass energies returns us to the present discussion's exploration of definitions of Afro-American 'modernism'. Locke's collection is not, however, the clearest instance of a full discursive engagement *with* such mass energies. Although his work set the stage for such an engagement, the editor left the task itself to a 'younger generation': 'Youth speaks, and the voice of the New Negro is heard. What stirs inarticulately in the masses is already vocal upon the lips of the talented few, and the future listens, however the present may shut its ears'. I want to suggest that a complete expressive modernity was achieved only when the 'Harlem Renaissance' gave way to what might be called – following the practices of Anglo-American and British moderns – 'renaissancism'. By this term, I want to suggest a *spirit* of nationalistic engagement that begins with intellectuals, artists, and spokespersons at the turn of the century and receives extensive definition and expression during the twenties. This spirit is one that prompts the black artist's awareness that his or her only possible foundation for authentic and modern expressivity resides in a discursive field marked by formal mastery and sounding deformation. Further, I want to suggest that 'renaissancism' connotes something quite removed from a single, exotic set of 'failed' high jinks confined to less than a decade. It signals in fact a resonantly and continuously productive set of tactics, strategies,and syllables that takes form at the turn of the century and extends to our own day. One of the most obvious cullings of renaissancism's fruits occurs in the thirties and situates itself firmly in accord with deformative possibilities inherent in *The New Negros'* validation of the folk, or, the vernacular.

Gone in the work of a poet like Sterling Brown is the felt necessity to produce only *recognizably* standard forms. What replaces this drive is an unashamed and bold dedication (a dedication that remains, for the most part, implicit in the *sotto voce* urgings of the Harlem twenties) to rendering the actual folk voice in its simple, performative eloquence. If a black, folk, national voice existed, the thirties seemed to realize that it was not far to seek. Gertrude 'Ma' Rainey, Bessie Smith, Mamie Smith, Victoria Spivey, Ida Cox, Alberta Hunter, Sleepy John Estes, Barbecue Bob, Robert Johnson, Blind Boy Fuller, Big Bill Broonzy, and other vernacular singers from the 'New Orleans Delta on Down' had taken the United States – and the Afro-American masses – by storm.

Similarly, spirituals and jazz, Afro-American 'terribleness' and flair had received rave reviews and serious attention from a second decade white population somehow 'desolate and sick of an old passion'. Blues releases sold by the tens of thousands in the twenties, and the folk energy and achievement that they represented gained global recognition for what can only be called a black and classical sound of the self-in-marronage.[2] A college-bred black man like Sterling Brown, standing as a member of a second (or even a third) twentieth-century Afro-American intellectual generation, could readily set himself the task of knowing the score where the folk nation (blues) voice was concerned. The inroads on myths and shibboleths, nonsense and exclusion, made by a first (and perhaps second) generation ensured Brown the necessary emotional and intellectual confidence to mine a southern Afro-American tradition with dedicated genius.

The indisputably modern moment in Afro-American discourse arrives, I believe, when the *intellectual* poet Brown, masterfully mantled in the wisdom of his Williams College Phi Beta Kappa education, gives forth the deformative sounds of Ma Rainey. (The actual meeting between the poet and Ma Rainey occurred in Nashville in 1928, at a Cedar Street theater.[3] The musicologist John Work provided what today must seem a fitting third in this historic encounter.) The blending, I want to suggest, of class and mass – *poetic* mastery discovered as a function of deformative *folk* sound – constitutes the essence of black discursive modernism. This blend is achieved within a fluid field. Indeed, if you have ever heard the blues righteously sung, you know that it sounds of and from fields burning under torpid Southern suns, or lands desolately drenched by too high rivers. The intended audience is black people themselves defined by the very blues tones and lyrics as sharers in a nation of common concern and culturally specific voice.

Renaissancism's success consists in a fruitfully resounding merger. We listen as what the critic Stephen Henderson[4] calls a religious rite and cultural performance takes place in the soundings of Sterling Brown:

Ma Rainey
I
When Ma Rainey
Comes to town,
Folks from anyplace

Miles aroun',
From Cape Girardeau,
Poplar Bluff,
Flocks in to hear
Ma do her stuff;
Comes flivverin' in,
Or ridin' mules,
Or packed in trains,
Picknickin' fools . . .
That's what it's like,
Fo' miles on down,
To New Orleans delta
An' Mobile town,
When Ma hits
Anywheres aroun'.

II

Dey comes to hear Ma Rainey from de little river settlements,
From blackbottom cornrows and from lumber camps;
Dey stumble in de hall, jes a-laughin' an'a-cacklin',
Cheerin' lak roarin' water, lak wind in river swamps.
An' some jokers keeps deir laughs a-goin' in de crowded aisles,
An' some folks sits dere waitin' wid deir aches an' miseries,
Till Ma comes out before dem, a-smilin' gold-toofed smiles
An' Long Boy ripples minors on de black an' yellow keys.

III

O Ma Rainey,
Sing yo' song;
Now you's back
Whah you belong,
Git way inside us,
Keep us strong . . .
O Ma Rainey,
Li'l an' low;
Sing us 'bout de hard luck
Roun' our do';
Sing us 'bout de lonesome road
We mus' go . . .

IV

I talked to a fellow, an' the fellow say,
'She jes' catch hold of us, somekindaway.
She sang Backwater Blues one day:

"It rained fo' days an' de skies was dark as night,
Trouble taken place in de lowlands at night.
"Thundered an' lightened an' the storm begin to roll
Thousan's of people ain't got no place to go.
"Den I went an' stood upon some high ol' lonesome hill,
An' looked down on the place where I used to live."
An' den de folks, dey natchally bowed dey heads an' cried,
Bowed dey heavy heads, shet dey moufs up tight an'cried,
An' Ma lef' de stage, an' followed some de folks outside.'

Dere wasn't much more de fellow say:
She jes' gits hold of us dataway.[5]

And, indeed, after hearing a Sterling Brown performance of 'Ma Rainey'
there is not much a fellow can say, except perhaps that Zora Neale
Hurston and Richard Wright move to the same rhythms witnessed in
Brown's ritual. Or perhaps that Brown's discursive gesture implies that
the modernity and effectiveness of Afro-American expression always
summon to view and to audition black sufferers of marginalization and
dispossession. The image of renaissancism *par excellence* is a mass image.
It stands opposed to an economics of slavery that has always attempted
to figure us as the mindlessly deformed, fit only for brutal servitude.

Renaissancism not only summons a mass image but converts it into a
salvific sound that becomes a spirit house and space of black habitation.
For the very sufferers imaged are a people of will and strength who
convert *marronage* into song, story, arts of liberation, and guerrilla war.
There is quite frequently among them a communicating by horns. And
their image translates at last into the mask of a resounding and venerable
ancestry of fields. The task of the spokesperson who would engage the
sound of folk conversion is to situate himself or herself in productive
relationship to a field marked by awesome strategies of deformation and
mastery. It is this discursive field that links us bone of the bone, flesh of
the flesh, and note by resounding blue note to contours of those
transforming African masks that constitute our beginnings.

Perhaps all of this is implicit in the statement by Marcus Garvey that
Professor Robert Hill was kind enough to share with me.[6] In one of his
Liberty Hall speeches, the indefatigable leader of the twenties warned
opponents that he could not be tampered with or harmed because, as he
said, 'I am a *modern.*' And if we of the present generation comprehend
the success constituted by Harlem's production of a tome such as *The
New Negro* and are happily successful in our own renaissancism, we may
share the confidence, indeed, the critical invulnerability claimed by
Garvey. *The New Negro* constitutes a national reference point and treasure
that will be summoned (perhaps 'by horns') whenever there is a

genuinely national surge among us, or whenever we reflect on our mission of African liberation, or whenever we acknowledge, in bold terms, that the massed folk are rank and file leaders of any group movement forward that we might make. It is no surprise that 1955 witnessed the publication at Howard University of Rayford Logan's collection dedicated to Alain Locke and entitled *The New Negro Thirty Years Afterward*, nor is it uncanny that Afro-American cultural nationalism and radical activism of the sixties and seventies styled itself 'Renaissance II'.

Notes

1. *The New Negro*, ed. Alain Locke (New York: Atheneum, 1968).

2. The sign 'self-in-*marronage*' comes from the work of Edward Braithwaite of Jamaica who has produced his own study of the phenomenon of *marronage* in the Caribbean. I encountered the term most recently in a study by Gordon Rohlehr entitled 'Articulating a Caribbean Aesthetic'. The paper was a handout at a lecture on Calypso presented by Professor Rohlehr at the University of Pennsylvania on 25 November 1985. What the term seems to imply is the always already AFRICAN SELF that has its being in community and cultural/racial/tribal interiority.

3. I am indebted to two people for information on the encounter between Brown and Ma Rainey – Eleanor Jones Baker, my sister-in-law, who first brought the matter to my attention, and Professor Joanne V. Gabbin, Brown's biographer, who went to the source to confirm my sister-in-law's memory that she had read about such an encounter during her research on minstrelsy. 'How did you find the information?' I asked Professor Gabbin. 'I called Sterling up and asked him', she responded. My gratitude.

4. See Stephen E. Henderson, 'The heavy Blues of Sterling Brown; A Study of Craft and Tradition', *Black American Literature Forum*, 14 (Spring 1980): 32–44.

5. *The Collected Poems of Sterling A. Brown*, selected by Michael S. Harper (New York: Harper, 1980), pp. 62–3.

6. Professor Hill wrote of his own interest in black modernism as follows in his 25 July 1985 letter:

   > In terms of the larger issue of modernism, my interest stems from the fact that in one of his Liberty Hall speeches Garvey directs a cautionary word at his opponents and informs them that he can't be tampered with because, as he says, 'I am a *modern*.' That intrigued me greatly. What did he mean by that? What, in fact, did it mean in the context of the early 1920s for someone to lay claim to being 'a modern'?

   I shared my own ideas on the matter with Professor Hill whose agreement seemed implicit in his notion that only an exploration of 'folk types' and iconographies (e.g., Garvey as Anancy, a trickster in competition with Washington as Brer Rabbit,a trickster of a different sort) could reveal the nature of the black modern to us. Professor Hill is the editor of the Garvey papers.

9 Laleen Jayamanne, Geeta Kapur, Yvonne Rainer, from 'Discussing Modernity, "Third World" and *The Man Who Envied Women*'*

The following interview rehearses many of the topics raised in previous selections – modernism, modernity, the metropolis, the avant-garde, class, gender and ethnicity. The three participants refer also to film, art, and dance rather than literature, and the item is included as a reminder of the different cultural practices to which the general categories are applied. Chiefly, however, it demonstrates the sharp and subtle differences marking First and Third World perspectives. (Laleen Jayamanne lives in Australia, Geeta Kapur is Indian and Yvonne Rainer North American.) Their discussion reveals a very real dialogical complexity, one in which the detail of theoretical, critical and practical artistic projects is shaped within a series of conditions. These include the conventions of different media, of course, but also different personal, social and cultural histories, as well as the discourses of power and oppositional cultural politics developed in the West and the East. The play of these factors and their uneven realisation make it difficult to think of modernism's 'survival' as a simple repetition or recovery of its original conditions and energies. For Geeta Kapur, Anglo-American modernism has metamorphosed from a dominant and problematical cultural inheritance to become one possible tradition amongst others. For the film-maker Yvonne Rainer, similarly, strategies associated with the historical avant-garde remain available techniques, open to fresh polemics. Kapur's witty 'eclecticism' and Rainer's ironic 'rewriting' suggest a common, productive relationship to these past modernisms. At the same time the differences in their experiences and political identities as women are striking.

The interview took place at the Edinburgh Festival in August 1986. The present extract omits some points of information and related discussion of Rainer's films.

---

* Reprinted from *Art and Text*, **23**, Part 4 (1987): 41–51.

Laleen Jayamanne: In all your work you have constantly traversed and perhaps tried to negotiate different cultures. In this context, can you comment on the notions of tradition, modernity and modernism in relation to Indian art. Also, can you tell us if the notion of postmodernism, which in the West has provoked opposing descriptions and definitions, has any relevance to contemporary Indian art.

Geeta Kapur: As a matter of fact, my own investigations into the role of tradition in art came a little late. As a student in New York in the early sixties I was persuaded by the claims of modernism, which at that time were particularly strong: the heyday of Clement Greenberg. Returning home to India to involve myself in contemporary art practice in the mid-sixties, which is when I started to write, I had to come to terms with the history around me. This is something that needs to be stressed: that art practice in modern India, which from the Western point of view may appear retarded or eclectic, has a history within our cultural tradition. So even the theoretical questions of modernism and modernist art have to be re-evaluated within our own context. A pragmatic re-evaluation, to suit our own purposes, but also an ideological one, on behalf of the West, shall we say. At any rate, for the Indian artist modernism has become part of the social and everyday experience in India; it has also become the language in which he or she speaks. Included in all this is the critique of modernity, and of tradition.

It was at this time that I went abroad again, in 1968, to study in London. It was an important time, and although I was not expressly politicised, ideology had become so much a part of the cultural question that any proposition, even in aesthetics, had to be so formulated as to include politics. Now I think it was at that time that modernism became properly problematised. In India the problematic was different: here it concerned the imperialist implications of modernism, and possible correctives in terms of our own cultural traditions. In England or Europe at the end of the sixties, the question being asked was how the West and its cultural practice, including ideologies such as modernism, related to other cultures. Coming from India this was my concern in reverse so to speak, and I felt then that the questions had come full circle and that I was being thrown into the arena. In fact, I saw for the first time that the question of cultural adaptation in India was ideologically problematic in several ways. In any case, on returning to India I worked more closely with my own generation of artists, many of whom had either studied or been overseas and were in constant critical dialogue with the West. Roughly speaking, in retrospect it seemed that modernism had come to us first via Paris and then somewhat tangentially from America. But since this legacy had been predominantly mediated by English critical practice, and considering that English art was seldom in the vanguard in this century, the impact was in a sense tame. Now in the mid-sixties a group of Indian artists, led by a colleague, J. Swanunathan, who had been a political activist for a very long time, a communist, quite spontaneously and perhaps not quite consciously linked themselves to the rhetoric of liberation movements. Swanunathan, outstandingly articulate, was a friend of Octavio Paz who was at that time in India. The kind of self-image developed by the Indian artist of the sixties was analogous to that adopted by artists and intellectuals from nations that were still colonised or which were now progressively subsumed by neo-colonialism. In India the simulation, if that is what it was, was vivid and even necessary. And once we had injected into the art debates at home the politics of liberation, it brought with it a kind of avantgardism which had not existed before. It was not avantgardism in terms of language – Indian art has not, formally, been part of the vanguard, not in the sense in which the word has been used in the West. But it had recognised poets, artists who are in the vanguard. In any event, by virtue of the fact that now questions of culture had to be seen in relation to politics, whether or not the work fitted into the current avant-garde art, consciousness was radicalised. Our generation inherited this moment.

By the seventies the necessity of posing modernity and tradition in solely oppositional terms was being questioned, as well as the whole polemic with the West. Increasingly it was felt that there is a sufficiently developed modern cultural context in India to allow the problematic to be addressed to ourselves, and this was very different from any kind of indigenism. It was not in order to be more Indian that this arose, not in order to be more authentically Indian. In fact, the whole question of authenticity was perhaps jettisoned at this point because authenticity had led us into an essentialism. To be authentic for the generation of the fifties was to be authentic in terms of self; the expressions used when they spoke of their work were almost always within the terms of existentialist literature. Alongside this there was the perennial question of Indian cultural development in terms of its tradition which supposed that you are authentic if you have roots, if you are firmly rooted within a fairly homogeneous culture; whereas, of course, Indian culture is not homogeneous, certainly not in any way monolithic. Anyhow, once modernism had been problematised the questions raised referred to our social and political existence in urban India: this was the area to which my generation could address itself. It was reflected in the subject matter, but not that alone. It was not simply a question of finding subject matter, but of finding new equations within the entire gamut of the language available, the modern art language which is more varied than any purified modernism will acknowledge. For instance, a progressivist chronology is imposed on Western artists – if you are part of the mainstream art scene, you are also part of an inevitable and quite overwhelming chronology of styles and movements.

Now, at this point in my relay of Indian art, there was an active disengagement from this kind of chronologised modernism. And for the first time, a fairly aggressive stance was taken on eclecticism. If one could disengage oneself from the art movements' stylistic imperatives, then you could quite clearly be eclectic, borrowing freely from your own tradition, from the West, from whichever tradition you like. I think if anything defines the idelogical positions of Indian artists today, it is an enligthened eclecticism.

And this brings us to the question of postmodernism. I believe Indian art to be eclectic but not postmodern. The word 'appropriation' is important to postmodernism, but probably it can only be used in a Western context. There is a long cultural history behind the idea of appropriation; it really belongs to the Western consciousness, especially in its colonising phase. When today it moves to the area of pastiche, which is also one of the elements of postmodernist art, it must be seen as arising from a condition of surplus, from one of saturation. If there is a surfeit of cultural input and output, you appropriate, jettison and parody, you make blatant pastiche because the options are too many. In all this the only element that interests me, and I think many of us, is the one of play. I think that aspect, that of playfuless, which is part of postmodernism, can be usefully assimilated.

Laleen: Why?

Geeta: Because if we retain the word 'eclecticism' for ourselves, then that must work itself out through an element of wit. Without wit we should merely be patching together an academic and lugubrious activity. Irony, or wit, requires a cunning set of relationships, not only in the subject but also in the elements of the language used. To the extent that postmodernist art has opened up that area, opened it up beyond what was available, what had hardened into the modernist position – I think to that extent postmodernism would interest us.

Laleen: Would you comment on the distinctions between modernity as a wider cultural concept and modernism as an aesthetic movement.

Geeta: I think we would agree that the modernity deriving from modernisation is a sociological term, and to that extent has more meaning than perhaps the discussion of tradition and modernity; then the reference is to 'a clash of cultures'. Modernity would be a learning process, for better or worse as the case may be. The experiential aspect might take some time to formulate, to transform itself into any kind of art form. Conversely, it may be possible to be quite advanced in one's understanding of modernism as a cultural phenomenon, without necessarily being part of a highly developed society. You can receive through the existing literature and art forms the wager of modernism, and this I think is what happened with the Indian artists. They were not always or necessarily committed to the process of modernisation as such, not at least in any quantifiable way from the point of view of sociology. But the possibility of assimilation through art practice, an almost unconscious assimilation of modernist beliefs, is the basis on which Indian modern art has developed. I think even the best of our cinema developed like this, for example in Ritwik Ghatak. He is in fact sometimes in advance of the quantifiable social aspects of modernisation, sometimes in opposition to it.

Ironically, the professional Indian, although she may be more directly part of the modernising process, is often less able to grasp the experiential or even political premises on which modernism is based; whereas an artist, by virtue of her language and practice, may arrive more acutely at the implications of what it means to be modern.

Let me refer the question back to you. In your experience, is it a viable proposition to say that the social processes of modernisation find their articulation within the middle classes only later, that the cultural manifestation of it may sometimes jump several steps ahead? Would you support that possibility? Because that is the only way one can explain the cultural telescoping in India, and I should think in Asia as well and in every culture outside the so-called mainstream. That is the only way we could explain the high incidence of critical awareness, of the various attempts to adopt, transform, or recycle the elements of modernist experience and language. Otherwise we would only be trudging along in a rather pedantic way, trying everything out piecemeal and always tardily pursuing modern art forms.

Laleen: I'd agree that the two processes are quite out of synch and that your formulation is most congenial and hopeful for the so-called 'developing countries'. For it means that the cultural work produced there does not *ipso facto* have to bear the burden of 'underdevelopment' or remain backward with regard to the 'developed' world.

Geeta: Questions of modernity such as they are discussed by Indian sociologists often seem to me to be woefully pedantic. A degree of empiricism is necessary for the social sciences, but any kind of transference to what is possible within the cultural situation is quite inadequate. I am not only speaking of the familiar argument of superstructural elasticity, or even of autonomy; I am speaking of creative flexibility, of the specific talent of the artist to transform . . ..

[At this point Yvonne Rainer joined the group]

117

Laleen to Yvonne: Why did you choose an Australian text, Meaghan Morris' 'The Pirate's Fiancée', for what I believe to be the central scene in your film, *The Man Who Envied Women*, when in fact there is an abundance of material on Foucault's ideas in the US? The place from which texts are written interests me because of the peculiar position of Australia with regard to the rest of the Anglophone world.

Yvonne: I don't read such critical material in any systematic way. I came upon this text and the book in which it was published, *Michel Foucault: Power, Truth, Strategy*, through the recommendation of Tom Zummer, who was a former research assistant to Foucault. All of the texts recited in the corridor are from this book, including interviews with Foucault and the Meaghan Morris text. I was quite struck by the far-reaching aspects of her text, the way that it covers Lacan and Derrida and Foucault and feminist ideas, the ironies of these, and the dilemmas of identity, of female identity in relation to psychoanalysis and Marxism that she poses in a very light-hearted way, by seeming to touch on all the basic problems without being heavy-handed or going into depth, and for a film in which I could not begin to go into such issues in any depth. It seemed a very recitable, entertaining treatment of some of these issues. Also, the usefulness of the text was to have an Australian voice referring obliquely to French feminism that is delivered in English by Jackie Raynal, a French woman and film-maker in her own right who has a heavy accent. It is the problematised voice of feminist theory itself.

Laleen: Geeta and I have just been discussing the distinction between appropriation and the eclectic, and she insisted that in the Indian context the word appropriation does not seem very appropriate.

Geeta: We prefer the word eclectic, even though our Marxist friends are very critical of it and say that the word is being used incorrectly, that eclecticism functions negatively. I was just now trying to suggest that we find the word more comfortable because it allows – or we would like to allow – for play, playfulness, by taking and transforming and changing; whereas appropriation as a term has a kind of aggressiveness which is perhaps endemic to Western thought and culture. I think we would prefer the kind of manoeuvrability which the term eclecticism allows. Besides, the word appropriation would inevitably lead, as it does in postmodernist discourse, to art which is pastiche. For us, pastiche has little purpose; it is just decorative, with only a one-dimensional form of irony. It does not really allow for any significant level of paradox . . . .

Yvonne: The word that occurs to me is 're-reading'. The only reason to dredge up familiar images is to re-read them in terms of current knowledges, experience.

Laleen: So the function of re-reading might apply to the way that Meaghan's essay is structured around quotations from Valerie Solanus's SCUM manifesto, an American text, one of those extreme feminist texts . . .

Yvonne: . . . infamous, incendiary!

Laleen: Solanus's text is inserted within the domain of 'high feminist theory' in a manner which enables one to question some of its certainties. One of the problems with some current feminist work, especially in the area of cinema, is the way that theory is stressed to the detriment of writing. A consequence of this is a dull, earnest kind of writing that simply applies, repetitively, the theoretical positions. Whereas the Meaghan Morris text is exemplary in its agility, wit and, crucially, in its departure from simply echoing the theoretical propositons of a master thinker. It is interesting to observe how you take this text and turn it into an incantatory utterance by your female character, who is caught in a tight spot.

Yvonne: I did a lot of condensing and in at least one spot made an addition. Meaghans' statement: 'If a girl takes her eyes off Lacan and Derrida long enough to look – a parenthetical aside in her original essay, I completed with: 'she may discover she is the Invisible Man', which goes right back to all those questions about autonomous or essential feminity within a partriarchal structure. I was sure Meaghan would have appreciated the cinematic reference.

Laleen: As women, one Indian and the other American, who have both attempted to redefine the very parameters of your chosen fields, are the questions of gender and nationality important in your work?

Geeta: I must confess that I have not worked critically with the question of gender. There are a number of very important women artists in India, all in their thirties and forties. Once there were very few Indian women artists, suddenly there are many. But most do not position themselves ideologically as women artists; they might even resist being placed in a women's show as a matter of fact, saying that neither their work nor their circumstance warrants any special consideration as they have been in a privileged class or cultural situation from the start. To present them as a minority group that had struggled more than their male counterparts and whose subject matter or language was in some way distinct, would not be something they would agree to. For instance, if you come from an enlightened middle-class educated family, if you had the finance to go to art school, if you didn't need to seek a mediocre job for economic reasons, then such women find themselves not just equal to, but possibly a little better off than male artists, whom they often marry and in whom they often find a congenial partner. They may even be pampered.

Yvonne: That's a potentially deadly combination in my culture, a female artist married to a male artist.

Geeta: In India it seems to work extremely well. Of course, the woman artist may not be overtly ambitious and may not be in the forefront of conferences, institutions and critical debates. Many of them have to raise families, and so have to ration their time with regard to studio time. Women artists would feel, as most women professionals in India would feel, that if they have made the initial crossover, if they have been able to escape the stereotype by entering a university education, then there is quite considerable freedom. I have lived for short periods abroad, and it is my belief that in India women have very many more options, that the number of professions open to an Indian woman are more varied.

As for the problem of nationality, you have to remember that we are a composite culture, that we never simply identify ourselves as Indian. But I do think that we need to probe further the category of nationality, to ask more questions amongst ourselves. With regard to the West, yes, national identity does concern its polemical or combative stance. We constantly try to break that, to turn it over, and even jettison it within our own debates.

Laleen: In order to avoid an essentialist identity?

Geeta: An essentialist identity based on the notion of indigenism. Quite obviously, all cultural discussion in India during the colonial struggle sprang from this notion. The national 'cultural resistance' beginning in the mid-nineteenth century was based entirely on the clash between Indian and Western identity. It remained alive right up to the sixties. It is only recently, I think, that another political dimension has been brought to it. The view of liberation is not only linked to nationalism; internationalism is now discussed critically but also from the potential of socialism. Until very recently the word internationalism made us very defensive because it signified a blatant misappropriation of our cultures, as with the international avant-garde and its affiliates . . .

Yvonne: The avant-garde is controlled by the West.

Geeta: Well, both the concept and its practice originated in the West, and it is naturally the prerogative of the West. But then any ideological analysis of the avant-garde for the last so many years would reveal its contradictions. After World War II the avant-garde is often a manufactured one; it is linked with advanced capitalism and its constant need for new commerce, whereas before it was clearly much more confrontational . . ..

*Yvonne:*Yes, I absolutely agree. For all practical purposes, the notion of avant-garde has become hopelessly debased through its ties with commodity speculation, the (dis)information apparatus, and cultural imperialism. But in principle I still cling to the somewhat romantic ideas of the avant-garde that launched my own creative efforts: ideas about marginality, intervention, an adversative subculture, a confrontation with the complacent past, the art of resistance, etc. Of course, these ideas must be constantly reassessed in terms of class, gender and race. On a personal level I could describe my development as a gradual discovery of the subtleties of my own privilege, which I took for granted when I began as a dancer – not realising that I had an automatic entry into the cultural space of New York's avant-garde milieu, primarily through male artists because I was involved in a 'feminised' art form that posed no threat. Later on feminism became central to my work by transferring my own personal feelings of victimisation to a more social articulation of the way women can be defined as a class. This is an on-going process and I feel I have just begun to scratch the surface: not to try to escape my class or my sex, but to constantly confront the facts of them. However, I still use in my work the avant-garde formal trappings and background which enabled me to start making art in the first place.

Geeta: Which are?

Yvonne: The things that belong to modernism and what I long ago called postmodern dance and what is now called postmodernism, which originated in collage and the strategies of radical juxtaposition. You might call it Brechtian, although Brecht was not my immediate influence. My gender is related to my sense of nationality, to feelings of being trapped in this country which again has become a world ogre. That, I feel, can only be dealt with by confronting it in very concrete ways, in terms of immediate social issues, or, in my case, a particular urban milieu.

Part Two

Postmodern Narratives

10 Jürgen Habermas, 'Modernity – an Incomplete Project'*

Habermas's essay was first given as a lecture in September 1980 when he was awarded the Theodor W. Adorno prize by the city of Frankfurt, and first printed under the title 'Modernity versus Post-modernity' (*New German Critique*, **22**, Winter 1981). The essay's two titles indicate the direction of Habermas's polemic. Firstly, he was responding to the 'neo-conservatism' of the American sociologist Daniel Bell, whose talk of a 'post-industrial' or postmodern society had, Habermas felt, over-identified the effects of capitalist modernisation with cultural modernism. Secondly he was replying to the critique of rationality and social progress at the heart of the Enlightenment project made by the French poststructuralists Foucault and Derrida. The latter Habermas describes as 'young conservatives' and as 'anti-modernists' (they nevertheless depended, he felt, upon both modernism and rationality).

'Modernity' in these debates designates a combined aesthetic, ethical and political outlook, unified in eighteenth century thought but splintered in the subsequent development of western societies. Habermas argues that reason has been wrongly identified in this tradition with the individual human subject. He shares this critique of a 'subject-centred' philosophy with poststructuralism but argues that the Enlightenment project of understanding, justice and democracy can be realised through the operation of an intersubjective 'communicative reason', socially situated and underpinned by a common commitment to the goals of truth, right and sincerity. This theory he developed especially in *Legitimation Crisis* (1976); *The Theory of Communicative Action* (2 vols, 1985, 1988); and *The Philosophical Discourse of Modernity* (1988).

The debate between Habermas and poststructuralist or post-modernist theory is at one level a debate about Marxism as a viable

---

* Reprinted from Hal Foster (ed.), *Postmodern Culture* (London: Pluto Press, 1985), trans. Seyla Ben-Habib, pp. 3–15. Notes to this essay are supplied by Hal Foster.

social and political philosophy. In this debate Habermas's evolutionary version of historical materialism is opposed by both the revolutionary class politics of classical Marxism and the postmodernist 'incredulity' towards all such 'metanarratives' of human history.

See the Introduction, pp. 20–1, and for further discussion, including additional essays by Habermas: J. Bernstein (ed.), *Habermas and Modernilty* (1985); B.S. Turner (ed.), *Theories of Modernity and Postmodernity* (1990); Callinicos, *Against Postmodernism* (1989); and L. Nicholson (ed.), *Feminism/Postmodernism* (1990). Also Nancy Fraser 'What's Critical about Critical Theory? The Case of Habermas and Gender', *New German Critique*, **35** (1985): 109–33.

In 1980, architects were admitted to the Biennial in Venice, following painters and filmmakers. The note sounded at this first Architecture Biennial was one of disappointment. I would describe it by saying that those who exhibited in Venice formed an avant-garde of reversed fronts. I mean that they sacrificed the tradition of modernity in order to make room for a new historicism. Upon this occasion, a critic of the German newspaper, *Frankfurter Allgemeine Zeitung*, advanced a thesis whose significance reaches beyond this particular event; it is a diagnosis of our times: 'Postmodernity definitely presents itself as Antimodernity.' This statement describes an emotional current of our times which has penetrated all spheres of intellectual life. It has placed on the agenda theories of postenlightenment, postmodernity, even of posthistory.

From history we know the phrase, 'The Ancients and the Moderns'. Let me begin by defining these concepts. The term 'modern' has a long history, one which has been investigated by Hans Robert Jauss.[1] The word 'modern' in its Latin form *'modernus'* was used for the first time in the late fifth century in order to distinguish the present, which had become officially Christian, from the Roman and pagan past. With varying content, the term 'modern' again and again expresses the consciousness of an epoch that relates itself to the past of antiquity, in order to view itself as the result of a transition from the old to the new.

Some writers restrict this concept of 'modernity' to the Renaissance, but this is historically too narrow. People considered themselves modern during the period of Charles the Great in the twelfth century, as well as in France of the late seventeenth century at the time of the famous 'Querelle des Anciens et des Modernes'. That is to say, the term 'modern' appeared and reappeared exactly during those periods in Europe when the consciousness of a new epoch formed itself through a renewed relationship to the ancients – whenever, moreover, antiquity was considered a model to be recovered through some kind of imitation.

The spell which the classics of the ancient world cast upon the spirit of later times was first dissolved with the ideals of the French Enlightenment. Specifically, the idea of being 'modern' by looking back to the ancients changed with the belief, inspired by modern science, in the infinite progress of knowledge and in the infinite advance towards social and moral betterment. Another form of modernist consciousness was formed in the wake of this change. The romantic modernist sought to oppose the antique ideals of the classicists; he looked for a new historical epoch and found it in the idealised Middle Ages. However, this new ideal age, established early in the nineteenth century, did not remain a fixed ideal. In the course of the nineteenth century, there emerged out of this romantic spirit that radicalised consciousness of modernity which freed itself from all specific historical ties. This most recent modernism simply makes an abstract opposition between tradition and the present; and we are, in a way, still the contemporaries of that kind of aesthetic modernity which first appeared in the midst of the nineteenth century. Since then the distinguishing mark of works which count as modern is 'the new' which will be overcome and made obsolete through the novelty of the next style. But, while that which is merely 'stylish' will soon become outmoded, that which is modern preserves a secret tie to the classical. Of course, whatever can survive time has always been considered to be a classic. But the emphatically modern document no longer borrows this power of being a classic from the authority of a past epoch; instead, a modern work becomes a classic because it has once been authentically modern. Our sense of modernity creates its own self-enclosed canons of being classic. In this sense we speak, e.g., in view of the history of modern art, of classical modernity. The relation between 'modern' and 'classical' has definitely lost a fixed historical reference.

The discipline of aesthetic modernity

The spirit and discipline of aesthetic modernity assumed clear contours in the work of Baudelaire. Modernity then unfolded in various avant-garde movements and finally reached its climax in the Café Voltaire of the Dadaists and in Surrealism. Aesthetic modernity is characterised by attitudes which find a common focus in a changed consciousness of time. This time consciousness expresses itself through metaphors of the vanguard and the avant-garde. The avant-garde understands itself as invading unknown territory, exposing itself to the dangers of sudden, shocking encounters, conquering an as yet unoccupied future. The avant-garde must find a direction in a landscape into which no one seems to have yet ventured.

But these forward gropings, this anticipation of an undefined future and the cult of the new mean in fact the exaltation of the present. The new time consciousness, which enters philosophy in the writings of Bergson, does more than express the experience of mobility in society, of acceleration in history, of discontinuity in everyday life. The new value placed on the transitory, the elusive and the ephermeral, the very celebration of dynamism, discloses a longing for an undefiled, immaculate and stable present.

This explains the rather abstract language in which the modernist temper has spoken of the 'past'. Individual epochs lose their distinct forces. Historical memory is replaced by the heroic affinity of the present with the extremes of history – a sense of time wherein decadence immediately recognises itself in the barbaric, the wild and the primitive. We observe the anarchistic intention of blowing up the continuum of history, and we can account for it in terms of the subversive force of this new aesthetic consciousness. Modernity revolts against the normalising functions of tradition; modernity lives on the experience of rebelling against all that is normative. This revolt is one way to neutralise the standards of both morality and utility. This aesthetic consciousness continuously stages a dialectical play between secrecy and public scandal; it is addicted to a fascination with that horror which accompanies the act of profaning, and yet is always in flight from the trivial results of profanation.

On the other hand, the time consciousness articulated in avant-garde art is not simply ahistorical; it is directed against what might be called a false normativity in history. The modern, avant-garde spirit has sought to use the past in a different way; it disposes those pasts which have been made available by the objectifying scholarship of historicism, but it opposes at the same time a neutralised history which is locked up in the museum of historicism.

Drawing upon the spirit of Surrealism, Walter Benjamin constructs the relationship of modernity to history in what I would call a posthistoricist attitude. He reminds us of the self-understanding of the French Revolution: 'The Revolution cited ancient Rome, just as fashion cites an antiquated dress. Fashion has a scent for what is current, whenever this moves within the thicket of what was once.' This is Benjamin's concept of the *Jetztzeit*, of the present as a moment of revelation; a time in which splinters of a messianic presence are enmeshed. In this sense, for Robespierre, the antique Rome was a past laden with momentary revelations.[2]

Now, this spirit of aesthetic modernity has recently begun to age. It has been recited once more in the 1960s; after the 1970s, however, we must admit to ourselves that this modernism arouses a much fainter response today than it did fifteen years ago. Octavio Paz, a fellow-traveller of modernity, noted already in the middle of the 1960s that 'the avant-garde of 1967 repeats the deeds and gestures of those of 1917. We are experiencing the end of the idea of modern art.' The work of Peter Bürger has since taught us to speak of 'post-avant-garde' art; this term is chosen to indicate the failure of the Surrealist rebellion.[3] But what is the meaning of this failure? Does it signal a farewell to modernity? Thinking more generally, does the existence of a post-avant-garde mean there is a transition to that broader phenomenon called postmodernity?

This is in fact how Daniel Bell, the most brilliant of the American neoconservatives, interprets matters. In his book, *The Cultural Contradictions of Capitalism*, Bell argues that the crises of the developed societies of the West are to be traced back to a split between culture and society. Modernist culture has come to penetrate the values of everyday life; the life-world is infected by modernism. Because of the forces of modernism, the principle of unlimited self-realisation, the demand for authentic self-experience and the subjectivism of a hyperstimulated sensitivity have come to be dominant. This temperament unleashes hedonistic motives irreconcilable with the discipline of professional life in society, Bell says. Moreover, modernist culture is altogether incompatible with the moral basis of a purposive, rational conduct of life. In this manner, Bell places the burden of responsibility for the dissolution of the protestant ethic (a phenomenon which had already disturbed Max Weber) on the 'adversary culture'. Culture in its modern form stirs up hatred against the conventions and virtues of everyday life, which has become rationalised under the pressures of economic and administrative imperatives.

I would call your attention to a complex wrinkle in this view. The impulse of modernity, we are told on the other hand, is exhausted; anyone who considers himself avant-garde can read his own death warrant. Although the avant-garde is still considered to be expanding, it is supposedly no longer creative. Modernism is dominant but dead. For the neoconservative the question then arises: how can norms arise in society which will limit libertinism, reestablish the ethic of discipline and work? What new norms will put a brake on the levelling caused by the social welfare state so that the virtues of individual competition for achievement can again dominate? Bell sees a religious revival to be the only solution. Religious faith tied to a faith in tradition will provide individuals with clearly defined identities and existential security.

Cultural modernity and societal modernisation

One can certainly not conjure up by magic the compelling beliefs which
command authority. Analyses like Bell's, therefore, only result in an
attitude which is spreading in Germany no less than in the States: an
intellectual and political confrontation with the carriers of cultural
modernity. I cite Peter Steinfels, an observer of the new style which the
neoconservatives have imposed upon the intellectual scene in the 1970s:

> The struggle takes the form of exposing every manifestation of what
> could be considered an oppositionist mentality and tracing its 'logic' so
> as to link it to various forms of extremism: drawing the connection
> between modernism and nihilism . . . between government regulation
> and totalitarianism, between criticism of arms expenditures and
> subservience to communism, between Women's liberation or
> homosexual rights and the destruction of the family . . . between the
> Left generally and terrorism, anti-semitism, and fascism . . ..[4]

The *ad hominem* approach and the bitterness of these intellectual
accusations have also been trumpeted loudly in Germany. They should
not be explained so much in terms of the psychology of neoconservative
writers; rather, they are rooted in the analytical weaknesses of
neoconservative doctrine itself.

Neoconservatism shifts onto cultural modernism the uncomfortable
burdens of a more or less successful capitalist modernisation of the
economy and society. The neoconservative doctrine blurs the
relationship between the welcomed process of societal modernisation on
the one hand, and the lamented cultural development on the other. The
neoconservative does not uncover the economic and social causes for the
altered attitudes towards work, consumption, achievement and leisure.
Consequently, he attributes all of the following – hedonism, the lack of
social identification, the lack of obedience, narcissism, the withdrawal
from status and achievement competition – to the domain of 'culture'. In
fact, however, culture is intervening in the creation of all these problems
in only a very indirect and mediated fashion.

In the neoconservative view, those intellectuals who still feel
themselves committed to the project of modernity are then presented as
taking the place of those unanalysed causes. The mood which feeds
neoconservatism today in no way originates from discontent about the
antinomian consequences of a culture breaking from the museums into
the stream of ordinary life. This discontent has not been called into life
by modernist intellectuals. It is rooted in deep-seated reactions against
the process of *societal* modernisation. Under the pressures of the
dynamics of economic growth and the organisational accomplishments of

the state, this social modernisation penetrates deeper and deeper into previous forms of human existence. I would describe this subordination of the life-worlds under the system's imperatives as a matter of disturbing the communicative infrastructure of everyday life.

Thus, for example, neopopulist protests only express in pointed fashion a widespread fear regarding the destruction of the urban and natural environment and of forms of human sociability. There is a certain irony about these protests in terms of neoconservatism. The tasks of passing on a cultural tradition, of social integration and of socialisation require adherence to what I call communicative rationality. But the occasions for protest and discontent originate precisely when spheres of communicative action, centered on the reproduction and transmission of values and norms, are penetrated by a form of modernisation guided by standards of economic and adminstrative rationality – in other words, by standards of rationalisation quite different from those of communicative rationality on which those spheres depend. But neoconservative doctrines turn our attention precisely away from such societal processes: they project the causes, which they do not bring to light, onto the plane of a subversive culture and its advocates.

To be sure, cultural modernity generates its own aporias as well. Independently from the consequences of *societal* modernisation and within the perspective of *cultural* development itself, there originate motives for doubting the project of modernity. Having dealt with a feeble kind of criticism of modernity – that of neoconservatism – let me now move our discussion of modernity and its discontents into a different domain that touches on these aporias of cultural modernity – issues that often serve only as a pretense for those positions which either call for a postmodernity, recommend a return to some form of premodernity, or throw modernity radically overboard.

The project of enlightenment

The idea of modernity is intimately tied to the development of European art, but what I call 'the project of modernity' comes only into focus when we dispense with the usual concentration upon art. Let me start a different analysis by recalling an idea from Max Weber. He characterised cultural modernity as the separation of the substantive reason expressed in religion and metaphysics into three autonomous spheres. They are:science, morality and art. These came to be differentiated because the unified world-views of religion and metaphysics fell apart. Since the eighteenth century, the problems inherited from these older world-views could be arranged so as to fall under specific aspects of validity; truth, normative rightness, authenticity and beauty. They could then be handled as questions of knowledge, or of justice and morality, or of taste. Scientific discourse, theories of morality, jurisprudence, and the production and criticism of art could in turn be institutionalised. Each domain of culture could be made to correspond to cultural professions in which problems could be dealt with as the concern of special experts. This professionalised treatment of the cultural tradition brings to the fore the intrinsic structures of each of the three dimensions of culture. There appear the structures of cognitive-instrumental, or moral-practical and of aesthetic-expressive rationality, each of these under the control of specialists who seem more adept at being logical in these particular ways than other people are. As a result, the distance grows between the culture of the experts and that of the larger public. What accrues to culture through specialised treatment and reflection does not immediately and necessarily become the property of everyday praxis. With cultural rationalisation of this sort, the threat increases that the life-world, whose traditional substance has already been devalued, will become more and more impoverished.

The project of modernity formulated in the eighteenth century by the philosophers of the Enlightenment consisted in their efforts to develop objective science, universal morality and law, and autonomous art according to their inner logic. At the same time, this project intended to release the cognitive potentials of each of these domains from their esoteric forms. The Enlightenment philosophers wanted to utilise this accumulation of specialised culture for the enrichment of everyday life – that is to say, for the rational organisation of everyday social life.

Enlightenment thinkers of the cast of mind of Condorcet still had the extravagant expectation that the arts and sciences would promote not only the control of natural forces but also understanding of the world and of the self, moral progress, the justice of institutions and even the happiness of human beings. The twentieth century has shattered this optimism. The differentiation of science, morality and art has come to mean the autonomy of the segments treated by the specialist and their separation from the hermeneutics of everyday communication. This splitting off is the problem that has given rise to efforts to 'negate' the culture of expertise. But the problem won't go away: should we try to hold on to the *intentions* of the Enlightenment, feeble as they may be, or should we declare the entire project of modernity a lost cause? I now want to return to the problem of artistic culture, having explained why, historically, aesthetic modernity is only a part of cultural modernity in general.

The false programs of the negation of culture

Greatly oversimplifying, I would say that in the history of modern art one can detect a trend towards ever greater autonomy in the definition and practice of art. The category of 'beauty' and the domain of beautiful objects were first constituted in the Renaissance. In the course of the eighteenth century, literature, the fine arts and music were institutionalised as activities independent from sacred and courtly life. Finally, around the middle of the nineteenth century an aestheticist conception of art emerged, which encouraged the artist to produce his work according to the distinct consciousness of art for art's sake. The autonomy of the aesthetic sphere could then become a deliberate project: the talented artist could lend authentic expression to those experiences he had in encountering his own decentered subjectivity, detached from the constraints of routinised cognition and everyday action.

In the mid-nineteenth century, in painting and literature, a movement began which Octavio Paz finds epitomised already in the art criticism of Baudelaire. Color, lines, sounds and movement ceased to serve primarily the cause of representation; the media of expression and the techniques of production themselves became the aesthetic object. Theodor W. Adorno could therefore begin his *Aesthetic Theory* with the following sentence: 'It is now taken for granted that nothing which concerns art can be taken for granted any more: neither art itself, nor art in its relationship to the whole, nor even the right of art to exist.' And this is what Surrealism then denied: *das Existenzrecht der Kunst als Kunst*. To be sure, Surrealism would not have challenged the right of art to exist, if modern art no longer had advanced a promise of happiness concerning its own relationship 'to the whole' of life. For Schiller, such a promise was delivered by aesthetic intuition, but not fulfilled by it. Schiller's *Letters on the Aesthetic Education of Man* speaks to us of a utopia reaching beyond art itself. But by the time of Beaudelaire, who repeated this *promesse de bonheur* via art, the utopia of reconciliation with society had gone sour. A relation of opposites had come into being; art had become a critical mirror, showing the irreconcilable nature of the aesthetic and the social worlds. This modernist transformation was all the more painfully realised, the more art alienated itself from life and withdrew into the untouchableness of complete autonomy. Out of such emotional currents finally gathered those explosive energies which unloaded in the Surrealist attempt to blow up the autarkical sphere of art and to force a reconciliation of art and life.

But all those attempts to level art and life, fiction and praxis, appearance and reality to one plane; the attempts to remove the distinction between artifact and object of use, between conscious staging and spontaneous excitement; the attempts to declare everything to be art and everyone to be an artist, to retract all criteria and to equate aesthetic judgement with the expression of subjective experiences – all these undertakings have proved themselves to be sort of nonsense experiments. These experiments have served to bring back to life, and to illuminate all the more glaringly, exactly those structures of art which they were meant to dissolve. They gave a new legitimacy, as ends in themselves, to appearance as the medium of fiction, to the transcendence of the artwork over society, to the concentrated and planned character of artistic production as well as to the special cognitive status of judgments of taste. The radical attempt to negate art has ended up ironically by giving due exactly to these categories through which Enlightenment aesthetics had circumscribed its object domain. The Surrealists waged the most extreme warfare, but two mistakes in particular destroyed their revolt. First, when the containers of an autonomously developed cultural sphere are shattered, the contents get dispersed. Nothing remains from a desublimated meaning or a destructured form; an emancipatory effect does not follow.

Their second mistake has more important consequences. In everyday communication, cognitive meanings, moral expectations, subjective expressions and evaluations must relate to one another. Communication processes need a cultural tradition covering all spheres – cognitive, moral-practical and expressive. A rationalised everyday life, therefore, could hardly be saved from cultural impoverishment through breaking open a single cultural sphere – art – and so providing access to just one of the specialised knowledge complexes. The Surrealist revolt would have replaced only one abstraction.

In the spheres of theoretical knowledge and morality, there are parallels to this failed attempt of what we might call the false negation of culture. Only they are less pronounced. Since the days of the Young Hegelians, there has been talk about the negation of philosophy. Since Marx, the question of the relationship of theory and practice has been posed. However, Marxist intellectuals joined a social movement; and only at its peripheries were there sectarian attempts to carry out a program of the negation of philosophy similar to the Surrealist program to negate art. A parallel to the Surrealist mistakes becomes visible in these programs when one observes the consequences of dogmatism and of moral rigorism.

A reified everyday praxis can be cured only by creating unconstrained interaction of the cognitive with the moral-practical and the aesthetic-expressive elements. Reification cannot be overcome by forcing just one of those highly stylised cultural spheres to open up and become more accessible. Instead, we see under certain circumstances a relationship emerge between terroristic activities and the over-extension of any one of these spheres to other domains: examples would be tendencies to aestheticise politics, or to replace politics by moral rigorism or to submit it to the dogmatism of a doctrine. These phenomena should not lead us, however, into denouncing the intentions of the surviving Enlightenment tradition as intentions rooted in a 'terroristic reason'.[5] Those who lump together the very project of modernity with the state of consciouness and the spectacular action of the individual terrorist are no less short-sighted than those who would claim that the incomparably more persistent and extensive bureacratic terror practiced in the dark, in the cellars of the military and secret police, and in camps and institutions, is the *raison d'être* of the modern state, only because this kind of adminstrative terror makes use of the coercive means of modern bureaucracies.

Alternatives

I think that instead of giving up modernity and its project as a lost cause, we should learn from the mistakes of those extravagant programs which have tried to negate modernity. Perhaps the types of reception of art may offer an example which at least indicates the direction of a way out.

Bourgeois art had two expectations at once from its audiences. On the one hand, the layman who enjoyed art should educate himself to become an expert. On the other hand, he should also behave as a competent consumer who uses art and relates aesthetic experiences to his own life problems. This second, and seemingly harmless, manner of experiencing art has lost its radical implications exactly because it had a confused relation to the attitude of being expert and professional.

To be sure, artistic production would dry up, if it were not carried out in the form of a specialised treatment of autonomous problems and if it were to cease to be the concern of experts who do not pay so much attention to exoteric questions. Both artists and critics accept thereby the fact that such problems fall under the spell of what I earlier called the 'inner logic' of a cultural domain. But this sharp delineation, this exclusive concentration on one aspect of validity alone and the exclusion of aspects of truth and justice, break down as soon as aesthetic experience is drawn into an individual life history and is absorbed into ordinary life. The reception of art by the layman, or by the 'everyday expert', goes in a rather different direction than the reception of art by the professional critic.

Albrecht Wellmer has drawn my attention to one way that an aesthetic experience which is not framed around the experts' critical judgments of taste can have its significance altered: as soon as such an experience is used to illuminate a life-historical situation and is related to life problems, it enters into a language game which is no longer that of the aesthetic critic. The aesthetic experience then not only renews the interpretation of our needs in whose light we perceive the world. It permeates as well our cognitive significations and our normative expectations and changes the manner in which all these moments refer to one another. Let me give an example of this process.

This manner of receiving and relating to art is suggested in the first volume of the work *The Aesthetics of Resistance* by the German-Swedish writer Peter Weiss. Weiss describes the process of reappropriating art by presenting a group of politically motivated, knowledge-hungry workers in 1937 in Berlin.[6] These were young people who, through an evening high-school education, acquired the intellectual means to fathom the general and social history of European art. Out of the resilient edifice of this objective mind, embodied in works of art which they saw again and again in the museums in Berlin, they started removing their own chips of stone, which they gathered together and reassembled in the context of their own milieu. This milieu was far removed from that of traditional education as well as from the then existing regime. These young workers went back and forth between the edifice of European art and their own milieu until they were able to illuminate both.

In examples like this which illustrate the reappropriation of the expert's culture from the standpoint of the life-world, we can discern an element which does justice to the intentions of the hopeless Surrealist revolts, perhaps even more to Brecht's and Benjamin's interest in how art works, which having lost their aura, could yet be received in illuminating ways. In sum, the project of modernity has not yet been fulfilled. And the reception of art is only one of at least three of its aspects. The project aims at a differentiated relinking of modern culture with an everyday praxis that still depends on vital heritages, but would be impoverished through mere traditionalism. This new connection, however, can only be established under the condition that societal modernisation will also be steered in a different direction. The life-world has to become able to develop institutions out of itself which set limits to the internal dynamics and imperatives of an almost autonomous economic system and its administrative complements.

If I am not mistaken, the chances for this today are not very good. More or less in the entire Western world a climate had developed that furthers capitalist modernisation processes as well as trends critical of cultural modernism. The disillusionment with the very failures of those programs that called for the negation of art and philosophy has come to serve as a pretense for conservative positions. Let me briefly distinguish the anti-modernism of the 'young conservatives' from the premodernism of the 'old conservatives' and from the postmodernism of the neoconservatives.

The 'young conservatives' recapitulate the basic experience of aesthetic modernity. They claim as their own the revelations of a decentered subjectivity, emancipated from the imperatives of work and usefulness, and with this experience they step outside the modern world. On the basis of modernistic attitudes they justify an irreconcilable antimodernism. They remove into the sphere of the far-away and the archaic the spontaneous powers of imagination, self-experience and emotion. To instrumental reason they juxtapose in Manichean fashion a principle only accessible through evocation, be it the will to power or sovereignty, Being or the Dionysiac force of the poetical. In France this line leads from Georges Bataille via Michel Foucault to Jacques Derrida.

The 'old conservatives' do not allow themselves to be contaminated by cultural modernism. They observe the decline of substantive reason, the differentiation of science, morality and art, the modern world view and its merely procedural rationality, with sadness and recommend a withdrawal to a position *anterior* to modernity. Neo-Aristotelianism, in particular, enjoys a certain success today. In view of the problematic of ecology, it allows itself to call for a cosmological ethic. (As belonging to this school, which originates with Leo Strauss, one can count the interesting works of Hans Jonas and Robert Spaemann.)

Finally, the neoconservatives welcome the development of modern science, as long as this only goes beyond its sphere to carry forward technical progress, capitalist growth and rational administration. Moreover, they recommend a politics of defusing the explosive content of cultural modernity. According to one thesis, science, when properly understood, has become irrevocably meaningless for the orientation of the life-world. A further thesis is that politics must be kept as far aloof as possible from the demands of moral-practical justification. And a third thesis asserts the pure immanence of art, disputes that it has a utopian content, and points to its illusory character in order to limit the aesthetic experience to privacy. (One could name here the early Wittgenstein, Carl Schmitt of the middle period, and Gottfried Benn of the late period.) But with the decisive confinement of science, morality and art to autonomous spheres separated from the life-world and administered by experts, what remains from the project of cultural modernity is only what we would have if we were to give up the project of modernity altogether. As a replacement one points to traditions which, however, are held to be immune to demands of (normative) justification and validation.

This typology is like any other, of course, a simplification, but it may not prove totally useless for the analysis of contemporary intellectual and political confrontations. I fear that the ideas of antimodernity, together with an additional touch of premodernity, are becoming popular in the circles of alternative culture. When one observes the transformations of consciousness within political parties in Germany, a new ideological shift (*Tendenzwende*) becomes visible. And this is the alliance of postmodernists with premodernists. It seems to me that there is no party in particular that monopolises the abuse of intellectuals and the position of neoconservatism. I therefore have good reason to be thankful for the liberal spirit in which the city of Frankfurt offers me a prize bearing the name of Theodor Adorno, a most significant son of this city, who as philosopher and writer has stamped the image of the intellectual in our country in incomparable fashion, who, even more, has become the very image of emulation for the intellectual.

Notes

1. Jauss is a prominent German literary historian and critic involved in 'the aesthetics of reception', a type of criticism related to reader-response criticism in this country. For a discussion of 'modern' see Jauss, *Asthetische Normen und geschichtliche Reflexion in der Querelle des Anciens et des Modernes* (Munich, 1964). For a reference in English see Jauss, 'History of Art and Pragmatic History', *Toward an Aesthetic of Reception*, trans. Timothy Bahti (Minneapolis: University of Minnesota Press, 1982)l, pp. 46–8.

2. See BENJAMIN, 'Theses on the Philosophy of History', *Illuminations*, trans. Harry Zohn (New York: Schocken, 1969), p. 261.

3. For Paz on the avant-garde see in particular *Children of the Mire: Modern Poetry from Romanticism to the Avant-Garde* (Cambridge: Harvard University Press, 1974), pp. 148–64. For Bürger see *Theory of the Avant-Garde* (Minneapolis: University of Minnesota Press, Fall 1983).

4. PETER STEINFELS, *The Neoconservatives* (New York: Simon and Schuster, 1979), p. 65.

5. The phrase 'to aestheticise politics' echoes Benjamin's famous formulation of the false social program of the fascists in 'The Work of Art in the Age of Mechanical Reproduction'. Habermas's criticism here of Enlightenment critics seems directed less at Adorno and Max Horkheimer than at the contemporary *nouveaux philosophes* (Bernard-Henri Lèvy, etc.) and their German and American counterparts.

6. The reference is to the novel *Die Asthetik des Widerstands* (1975–78) by the author perhaps best known here for his 1965 play *Marat/Sade*. The work of art 'reappropriated' by the workers is the Pergamon altar, emblem of power, classicism and rationality.

11 Jean-François Lyotard, 'Answering the Question: What is Postmodernism?'*

The present essay appeared in *Critique*, **419** (April 1982), then in translation in Hassan and Hassan (eds) *Innovation/Renovation* (1983), and subsequently as an appendix to the English translation of Lyotard's *The Postmodern Condition*. This text has proved a major focus in debates on cultural postmodernism. Whereas Habermas continues the search for a social ethics based on reason, Lyotard draws on Nietzsche's critique of the totalising claims of reason to argue that this goal is without moral or philosophical grounds, or 'legitimation'. Secondly, drawing upon Wittgenstein, Lyotard argues that the criteria regulating the 'truth claims' of knowledge derive from discrete, context-dependent 'language games' not absolute rules or standards. His major example concerns the different procedures and effects marking scientific and narrative knowledge. In its 'modern' phase, science sought legitimation from either of two narrative types: the narrative of human liberation associated with the Enlightenment and the revolutionary tradition, or of the prospective unity of all knowledge associated with Hegelianism.

Neither of these legitimating 'metanarratives' or '*grands récits*', says Lyotard, now has credibility. Instead, 'postmodern' science pursues the technical and commercial aims of optimal performance; a change reinforced by new computerised technologies which make information a political quantity. But yet this technocratic order is at odds with an internal experimental drive which questions the paradigms of 'normal science'. What Lyotard calls the activity of paralogism – exercised in illogical or contradictory reasoning – produces a breakthrough into

---

* Trans. Régis Durand, reprinted from *The Postmodern Condition: a Report on Knowledge*, trans. G. Bennington and B. Massumi. Foreword by F. Jameson (Manchester: Manchester University Press, 1984), pp. 71–82.

the unknown of new knowledge. There thus emerges a new source of legitimation, invested in more modest '*petits récits*' and indebted to the radical avant-garde imperative to experiment and 'make it new'. The postmodern aesthetic, examined below, thus emerges as an investigative aesthetic of the 'sublime'. It does not sequentially follow modernism but describes its founding conditions. As Lyotard puts it, the postmodern 'is undoubtedly a part of the modern', it 'would be that which, in the modern, puts forward the unpresentable in presentation itself' (pp. 148, 149).

The implications of this are ambiguous. Thus Lyotard, along with deconstruction generally, can be said to have authorised a consciously decentred postmodernism and micropolitics, keyed to social heterogeneity, the local, provisional and pragmatic; its political or ethical judgements undecided in advance. On the other hand, his views appear to sponsor a romantic anarchism, large on rhetoric and low on concrete social transformation. Jameson's 'Foreword' to *The Postmodern Condition*, Honneth (in *Theory, Culture and Society*, 2, 3, 1985) and Connor (*Postmodernist Culture*, 1989) issue warnings along these lines. Fraser and Nicholson also (in Nicholson (ed.), *Feminism/Postmodernism*, 1990), while sympathetic to Lyotard's anti-foundationalism, note his failure to identify macrostructures of inequality and injustice, particularly concerning gender. For a sympathetic explication of Lyotard, see Bennington, *Lyotard: Writing the Event*, (1988).

A demand

This is a period of slackening – I refer to the color of the times. From every direction we are being urged to put an end to experimentation, in the arts and elsewhere. I have read an art historian who extols realism and is militant for the advent of a new subjectivity. I have read an art critic who packages and sells 'Transavantgardism' in the marketplace of painting. I have read that under the name of postmodernism, architects are getting rid of the Bauhaus project, throwing out the baby of experimentation with the bathwater of functionalism. I have read that a new philosopher is discovering what he drolly calls Judaeo-Christianism, and intends by it to put an end to the impiety which we are supposed to have spread. I have read in a French weekly that some are displeased with *Mille Plateaux* (by Deleuze and Guattari) because they expect, especially when reading a work of philosophy, to be gratified with a little sense. I have read from the pen of a reputable historian that writers and thinkers of the 1960 and 1970 avant-gardes spread a reign of terror in the use of language, and that the conditions for a fruitful exchange must be restored by imposing on the intellectuals a common way of speaking, that of the historians. I have been reading a young philosopher of language who complains that Continental thinking, under the challenge of speaking machines, has surrendered to the machines the concern for reality, that it has substituted for the referential paradigm that of 'adlinguisticity' (one speaks about speech, writes about writing, intertextuality), and who thinks that the time has now come to restore a solid anchorage of language in the referent. I have read a talented theatrologist for whom postmodernism, with its games and fantasies, carried very little weight in front of political authority, especially when a worried public opinion encourages authority to a politics of totalitarian surveillance in the face of nuclear warfare threats.

I have read a thinker of repute who defends modernity against those he calls the neoconservatives. Under the banner of postmodernism, the latter would like, he believes, to get rid of the uncompleted project of modernism, that of the Enlightenment. Even the last advocates of *Aufklärung*, such as Popper or Adorno, were only able, according to him, to defend the project in a few particular spheres of life – that of politics for the author of *The Open Society*, and that of art for the author of *Ästhetische Theorie*. Jürgen Habermas (everyone had recognised him) thinks that if modernity has failed, it is in allowing the totality of life to be splintered into independent specialities which are left to the narrow competence of experts, while the concrete individual experiences 'desublimated meaning' and 'destructured form', not as a liberation but in the mode of that immense *ennui* which Baudelaire described over a century ago.

Following a prescription of Albrecht Wellmer, Habermas considers that the remedy for this splintering of culture and its separation from life can only come from 'changing the status of aesthetic experience when it is no longer primarily expressed in judgments of taste', but when it is 'used to explore a living historical situation', that is, when 'it is put in relation with problems of existence'. For this experience then 'becomes a part of a language game which is no longer that of aesthetic criticism'; it takes part 'in cognitive processes and normative expectations'; 'it alters the manner in which those different moments *refer* to one another'. What Habermas requires from the arts and the experiences they provide is, in short, to bridge the gap between cognitive, ethical, and political discourse, thus opening the way to a unity of experience.

My question is to determine what sort of unity Habermas has in mind. Is the aim of the project of modernity the consitituion of sociocultural unity within which all the elements of daily life and of thought would take their places as in an organic whole? Or does the passage that has to be charted between heterogeneous language games – those of cognition, of ethics, of politics – belong to a different order from that? And if so, would it be capable of effecting a real synthesis between them?

The first hypothesis, of a Hegelian inspiration, does not challenge the notion of a dialectically totalising *experience*; the second is closer to the spirit of Kant's *Critique of Judgment*; but must be submitted, like the *Critique*, to that severe reexamination which postmodernity imposes on the thought of the Enlightenment, on the idea of a unitary end of history and of a subject. It is this critique which not only Wittgenstein and Adorno have initiated, but also a few other thinkers (French or other) who do not have the honor to be read by Professor Habermas – which at least saves them from getting a poor grade for their neoconservatism.

Realism

The demands I began by citing are not all equivalent. They can even be contradictory. Some are made in the name of postmodernism, others in order to combat it. It is not necessarily the same thing to formulate a demand for some referent (and objective reality), for some sense (and credible transcendence), for an addressee (and audience), or an addressor (and subjective expressiveness) or for some communicational consensus (and a general code of exchanges, such as the genre of historical discourse). But in the diverse invitations to suspend artistic experimentation, there is an identical call for order, a desire for unity, for identity, for security, or popularity (in the sense of *Öffentlichkeit*, of 'finding a public'). Artists and writers must be brought back into the bosom of the community, or at least, if the latter is considered to be ill, they must be assigned the task of healing it.

There is an irrefutable sign of this common disposition: it is that for all those writers nothing is more urgent than to liquidate the heritage of the avant-gardes. Such is the case, in particular, of the so-called transavantgardism. The answers given by Achille Bonito Oliva to the questions asked by Bernard Lamarche-Vadel and Michel Enric leave no room for doubt about this. By putting the avant-gardes through a mixing process, the artist and critic feel more confident that they can suppress them than by launching a frontal attack. For they can pass off the most cynical eclecticism as a way of going beyond the fragmentary character of the preceding experiments; whereas if they openly turned their backs on them, they would run the risk of appearing ridiculously neoacademic. The *Salons* and the *Académies*, at the time when the bourgeoisie was establishing itself in history, were able to function as purgation and to grant awards for good plastic and literary conduct under the cover of realism. But capitalism inherently possesses the power to derealise familiar objects, social roles, and institutions to such a degree that the so-called realistic representations can no longer evoke reality except as nostalgia or mockery, as an occasion for suffering rather than for satisfaction. Classicism seems to be ruled out in a world in which reality is so destabilised that it offers no occasion for experience but one for ratings and experimentation.

This theme is familiar to all readers of Walter Benjamin. But it is necessary to assess its exact reach. Photography did not appear as a challenge to painting from the outside, any more than industrial cinema did to narrative literature. The former was only putting the final touch to the program of ordering the visible elaborated by the quattrocento; while the latter was the last step in rounding off diachronies as organic wholes, which had been the ideal of the great novels of education since the eighteenth century. That the mechanical and the industrial should appear as substitutes for hand or craft was not in itself a disaster – except if one believes that art is in its essence the expression of an individuality of genius assisted by an elite craftsmanship.

The challenge lay essentially in that photographic and cinematographic processes can accomplish better, faster, and with a circulation a hundred thousand times larger than narrative or pictorial realism, the task which academicism had assigned to realism: to preserve various consciousnesses from doubt. Industrial photography and cinema will be superior to painting and the novel whenever the objective is to stabilise the referent, to arrange it according to a point of view which endows it with a recognisable meaning, to reproduce the syntax and vocabulary which enable the addressee to decipher images and sequences quickly, and so to arrive easily at the consciousness of his own identity as well as the approval which he thereby receives from others – since such structures of images and sequences constitute a communication code among all of them. This is the way the effects of reality, or if one prefers, the fantasies of realism, multiply.

If they too do not wish to become supporters (of minor importance at that) of what exists, the painter and novelist must refuse to lend themselves to such therapeutic uses. They must question the rules of the art of painting or of narrative as they have learned and received them from their predecessors. Soon those rules must appear to them as a means to deceive, to seduce and to reassure, which makes it impossible for them to be 'true'. Under the common name of painting and literature, an unprecedented split is taking place. Those who refuse to re-examine the rules of art pursue successful careers in mass conformism by communicating, by means of the 'correct rules', the endemic desire for reality with objects and situations capable of gratifying it. Pornography is the use of photography and film to such an end. It is becoming a general model for the visual or narrative arts which have not met the challenge of the mass media.

As for the artists and writers who question the rules of plastic and narrative arts and possibly share their suspicions by circulating their work, they are destined to have little credibility in the eyes of those concerned with 'reality' and 'identity'; they have no guarantee of an audience. Thus it is possible to ascribe the dialectics of the avant-gardes to the challenge posed by the realisms of industry and mass communication to painting and the narrative arts. Duchamp's 'ready made' does nothing but actively and parodistically signify this constant process of dispossession of the craft of painting or even of being an artist. As Thierry de Duve penetratingly observes, the modern aesthetic question is not 'What is beautiful?' but 'What can be said to be art (and literature)?'

Realism, whose only definition is that it intends to avoid the question of reality implicated in that of art, always stands somewhere between academicism and kitsch. When power assumes the name of a party, realism and its neoclassical complement triumph over the experimental avant-garde by slandering and banning it – that is, provided the 'correct' images, the 'correct' narratives, the 'correct' forms which the party requests, selects, and propagates can find a public to desire them as the appropriate remedy for the anxiety and depression that public experiences. The demand for reality – that is, for unity, simplicity, communicability, etc. – did not have the same intensity nor the same continuity in German society between the two world wars and in Russian society after the Revolution: this provides a basis for a distinction between Nazi and Stalinist realism.

What is clear, however, is that when it is launched by the political apparatus, the attack on artistic experimentation is specifically reactionary: aesthetic judgment would only be required to decide whether such or such work is in conformity with the established rules of the beautiful. Instead of the work of art having to investigate what makes it an art object and whether it will be able to find an audience, political academicism possesses and imposes *a priori* criteria of the beautiful, which designate some works and a public at a stroke and forever. The use of categories in aesthetic judgment would thus be of the same nature as in cognitive judgment. To speak like Kant, both would be determining judgments: the expression is 'well formed' first in the understanding, then the only cases retained in experience are those which can be subsumed under this expression.

When power is that of capital and not that of a party, the 'transavantgardist' or 'postmodern' (in Jencks's sense) solution proves to be better adapted than the antimodern solution. Eclecticism is the degree zero of contemporary general culture: one listens to reggae, watches a western, eats McDonald's food for lunch and local cuisine for dinner, wears Paris perfume in Tokyo and 'retro' clothes in Hong Kong; knowledge is a matter for TV games. It is easy to find a public for eclectic works. By becoming kitsch, art panders to the confusion which reigns in the 'taste' of the patrons. Artists, gallery owners, critics and public wallow together in the 'anything goes', and the epoch is one of slackening. But this realism of the 'anything goes' is in fact that of money; in the absence of aesthetic criteria, it remains possible and useful to assess the value of works of art according to the profits they yield. Such realism accommodates all tendencies, just as capital accommodates all 'needs', providing that the tendencies and needs have purchasing power. As for taste, there is no need to be delicate when one speculates or entertains oneself.

Artistic and literary research is doubly threatened, once by the 'cultural policy' and once by the art and book market. What is advised, sometimes through one channel, sometimes through the other, is to offer works which, first, are relative to subjects which exist in the eyes of the public they address, and second, works so made ('well made') that the public will recognise what they are about, will understand what is signified, will be able to give or refuse its approval knowingly, and if possible, even to derive from such work a certain amount of comfort.

The interpretation which has just been given of the contact between the industrial and mechanical arts, and literature and the fine arts is correct in its outline, but it remains narrowly sociologising and historicising – in other words, one-sided. Stepping over Benjamin's and Adorno's reticences, it must be recalled that science and industry are no more free of the suspicion which concerns reality than are art and writing. To believe otherwise would be to entertain an excessively humanistic notion of the mephistophelian functionalism of sciences and technologies. There is no denying the dominant existence today of techno-science, that is, the massive subordination of cognitive statements to the finality of the best possible performance, which is the technolgical criterion. But the mechanical and the industrial, especially when they enter fields traditionally reserved for artists, are carrying with them much more than power effects. The objects and the thoughts which originate in scientific knowledge and the capitalist economy convey with them one of the rules which supports their possibililty: the rule that there is no reality unless testified by a consensus between partners over a certain knowledge and certain commitments.

This rule is of no little consequence. It is the imprint left on the politics of the scientist and the trustee of capital by a kind of flight of reality out of the metaphysical, religious, and political certainties that the mind

believed it held. This withdrawal is absolutely necessary to the
emergence of science and capitalism. No industry is possible without a
suspicion of the Aristotelian theory of motion, no industry without a
refutation of corporatism, of mercantilism, and physiocracy. Modernity,
in whatever age it appears, cannot exist without a shattering of belief and
without discovery of the 'lack of reality' of reality, together with the
invention of other realities.

What does this 'lack of reality' signify if one tries to free it from a
narrowly historicised intepretation? The phrase is of course akin to what
Nietzsche calls nihilism. But I see a much earlier modulation of
Nietzschean perspectivism in the Kantian theme of the sublime. I think
in particular that it is in the aesthetic of the sublime that modern art
(including literature) finds its impetus and the logic of avant-gardes finds
its axioms.

The sublime sentiment, which is also the sentiment of the sublime, is,
according to Kant, a strong and equivocal emotion: it carries with it both
pleasure and pain. Better still, in it pleasure derives from pain. Within
the tradition of the subject, which comes from Augustine and Descartes
and which Kant does not radically challenge, this contradiction, which
some would call neurosis or masochism, develops as a conflict between
the faculties of a subject, the faculty to conceive of something and the
faculty to 'present' something. Knowledge exists if, first, the statement is
intelligible, and second, if 'cases' can be derived from the experience
which 'corresponds' to it. Beauty exists if a certain 'case' (the work of
art), given first by the sensibility without any conceptual determination,
the sentiment of pleasure independent of any interest the work may
elicit, appeals to the principle of a universal consensus (which may never
be attained).

Taste, therefore, testifies that between the capacity to conceive and the
capacity to present an object corresponding to the concept, an
undetermined agreement, without rules, giving rise to a judgment which
Kant calls reflective, may be experienced as pleasure. The sublime is a
different sentiment. It takes place, on the contrary, when the imagination
fails to present an object which might, if only in principle, come to match
a concept. We have the Idea of the world (the totality of what is), but we
do not have the capacity to show an example of it. We have the Idea of
the simple (that which cannot be broken down, decomposed), but we
cannot illustrate it with a sensible object which would be a 'case' of it. We
can conceive the infinitely great, the infinitely powerful, but every
presentation of an object destined to 'make visible' this absolute
greatness or power appears to us painfully inadequate. Those are Ideas
of which no presentation is possible. Therefore, they impart no
knowledge about reality (experience); they also prevent the free union of

the faculties which gives rise to the sentiment of the beautiful; and they prevent the formation and the stabilisation of taste. They can be said to be unpresentable.

I shall call modern the art which devotes its 'little technical expertise' (*son 'petit technique'*), as Diderot used to say, to present the fact that the unpresentable exists. To make visible that there is something which can be conceived and which can neither be seen nor made visible: this is what is at stake in modern painting. But how to make visible that there is something which cannot be seen? Kant himself shows the way when he names 'formlessness, the absence of form', as a possible index to the unpresentable. He also says of the empty 'abstraction' which the imagination experiences when in search for a presentation of the infinite (another unpresentable): this abstraction itself is like a presentation of the infinite, its 'negative presentation'. He cites the commandment, 'Thou shalt not make graven images' (*Exodus*), as the most sublime passage in the Bible in that it forbids all presentation of the Absolute. Little needs to be added to those observations to outline an aesthetic of sublime paintings. As painting, it will of course 'present' something though negatively; it will therefore avoid figuration or representation. It will be 'white' like one of Malevitch's squares; it will enable us to see only by making it impossible to see; it will please only by causing pain. One recognises in those instructions the axioms of avant-gardes in painting, inasmuch as they devote themselves to making an allusion to the unpresentable by means of visible presentations. The systems in the name of which, or with which, this task has been able to support or to justify itself deserve the greatest attention; but they can originate only in the vocation of the sublime in order to legitimise it, that is, to conceal it. They remain inexplicable without the incommensurability of reality to concept which is implied in the Kantian philosophy of the sublime.

It is not my intention to analyse here in detail the manner in which the various avant-gardes have, so to speak, humbled and disqualified reality by examining the pictorial techniques which are so many devices to make us believe in it. Local tone, drawing, the mixing of colors, linear perspective, the nature of the support and that of the instrument, the treatment, the display, the museum: the avant-gardes are perpetually flushing out artifices of presentation which make it possible to subordinate thought to the gaze and to turn it away from the unpresentable. If Habermas, like Marcuse, understands this task of derealisation as an aspect of the (repressive) 'desublimation' which characterises the avant-garde, it is because he confuses the Kantian sublime with Freudian sublimation, and because aesthetics has remained for him that of the beautiful.

The postmodern

What, then, is the postmodern? What place does it or does it not occupy in the vertiginous work of the questions hurled at the rules of image and narration? It is undoubtedly a part of the modern. All that has been received, if only yesterday (*modo, modo*, Petronius used to say), must be suspected. What space does Cézanne challenge? The Impressionists'. What object do Picasso and Braque attack? Cézanne's. What presupposition does Duchamp break with in 1912? That which says one must make a painting, be it Cubist. And Buren questions that other presupposition which he believes had survived untouched by the work of Duchamp: the place of presentation of the work. In an amazing acceleration, the generations precipitate themselves. A work can become modern only if it is first postmodern. Postmodernism thus understood is not modernism at its end but in the nascent state, and this state is constant.

Yet I would like not to remain with this slightly mechanistic meaning of the word. If it is true that modernity takes place in the withdrawal of the real and according to the sublime relation between the presentable and the conceivable, it is possible, within this relation, to distinguish two modes (to use the musician's language). The emphasis can be placed on the powerlessness of the faculty of presentation, on the nostalgia for presence felt by the human subject, on the obscure and futile will which inhabits him in spite of everything. The emphasis can be placed, rather, on the power of the faculty to conceive, on its 'inhumanity' so to speak (it was the quality Apollinaire demanded of modern artists), since it is not the business of our understanding whether or not human sensibility or imagination can match what it conceives. The emphasis can also be placed on the increase of being and the jubilation which result from the invention of new rules of the game, be it pictorial, artistic, or any other. What I have in mind will become clear if we dispose very schematically a few names on the chessboard of the history of avant-gardes: on the side of melancholia, the German Expressionists, and on the side of *novatio*, Braque and Picasso, on the former Malevitch and on the latter Lissitsky, on the one Chirico and on the other Duchamp. The nuance which distinguishes these two modes may be infinitesimal; they often coexist in the same piece, are almost indistinguishable; and yet they testify to a difference (*un différend*) on which the fate of thought depends and will depend for a long time, between regret and assay.

The work of Proust and that of Joyce both allude to something which does not allow itself to be made present. Allusion, to which Paolo Fabbri recently called my attention, is perhaps a form of expression indispensable to the works which belong to an aesthetic of the sublime. In Proust, what is being eluded as the price to pay for this allusion is the identity of consciousness, a victim to the excess of time (*au trop de temps*). But in Joyce, it is the identity of writing which is the victim of an excess of the book (*au trop de livre*) or of literature.

Proust calls forth the unpresentable by means of a language unaltered in its syntax and vocabulary and of a writing which in many of its operators still belongs to the genre of novelistic narration. The literary institution, as Proust inherits it from Balzac and Flaubert, is admittedly subverted in that the hero is no longer a character but the inner consciousness of time, and in that the diegetic diachrony, already damaged by Flaubert, is here put in question because of the narrative voice. Nevertheless, the unity of the book, the odyssey of that consciousness, even if it is deferred from chapter to chapter, is not seriously challenged: the identity of the writing with itself throughout the labyrinth of the interminable narration is enough to connote such unity, which has been compared to that of *The Phenomenology of Mind*.

Joyce allows the unpresentable to become perceptible in his writing itself, in the signifier. The whole range of available narrative and even stylistic operators is put into play without concern for the unity of the whole, and new operators are tried. The grammar and vocabulary of literary language are no longer accepted as given; rather, they appear as academic forms, as rituals originating in piety (as Nietzsche said) which prevent the unpresentable from being put forward.

Here, then, lies the difference: modern aesthetics is an aesthetic of the sublime, though a nostalgic one. It allows the unpresentable to be put forward only as the missing contents; but the form, because of its recognisable consistency, continues to offer to the reader or viewer matter for solace and pleasure. Yet these sentiments do not constitute the real sublime sentiment, which is in an intrinsic combination of pleasure and pain: the pleasure that reason should exceed all presentation, the pain that imagination or sensibility should not be equal to the concept.

The postmodern would be that which, in the modern, puts forward the unpresentable in presentation itself; that which denies itself the solace of good forms, the consensus of a taste which would make it possible to share collectively the nostalgia for the unattainable; that which searches for new presentations, not in order to enjoy them but in order to impart a stronger sense of the unpresentable. A postmodern artist or writer is in the position of a philosopher: the text he writes, the work he produces are not in principle governed by preestablished rules, and they cannot be judged according to a determining judgment, by applying familiar categories to the text or to the work. Those rules and categories are what the work of art itself is looking for. The artist and the writer, then, are working without rules in order to formulate the rules of what *will have been done*. Hence the fact that work and text have the characters of an *event*; hence also, they always come too late for their author, or, what amounts to the same thing, their being put into work, their realisation (*mise en oeuvre*) always begin too soon. *Post modern* would have to be understood according to the paradox of the future (*post*) anterior (*modo*).

It seems to me that the essay (Montaigne) is postmodern, while the fragment (*The Athaeneum*) is modern.

Finally, it must be clear that it is our business not to supply reality but to invent allusions to the conceivable which cannot be presented. And it is not to be expected that this task will effect the last reconciliation between language games (which, under the name of faculties, Kant knew to be separated by a chasm), and that only the transcendental illusion (that of Hegel) can hope to totalise them into a real unity. But Kant also knew that the price to pay for such an illusion is terror. The nineteenth and twentieth centuries have given us as much terror as we can take. We have paid a high enough price for the nostalgia of the whole and the one, for the reconciliation of the concept and the sensible, of the transparent and the communicable experience. Under the general demand for slackening and for appeasement, we can hear the mutterings of the desire for a return of terror, for the realisation of the fantasy to seize reality. The answer is: Let us wage a war on totality; let us be witnesses to the unpresentable; let us activate the differences and save the honor of the name.

12 Jean Baudrillard, from 'Simulacra and Simulations'*

Baudrillard's work has questioned the tenets of Marxism and structuralism to the point where, having argued for the relevance in modern capitalist societies of consumption over production and of the signifier over the signified, he has come to deny all models assuming a distinction between surface and depth. Postmodern communication technologies, principally television, are said to flood the world with self-generating, self-mirroring images; and experience, now thoroughly eclectic and superficial, to achieve its final, 'utopian' form in the instantaneous abundance and banality of a 'cultureless' North America.

Baudrillard's earlier, provocative but academically conventional, studies reworked the themes of poststructuralism and the French situationists (notably the findings of Guy Debord's *Society of the Spectacle*) in ways that signalled the 'retreat from politics' of Left intellectuals in the late seventies and eighties and made Baudrillard a popular guru. In 1988 the *Guardian* described him as the 'hottest property on the New York intellectual circuit'. One reason for this, perhaps, is the increasingly gnomic hyperbole, at once cool and apocalyptic, of his own and his disciples' utterances. The sensational message of 'the loss of the real', for example, (where there is no depth there can be no 'reality') comes with some of the combined shock and consolation of a headline or advertisement. Since, we are told, reality is gone for good there can be no grounds for remedial action, or for worry. Similarly, any anxieties over anonymous national and multinational structures of media and money power are offset by the wardrobe of new roles, images and codes they supply. At the

* Reprinted from *Selected Writings*, ed. and with Introduction by Mark Poster (Cambridge: Polity Press, 1988), pp. 170–4; 177–84.

same time, in an irony of postmodernism which foregrounds the popular, Baudrillard's popularity cannot be dismissed as a mere passing symptom, particularly by those of his critics committed to a rational analysis of 'real' historical change.

The present selection consolidates Baudrillard's argument on the dominance of the image or play of signs and inaugurates his view of American hyper-reality. His remarks on Disneyland might usefully be compared with Umberto Eco's in *Travels in Hyperreality* (1987). (See Introduction, pp. 17–20.)

The series *Culture Texts* has been particularly influenced by Baudrillard. See titles by Kroker and Cook under Further Reading. Of several further discussions see Douglas Kellner, *Jean Baudrillard. From Marxism to Post-Modernism and Beyond* (1988); Meagham Morris 'Room 101, Or A Few Worst Things in The World' in *The Pirate's Fiancée* (1988); and Christopher Norris, 'Lost in the Funhouse: Baudrillard and the Politics of Postmodernism' in Boyne and Rattansi (eds), *Postmodernism and Society* (1990), pp. 111–53.

All of Western faith and good faith was engaged in this wager on representation: that a sign could refer to the depth of meaning, that a sign could *exchange* for meaning and that something could guarantee this exchange – God, of course. But what if God himself can be simulated, that is to say, reduced to the signs which attest his existence? Then the whole system becomes weightless; it is no longer anything but a gigantic simulacrum: not unreal, but a simulacrum, never again exchanging for what is real, but exchanging in itself, in an uninterrupted circuit without reference or circumference.

So it is with simulation, in so far as it is opposed to representation. Representation starts from the principle that the sign and the real are equivalent (even if this equivalence is Utopian, it is a fundamental axiom). Conversely, simulation starts from the Utopia of this principle of equivalence, *from the radical negation of the sign as value*, from the sign as reversion and death sentence of every reference. Whereas representation tries to absorb simulation by interpreting it as false representation, simulation envelops the whole edifice of representation as itself a simulacrum.

These would be the successive phases of the image:

(1) It is the reflection of a basic reality.
(2) It masks and perverts a basic reality.
(3) It masks the *absence* of a basic reality.

(4) It bears no relation to any reality whatever: it is its own pure simulacrum.

In the first case, the image is a *good* appearance: the representation is of the order of sacrament. In the second, it is an *evil* appearance: of the order of malefice. In the third, it *plays at being* an appearance: it is of the order of sorcery. In the fourth, it is no longer in the order of appearance at all, but of simulation.

The transition from signs which dissimulate something to signs which dissimulate that there is nothing, marks the decisive turning point. The first implies a theology of truth and secrecy (to which the notion of ideology still belongs). The second inaugurates an age of simulacra and simulation, in which there is no longer any God to recognise his own, nor any last judgement to separate truth from false, the real from its artificial resurrection, since everything is already dead and risen in advance.

When the real is no longer what it used to be, nostalgia assumes its full meaning. There is a proliferation of myths of origin and signs of reality; of second-hand truth, objectivity and authenticity. There is an escalation of the true, of the lived experience; a resurrection of the figurative where the object and substance have disappeared. And there is a panic-stricken production of the real and the referential, above and parallel to the panic of material production. This is how simulation appears in the phase that concerns us: a strategy of the real, neo-real and hyperreal, whose universal double is a strategy of deterrence.

Hyperreal and imaginary

Disneyland is a perfect model of all the entangled orders of simulation. To begin with it is a play of illusions and phantasms: pirates, the frontier, future world, etc. This imaginary world is supposed to be what makes the operation successful. But, what draws the crowds is undoubtedly much more the social microcosm, the miniaturised and *religious* revelling in real America, in its delights and drawbacks. You park outside, queue up inside, and are totally abandoned at the exit. In this imaginary world the only phantasmagoria is in the inherent warmth and affection of the crowd, and in that sufficiently excessive number of gadgets used there to specifically maintain the multitudinous affect. The contrast with the absolute solitude of the parking lot – a veritable concentration camp – is total. Or rather: inside, a whole range of gadgets magnetise the crowd into direct flows; outside, solitude is directed onto a single gadget; the automobile. By an extraordinary coincidence (one that undoubtedly belongs to the peculiar enchantment of this universe), this deep-frozen infantile world happens to have been conceived and realised by a man who is himself now cryogenised; Walt Disney, who awaits his resurrection at minus 180 degrees centigrade.

The objective profile of the United States, then, may be traced throughout Disneyland, even down to the morphology of individuals and the crowd. All its values are exalted here, in miniature and comic-strip form. Embalmed and pacified. Whence the possibility of an ideological analysis of Disneyland (L. Marin does it well in *Utopies, jeux d'espaces*): digest of the American way of life, panegyric to American values, idealised transposition of a contradictory reality. To be sure. But this conceals something else, and that 'ideological' blanket exactly serves to cover over a *third-order simulation*: Disneyland is there to conceal the fact that it is the 'real' country, all of 'real' America, which *is* Disneyland (just as prisons are there to conceal the fact that it is the social in its entirety, in its banal omnipresence, which is carceral). Disneyland is presented as imaginary in order to make us believe that the rest is real, when in fact all of Los Angeles and the America surrounding it are no longer real, but of the order of the hyperreal and of simulation. It is no longer a question of a false representation of reality (ideology), but of concealing the fact that the real is no longer real, and thus of saving the reality principle.

The Disneyland imaginary is neither true nor false: it is a deterrence machine set up in order to rejuvenate in reverse the fiction of the real. Whence the debility, the infantile degeneration of this imaginary. It is meant to be an infantile world, in order to make us believe that the adults are elsewhere, in the 'real' world, and to conceal the fact that real childishness is everywhere, particularly among those adults who go there to act the child in order to foster illusions of their real childishness.

Moreover, Disneyland is not the only one. Enchanted Village, Magic Mountain, Marine World: Los Angeles is encircled by these 'imaginary stations' which feed reality, reality-energy, to a town whose mystery is precisely that it is nothing more than a network of endless, unreal circulation: a town of fabulous proportions, but without space or dimensions. As much as electrical and nuclear power stations, as much as film studios, this town, which is nothing more than an immense script and a perpetual motion picture, needs this old imaginary made up of childhood signals and faked phantasms for its sympathetic nervous system.

Political incantation

Watergate. Same scenario as Disneyland (an imaginary effect concealing that reality no more exists outside than inside the bounds of the artificial perimeter): though here it is a scandal-effect concealing that there is no difference between the facts and their denunciation (identical methods are employed by the CIA and the *Washington Post* journalists). Same operation, though this time tending towards scandal as a means to regenerate a moral and political principle, towards the imaginary as a means to regenerate a reality principle in distress.

The denunciation of scandal always pays homage to the law. And Watergate above all succeeded in imposing the idea that Watergate *was* a scandal – in this sense it was an extraordinary operation of intoxication: the reinjection of a large dose of political morality on a global scale. It could be said along with Bourdieu that: 'The specific character of every relation of force is to dissimulate itself as such, and to acquire all its force only because it is so dissimulated'; understood as follows: capital, which is immoral and unscrupulous, can only function behind a moral superstructure, and whoever regenerates this public morality (by indignation, denunciation, etc.) spontaneously furthers the order of capital, as did the *Washington Post* journalists.

But this is still only the formula of ideology, and when Bourdieu enunciates it, he takes 'relation of force' to mean the *truth* of capitalist domination, and he *denounces* this relation of force as itself a *scandal*: he therefore occupies the same deterministic and moralistic position as the *Washington Post* journalists. He does the same job of purging and reviving moral order, an order of truth wherein the genuine symbolic violence of the social order is engendered, well beyond all relations of force, which are only elements of its indifferent and shifting configuration in the moral and political consciousnesses of people.

All that capital asks of us is to receive it as rational or to combat it in the name of rationality, to receive it as moral or to combat it in the name of morality. For they are *identical*, meaning *they can be read another way*: before, the task was to dissimulate scandal; today, the task is to conceal the fact that there is none.

Watergate is not a scandal: this is what must be said at all cost, for this is what everyone is concerned to conceal, this dissimulation masking a strengthening of morality, a moral panic as we approach the primal (*mise-en-*)scene of capital: its instantaneous cruelty; its incomprehensible ferocity; its fundamental immorality – these are what are scandalous, unaccountable for in that system of moral and economic equivalence which remains the axiom of Leftist thought, from Enlightenment theory to communism. Capital doesn't give a damn about the idea of the contract which is imputed to it: it is a monstrous unprincipled

undertaking, nothing more. Rather, it is 'enlightened' thought which
seeks to control capital by imposing rules on it. And all that recrimination
which replaced revolutionary thought today comes down to reproaching
capital for not following the rules of the game. 'Power is unjust; its
justice is a class justice; capital exploits us; etc.' – as if capital were linked
by a contract to the society it rules. It is the Left which holds out the
mirror of equivalence, hoping that capital will fall for this
phantasmagoria of the social contract and fulfill its obligation towards the
whole of society (at the same time, no need for revolution: it is enough
that capital accept the rational formula of exchange).

Capital in fact has never been linked by a contract to the society it
dominates. It is a sorcery of the social relation, it is *a challenge to society*
and should be responded to as such. It is not a scandal to be denounced
according to moral and economic rationality, but a challenge to take up
according to symbolic law.

Strategy of the real

Of the same order as the impossibility of rediscovering an absolute level
of the real, is the impossibility of staging an illusion. Illusion is no longer
possible, because the real is no longer possible. It is the whole *political*
problem of the parody, of hypersimulation or offensive simulation,
which is posed here.

For example: it would be interesting to see whether the repressive
apparatus would not react more violently to a simulated hold-up than to
a real one? For a real hold-up only upsets the order of things, the right of
property, whereas a simulated hold-up interferes with the very principle
of reality. Transgression and violence are less serious, for they only
contest the *distribution* of the real. Simulation is infinitely more dangerous
since it always suggests, over and above its object, that *law and order
themselves might really be nothing more than a simulation.*

But the difficulty is in proportion to the peril. How to feign a violation
and put it to the test? Go and simulate a theft in a large department store:
how do you convince the security guards that it is a simulated theft?
There is no 'objective' difference: the same gestures and the same signs
exist as for a real theft; in fact the signs incline neither to one side nor the
other. As far as the established order is concerned, they are always of the
order of the real.

Go and organise a fake hold-up. Be sure to check that your weapons
are harmless, and take the most trustworthy hostage, so that no life is in
danger (otherwise you risk committing an offence). Demand ransom,
and arrange it so that the operation creates the greatest commotion

possible. In brief, stay close to the 'truth', so as to test the reaction of the apparatus to a perfect simlulation. But you won't succeed: the web of artificial signs will be inextricably mixed up with real elements (a police officer will really shoot on sight; a bank customer will faint and die of a heart attack; they will really turn the phoney ransom over to you). In brief, you will unwittingly find yourself immediately in the real, one of whose functions is precisely to devour every attempt at simulation, to reduce everything to some reality: that's exactly how the established order is, well before institutions and justice come into play.

In this impossibility of isolating the process of simulation must be seen the whole thrust of an order that can only see and understand in terms of some reality, because it can function nowhere else. The simulation of an offence, if it is patent, will either be punished more lightly (because it has no 'consequences') or be punished as an offence to public office (for example, if one triggered off a police operation 'for nothing') – but *never as simulation*, since it is precisely as such that no equivalence with the real is possible, and hence no repression either. The challenge of simulation is irreceivable by power. How can you punish the simulation of virtue? Yet as such it is as serious as the simulation of crime. Parody makes obedience and transgression equivalent, and that is the most serious crime, since it *cancels out the difference upon which the law is based*. The established order can do nothing against it, for the law is a second-order simulacrum whereas simulation is a third-order simulacrum, beyond true and false, beyond equivalences, beyond the rational distinctions upon which function all power and the entire social stratum. Hence, *failing the real*, it is here that we must aim at order.

This is why order always opts for the real. In a state of uncertainty, it always prefers this assumption (thus in the army they would rather take the simulator as a true madman). But this becomes more and more difficult, for it is practically impossible to isolate the process of simulation; through the force of inertia of the real which surrounds us, the inverse is also true (and this very reversibility forms part of the apparatus of simulation and of power's impotency): namely, *it is now impossible to isolate the process of the real*, or to prove the real.

Thus all hold-ups, hijacks and the like are now, as it were, simulation hold-ups, in the sense that they are inscribed in advance in the decoding and orchestration rituals of the media, anticipated in their mode of presentation and possible consequences. In brief, where they function as a set of signs dedicated exclusively to their recurrence as signs, and no longer to their 'real' goal at all. But this does not make them inoffensive. On the contrary, it is as hyperreal events, no longer having any particular contents or aims, but indefinitely refracted by each other (for that matter like so-called historical events: strikes, demonstrations, crises, etc.), [1] that they are precisely unverifiable by an order which can only exert itself on the real and the rational, on ends and means: a referential order which can only dominate referentials, a determinate power which can only dominate a determined world, but which can do nothing about that indefinite recurrence of simulation, about that weightless nebula no longer obeying the law of gravitation of the real – power itself eventually breaking apart in this space and becoming a simulation of power (disconnected from its aims and objectives, and dedicated to *power effects* and mass simulation).

The only weapon of power, its only strategy against this defection, is to reinject realness and referentiality everywhere, in order to convince us of the reality of the social, of the gravity of the economy and the finalities of production. For that purpose it prefers the discourse of crisis, but also – why not? – the discourse of desire. 'Take your desires for reality!' can be understood as the ultimate slogan of power, for in a nonreferential world even the confusion of the reality principle with the desire principle is less dangerous than contagious hyperreality. One remains among principles, and there power is always right.

Hyperreality and simulation are deterrents of every principle and of every objective; they turn against power this deterrence which is so well utilised for a long time itself. For, finally, it was capital which was the first to feed throughout its history on the destruction of every referential, of every human goal, which shattered every ideal distinction between true and false, good and evil, in order to establish a radical law of equivalence and exchange, the iron law of its power. It was the first to practice deterrence, abstraction, disconnection, deterritorialisation, etc.; and if it was capital which fostered reality, the reality principle, it was also the first to liquidate it in the extermination of every use value, of every real equivalence, of production and wealth, in the very sensation we have of the unreality of the stakes and the omnipotence of manipulation. Now, it is this very logic which is today hardened even more *against* it. And when it wants to fight this catastrophic spiral by secreting one last glimmer of reality, on which to found one last glimmer of power, it only multiplies the *signs* and accelerates the play of simulation.

As long as it was historically threatened by the real, power risked deterrence and simulation, disintegrating every contradiction by means of the production of equivalent signs. When it is threatened today by simulation (the threat of vanishing in the play of signs), power risks the real, risks crisis, it gambles on remanufacturing artificial, social, economic, political stakes. This is a question of life or death for it. But it is too late.

Whence the characteristic hysteria of our time: the hysteria of production and reproduction of the real. The other production, that of goods and commodities, that of *la belle epoque* of political economy, no longer makes any sense of its own, and has not for some time. What society seeks through production, and overproduction, is the restoration of the real which escapes it. That is why *contemporary 'material' production is itself hyperreal*. It retains all the features, the whole discourse of traditional production, but it is nothing more than its scaled-down refraction (thus the hyperrealists fasten in a striking resemblance a real from which has fled all meaning and charm, all the profundity and energy of representation). Thus the hyperrealism of simulation is expressed everywhere by the real's striking resemblance to itself.

Power, too, for some time now produces nothing but signs of its resemblance. And at the same time, another figure of power comes into play: that of a collective demand for *signs* of power – a holy union which forms around the disappearance of power. Everybody belongs to it more or less in fear of the collapse of the political. And in the end the game of power comes down to nothing more than the *critical* obsession with power: an obsession with its death; an obsession with its survival which becomes greater the more it disappears. When it has totally disappeared, logically we will be under the total spell of power – a haunting memory already foreshadowed everywhere, manifesting at one and the same time the satisfaction of having got rid of it (nobody wants it any more, everybody unloads it on others) and grieving its loss. Melancholy for societies without power: this has already given rise to fascism, that overdose of a powerful referential in a society which cannot terminate its mourning.

But we are still in the same boat: none of our societies know how to manage their mourning for the real, for power, for the *social itself*, which is implicated in this same breakdown. And it is by an artificial revitalisation of all this that we try to escape it. *Undoubtedly this will even end up in socialism*. By an unforeseen twist of events and an irony which no longer belongs to history, it is through the death of the social that socialism will emerge – as it is through the death of God that religions emerge. A twisted coming, a perverse event, an unintelligible reversion to the logic of reason. As is the fact that power is no longer present except to conceal that there is none. A simulation which can go on indefinitely, since – unlike 'true' power which is, or was, a structure, a strategy, a relation of force, a stake – this is nothing but the object of a social *demand*, and hence subject to the law of supply and demand, rather than to violence and death. Completely expunged from the *political* dimension, it is dependent, like any other commodity, on production and mass consumption. Its spark has disappeared; only the fiction of a political universe is saved.

Likewise with work. The spark of production, the violence of its stake no longer exists. Everybody still produces, and more and more, but work has subtly become something else: a need (as Marx ideally envisaged it, but not at all in the same sense), the object of a social 'demand', like leisure, to which it is equivalent in the general run of life's options. A demand exactly proportional to the loss of stake in the work process.[2] The same change in fortune as for power: the *scenario* of work is there to conceal the fact that the work-real, the production-real, has disappeared. And for that matter so has the strike-real too, which is no longer a stoppage of work, but its alternative pole in the ritual scansion of the social calendar. It is as if everyone has 'occupied' their work place or work post, after declaring the strike, and resumed production, as is the custom in a 'self-managed' job, in exactly the same terms as before, by declaring themselves (and virtually being) in a state of permanent strike.

This isn't a science-fiction dream: everywhere it is a question of a doubling of the work process. And of a double or locum for the strike process – strikes which are incorporated like obsolescence in objects, like crises in production. Then there are no longer any strikes or work, but both simultaneously, that is to say something else entirely: a wizardry of work, a *trompe-l'oeil*, a scenodrama (not to say melodrama) of production, collective dramaturgy upon the empty stage of the social.

It is no longer a question of the *ideology* of work – of the traditional ethic that obscures the 'real' labour process and the 'objective' process of exploitation – but of the scenario of work. Likewise, it is no longer a question of the ideology of power, but of the *scenario* of power. Ideology only corresponds to a betrayal of reality by signs; simulation corresponds to a short-circuit of reality and to its reduplication by signs. It is always the aim of ideological analysis to restore the objective process; it is always a false problem to want to restore the truth beneath the simulacrum.

This is ultimately why power is so in accord with ideological discourses and discourses on ideology, for these are all discourses of *truth* – always good, even and especially if they are revolutionary, to counter the mortal blows of simulation.

Notes

1. The entire current 'psychological' situation is characterised by this short-circuit.

   Doesn't emancipation of children and teenagers, once the initial phase of revolt is passed and once there has been established the *principle* of the *right* to emancipation, seem like the *real* emancipation of parents. And the young (students, high-schoolers, adolescents) seem to sense it in their always more insistent demand (though still as paradoxical) for the presence and advice of parents or of teachers. Alone at last, free and responsible, it seemed to them suddenly that other people possibly have absconded with their true liberty. Therefore, there is no question of 'leaving them be'. They're going to hassle them, not with any emotional or material spontaneous demand, but with an exigency that has been premeditated and corrected by an implicit oedipal knowledge. Hyperdependence (much greater than before) distorted by irony and refusal, *parody of libidinous original mechanisms*. Demand without content, without referent, unjustified, but for all that all the more severe – naked demand with no possible answer. The contents of knowledge (teaching) or of affective relations, the pedagogical or familial referent having been eliminated in the act of emancipation, there remains only a demand linked to the empty form of the institution – perverse demand, and for that reason all the more obstinate. 'Transferable' desire (that is to say non-referential, un-referential), desire that has been fed by lack, by the place left vacant, 'liberated', desire captured in its own vertiginous image, desire of desire, as pure form, hyperreal. Deprived of symbolic substance, it doubles back upon itself, draws its energy from its own reflection and its disappointment with itself. This is literally today the demand, and it is obvious that unlike the 'classical' objective or transferable relations this one here is insoluble and interminable.

Simulated Oedipus.

François Richard:

> Students asked to be seduced either bodily or verbally. But also they are aware of this and they play the game, ironically. 'Give us your knowledge, your presence, you have the word, speak, you are there for that.' Contestation certainly, but not only: the more authority is contested, vilified, the greater the need for authority as such. They play at Oedipus also, to deny it all the more vehemently. The 'teach', he's Daddy, they say; it's fun, you play at incest, malaise, the untouchable, at being a tease – in order to de-sexualise finally.

Like one under analysis who asks for Oedipus back again, who tells the 'oedipal' stories, who has the 'analytical' dreams to satisfy the supposed request of the analyst, or to resist him? In the same way the student goes through his oedipal number, his seduction number, gets chummy, close, approaches, dominates – but this isn't desire, it's simulation. Oedipal psychodrama of simulation (neither less real nor less dramatic for all that). Very different from the real libidinal stakes of knowledge and power or even of a real mourning for the absence of same (as could have happened after 1968 in the universities.) Now we've reached the phase of desperate reproduction, and where the stakes are nil, the simulacrum is maximal – exacerbated and parodied simulation at one and the same time – as interminable as psychoanalysis and for the same reasons.

The interminable psychoanalysis.

There is a whole chapter to add to the history of transference and countertransference: that of their liquidation by simulation, of the impossible psychoanalysis because it is itself, from now on, that produces and reproduces the unconscious as its institutional substance. Psychoanalysis dies also of the exchange of the *signs* of the unconscious. Just as revolution dies of the exchange of the critical signs of political economy. This short-circuit was well known to Freud in the form of the gift of the analytic dream, or with the 'uninformed' patients, in the form of the gift of their analytic knowledge. But this was still interpreted as resistance, as detour, and did not put fundamentally into question either the process of analysis or the principle of transference. It is another thing entirely when the unconscious itself, the discourse of the unconscious becomes unfindable – according to the same scenario of simulative anticipation that we have seen at work on all levels with the machines of the third order. The analysis then can no longer end, it becomes logically and historically interminable, since it stabilises on a puppet-substance of reproduction, an unconscious programmed on demand – an impossible-to-break-through point around which the whole analysis is rearranged. The messages of the unconscious have been short-circuited by the psychoanalysis 'medium'. This is libidinal hyperrealism. To the famous categories of the real, the symbolic and the imaginary, it is going to be necessary to add the hyperreal, which captures and obstructs the functioning of the three orders.

2. Athenian democracy, much more advanced than our own, had reached the point where the vote was considered as payment for a service, after all other repressive solutions had been tried and found wanting in order to insure a quorum.

13 Fredric Jameson, 'Postmodernism and Consumer Society'*

Fredric Jameson has consistently drawn attention to the questions of social, economic and cultural change raised by postmodernism, and thus to the changing nature of capitalism and the continued viability of Marxism. He takes issue with the view, advanced especially by the conservative sociologist Daniel Bell, that twentieth-century society has entered a 'post-industrial' phase, to argue, by way of Ernest Mandel's *Late Capitalism*, that capitalism has in fact expanded and consolidated its hegemony. He further asks how changes in capitalism's mode of production and class relations relate to new forms of cultural production. Both Habermas and Lyotard, in Jameson's view, are indebted to an earlier cultural modernism which he feels has failed, particularly on the evidence of its architecture.

The new forms and effects of postmodernism, in literature, music, film and new physical and psychic environments, Jameson characterises as matters of surface, pastiche and paranoia. But yet this depthless diaspora frustrates the analytic and political instincts of his Hegelian Marxism. The central problem in Jameson's accounts of postmodernism lies here. It may be summarised by saying that while he accepts Baudrillard's view of present society as a society of the simulacrum, free of reference to 'reality', and even accepts Lyotard's view of Marxism as a now threadbare metanarrative, he would retain a distinction between surface and depth, within a dialectical materialism which employs the concepts of totality and critical distance as necessary means to significant social and cultural transformation.

These questions are taken up most vigorously by Warren Montag in E. Ann Kaplan (ed.), *Postmodernism and its Discontents* (1988), pp. 88–103. In addition to the present Introduction and further references there (pp. 20–4), see the recent collection of essays,

---

* Reprinted from E. Ann Kaplan (ed.), *Postmodernism and its Discontents* (London and New York: Verso, 1988), pp. 13–29.

including Jameson's response to criticisms, in Douglas Kellner (ed.), *Postmodernism/Jameson/Critique* (1990). The essay 'Postmodernism and Consumer Society' appeared in an earlier form in Foster (ed.), *Postmodern Culture* (1985). The present version combines this with material from Jameson's major longer essay 'Postmodernism, or the Cultural Logic of Late Capitalism' in *New Left Review 146* (1984): 53–92; reprinted in the volume of that title.

The concept of postmodernism is not widely accepted or even understood today. Some of the resistance to it may come from the unfamiliarity of the works it covers, which can be found in all the arts: the poetry of John Ashbery, for instance, but also the much simpler talk poetry that came out of the reaction against complex, ironic, academic modernist poetry in the 1960s; the reaction against modern architecture and in particular against the monumental buildings of the International Style, the pop buildings and decorated sheds celebrated by Robert Venturi in his manifesto, *Learning from Las Vegas*; Andy Warhol and Pop Art, but also the more recent Photorealism; in music, the moment of John Cage but also the later synthesis of classical and 'popular' styles found in composers like Philip Glass and Terry Riley, and also punk and new-wave rock with such groups as the Clash, Talking Heads and the Gang of Four; in film, everything that comes out of Godard – contemporary vanguard film and video – but also a whole new style of commercial or fiction films, which has its equivalent in contemporary novels as well, where the works of William Burroughs, Thomas Pynchon and Ishmael Reed on the one hand, and the French new novel on the other, are also to be numbered among the varieties of what can be called postmodernism.

This list would seem to make two things clear at once: first, most of the postmodernisms mentioned above emerge as specific reactions against the established forms of high modernism, against this or that dominant high modernism which conquered the university, the museum, the art gallery network, and the foundations. Those formerly subversive and embattled styles – Abstract Expressionism; the great modernist poetry of Pound, Eliot or Wallace Stevens; the International Style (Le Corbusier, Frank Lloyd Wright, Mies); Stravinsky; Joyce, Proust and Mann – felt to be scandalous or shocking by our grandparents are, for the generation which arrives at the gate in the 1960s, felt to be the establishment and the enemy – dead, stifling, canonical, the reified monuments one has to destroy to do anything new. This means that there will be as many different forms of postmodernism as there were high modernisms in place, since the former are at least initially specific and local reactions *against* those models. That obviously does not make the job of describing postmodernism as a coherent thing any easier, since the unity of this new impulse – if it has one – is given not in itself but in the very modernism it seeks to displace.

The second feature of this list of postmodernisms is the effacement in it of some key boundaries or separations, most notably the erosion of the older distinction between high culture and so-called mass or popular culture. This is perhaps the most distressing development of all from an academic standpoint, which has traditionally had a vested interest in preserving a realm of high or élite culture against the surrounding environment of philistinism, of schlock and kitsch, of TV series and *Reader's Digest* culture, and in transmitting difficult and complex skills of reading, listening and seeing to its initiates. But many of the newer postmodernisms have been fascinated precisely by that whole landscape of advertising and motels, of the Las Vegas strip, of the late show and Grade-B Hollywood film, of so-called paraliterature with its airport paperback categories of the gothic and the romance, the popular biography, the murder mystery and the science fiction or fantasy novel. They no longer 'quote' such 'texts' as a Joyce might have done, or a Mahler; they incorporate them, to the point where the line between high art and commercial forms seems increasingly difficult to draw.

A rather different indication of this effacement of the older categories of genre and discourse can be found in what is sometimes called contemporary theory. A generation ago there was still a technical discourse of professional philosophy – the great systems of Sartre or the phenomenologists, the work of Wittgenstein or analytical or common language philosophy – alongside which one could still distinguish that quite different discourse of the other academic disciplines – of political science, for example, or sociology or literary criticism. Today, increasingly, we have a kind of writing simply called 'theory' which is all or none of those things at once. This new kind of discourse, generally associated with France and so-called French theory, is becoming widespread and marks the end of philosophy as such. Is the work of Michel Foucault, for example, to be called philosophy, history, social theory or political science? It's undecidable, as they say nowadays; and I will suggest that such 'theoretical discourse' is also to be numbered among the manifestations of postmodernism.

Now I must say a word about the proper use of this concept: it is not just another word for the description of a particular style. It is also, at least in my use, a periodizing concept whose function is to correlate the emergence of new formal features in culture with the emergence of a new type of social life and a new economic order – what is often euphemistically called modernization, postindustrial or consumer society, the society of the media or the spectacle, or multinational

165

capitalism. This new moment of capitalism can be dated from the post-war boom in the United States in the late 1940s and early 1950s or, in France, from the establishment of the Fifth Republic in 1958. The 1960s are in many ways the key transitional period, a period in which the new international order (neocolonialism, the Green Revolution, computerization and electronic information) is at one and the same time set in place and is swept and shaken by its own internal contradictions and by external resistance. I want here to sketch a few of the ways in which the new postmodernism expresses the inner truth of that newly emergent social order of late capitalism, but will have to limit the description to only two of its significant features, which I will call pastiche and schizophrenia; they will give us a chance to sense the specificity of the postmodernist experience of space and time respectively.

Pastiche eclipses parody

One of the most significant features or practices in postmodernism today is pastiche. I must first explain this term, which people generally tend to confuse with or assimilate to that related verbal phenomenon called parody. Both pastiche and parody involve the imitation or, better still, the mimicry of other styles and particularly of the mannerisms and stylistic twitches of other styles. It is obvious that modern literature in general offers a very rich field for parody, since the great modern writers have all been defined by the invention or production of rather unique styles: think of the Faulknerian long sentence or of D.H. Lawrence's characteristic nature imagery; think of Wallace Stevens's peculiar way of using abstractions; think also of the mannerisms of the philosophers, of Heidegger for example, or Sartre; think of the musical styles of Mahler or Prokofiev. All of these styles, however, different from each other, are comparable in this: each is quite unmistakable; once one is learned, it is not likely to be confused with something else.

Now parody capitalises on the uniqueness of these styles and seizes on their idiosyncrasies and eccentricities to produce an imitation which mocks the original. I won't say that the satiric impulse is conscious in all forms of parody. In any case, a good or great parodist has to have some secret sympathy for the original, just as a great mimic has to have the capacity to put himself/herself in the place of the person imitated. Still, the general effect of parody is – whether in sympathy or with malice – to cast ridicule on the private nature of these stylistic mannerisms and their excessiveness and eccentricity with respect to the way people normally speak or write. So there remains somewhere behind all parody the feeling that there is a linguistic norm in contrast to which the styles of the great modernists can be mocked.

But what would happen if one no longer believed in the existence of normal language, or ordinary speech, of the linguistic norm (the kind of clarity and communicative power celebrated by Orwell in his famous essay, say)? One could think of it in this way; perhaps the immense fragmentation and privatization of modern literature – its explosion into a host of distinct private styles and mannerisms – foreshadows deeper and more general tendencies in social life as a whole. Supposing that modern art and modernism – far from being a kind of specialized aesthetic curiosity – actually anticipated social developments along these lines; supposing that in the decades since the emergence of the great modern styles society has itself begun to fragment in this way, each group coming to speak a curious private language of its own, each profession developing its private code or idiolect, and finally each individual coming to be a kind of linguistic island, separated from everyone else? But then in that case, the very possibility of any linguistic norm in terms of which one could ridicule private languages and idiosyncratic styles would vanish, and we would have nothing but stylistic diversity and heterogeneity.

That is the moment at which pastiche appears and parody has become impossible. Pastiche is, like parody, the imitation of a peculiar or unique style, the wearing of a stylistic mask, speech in a dead langauge: but it is a neutral practice of such mimicry, without parody's ulterior motive, without the satirical impulse, without laughter, without that still latent feeling that there exists something *normal* compared to which chat is being imitated is rather comic. Pastiche is blank parody, parody that has lost its sense of humor: pastiche is to parody what that curious thing, the modern practice of a kind of blank irony, is to what Wayne Booth calls the stable and comic ironies of, say, the eighteenth century.

The death of the subject

But now we need to introduce a new piece into this puzzle, which may help to explain why classical modernism is a thing of the past and why postmodernism should have taken its place. This new component is what is generally called the 'death of the subject' or, to say it in more conventional language, the end of individualism as such. The great modernisms were, as we have said, predicated on the invention of a personal, private style, as unmistakable as your fingerprint, as imcomparable as your own body. But this means that the modernist aesthetic is in some way organically linked to the conception of a unique self and private identity, a unique personality and individuality, which can be expected to generate its own unique vision of the world and to forge its own unique, unmistakable style.

Yet today, from any number of distinct perspectives, the social theorists, the psychoanalysts, even the linguists, not to speak of those of us who work in the area of culture and cultural and formal change, are all exploring the notion that that kind of individualism and personal identity is a thing of the past; that the old individual or individualist subject is 'dead'; and that one might even describe the concept of the unique individual and the theoretical basis of individualism as ideological. There are in fact two positions on all this, one of which is more radical than the other. The first one is content to say: yes, once upon a time, in the classic age of competitive capitalism, in the heyday of the nuclear family and the emergence of the bourgeoisie as the hegemonic social class, there was such a thing as individualism, as individual subjects. But today, in the age of corporate capitalism, of the so-called organization man, of bureaucracies in business as well as in the state, of demographic explosion – today, that older bourgeois individual subject no longer exists.

Then there is a second position, the more radical of the two, what one might call the poststructuralist position. It adds: not only is the bourgeois individual subject a thing of the past, it is also a myth; it *never* really existed in the first place; there have never been autonomous subjects of that type. Rather, this construct is merely a philosophical and cultural mystification which sought to persuade people that they 'had' individual subjects and possessed this unique personal identity.

For our purposes, it is not particularly important to decide which of these positions is correct (or rather, which is more interesting and productive). What we have to retain from all this is rather an aesthetic dilemma: because if the experience and the ideology of the unique self, an experience and ideology which informed the stylistic practice of classical modernism, is over and done with, then it is no longer clear what the artists and writers of the present period are supposed to be doing. What is clear is merely that the older models – Picasso, Proust, T.S. Eliot – do not work any more (or are positively harmful), since nobody has that kind of unique private world and style to express any longer. And this is perhaps not merely a 'psychological' matter: we also have to take into account the immense weight of seventy or eighty years of classical modernism itself. There is another sense in which the writers and artists of the present day will no longer be able to invent new styles and worlds – they've already been invented; only a limited number of combinations are possible; the unique ones have been thought of already. So the weight of the whole modernist aesthetic tradition – now dead – also 'weighs like a nightmare on the brains of the living', as Marx said in another context.

Hence, once again, pastiche: in a world in which stylistic innovation is no longer possible, all that is left is to imitate dead styles, to speak through the masks and with the voices of the styles in the imaginary museum. But this means that contemporary or postmodernist art is going to be about art itself in a new kind of way; even more, it means that one of its essential messages will involve the necessary failure of art and the aesthetic, the failure of the new, the imprisonment in the past.

The nostalgia mode

As this may seem very abstract, I want to give a few examples, one of which is so omnipresent that we rarely link it with the kinds of developments in high art discussed here. This particular practice of pastiche is not high-cultural but very much within mass culture, and it is generally known as the 'nostalgia film' (what the French neatly call *la mode rétro* – retrospective styling). We must conceive of this category in the broadest way: narrowly, no doubt, it consists merely of films about the past and about specific generational moments of that past. Thus, one of the inaugural films in this new 'genre' (if that's what it is) was Lucas's *American Graffiti*, which in 1973 set out to recapture all the atmosphere and stylistic peculiarities of the 1950s United States, the United States of the Eisenhower era. Polanski's great film *Chinatown* does something similar for the 1930s, as does Bertolucci's *The Conformist* for the Italian and European context of the same period, the fascist era in Italy; and so forth. We could go on listing these films for some time: why call them pastiche? Are they not rather work in the more traditional genre known as the historical film – work which can more simply be theorised by extrapolating that other well-known form which is the historical novel?

I have my reasons for thinking that we need new categories for such films. But let me first add some anomalies: supposing I suggested that *Star Wars* is also a nostalgic film. What could that mean? I presume we can agree that this is not a historical film about our own intergalactic past. Let me put it somewhat differently: one of the most important cultural experiences of the generations that grew up from the 1930s to the 1950s was the Saturday afternoon serial of the Buck Rogers type – alien villains, true American heroes, heroines in distress, the death ray or the doomsday box, and the cliffhanger at the end whose miraculous resolution was to be witnessed next Saturday afternoon. *Star Wars* re-invents this experience in the form of a pastiche: that is, there is no longer any point to a parody of such serials since they are long extinct. *Star Wars*, far from being a pointless satire of such now dead forms, satisfies a deep (might I even say repressed?) longing to experience them again: it is a complex object in which on some first level children and adolescents can take the adventures straight, while the adult public is able to gratify a deeper and more properly nostalgic desire to return to that older period and to live its strange old aesthetic artifacts through once again. This film is thus *metonymically* a historical or nostalgia film: unlike *American Graffiti*, it does not reinvent a picture of the past in its lived totality; rather, by inventing the feel and shape of characteristic art objects of an older period (the serials), it seeks to reawaken a sense of the past associated with those objects. *Raiders of the Lost Ark*, meanwhile, occupies an intermediary position here: on some level it is *about* the 1930s and 1940s, but in reality it too conveys that period metonymically through its own characteristic adventure stories (which are no longer ours).

Now let me discuss another interesting anomaly which may take us further towards understanding nostalgia film in particular and pastiche generally. This one involves a recent film called *Body Heat*, which, as has abundantly been pointed out by the critics, is a kind of distant remake of *The Postman Always Rings Twice* or *Double Indemnity*. (The allusive and elusive plagiarism of older plots is, of course, also a feature of pastiche.) Now *Body Heat* is technically not a nostalgia film, since it takes place in a contemporary setting, in a little Florida village near Miami. On the other hand, this technical contemporaneity is most ambiguous indeed: the credits – always our first cue – are lettered and scripted in a 1930s Art-Deco style which cannot but trigger nostalgic reactions (first to *Chinatown*, no doubt, and then beyond it to some more historical referent). Then the very style of the hero himself is ambiguous: William Hurt is a new star but has nothing of the distinctive style of the preceding generation of male superstars like Steve McQueen or even Jack Nicholson, or rather, his persona here is a kind of mix of their characteristics with an older role of the type generally associated with Clark Gable. So here too there is a faintly archaic feel to all this. The spectator begins to wonder why this story, which could have been situated anywhere, is set in a small Florida town, in spite of its contemporary reference. One begins to realise after a while that the small town setting has a crucial strategic function: it allows the film to do without most of the signals and references which we might associate with the contemporary world, with consumer society – the appliances and artifacts, the high rises, the object world of late capitalism. Technically, then, its objects (its cars, for instance) are 1980s products, but everything in the film conspires to blur that immediate contemporary reference and to make it possible to receive this too as nostalgia work – as a narrative set in some indefinable nostalgic past, an eternal 1930s, say, beyond history. It seems to me exceedingly symptomatic to find the very style of nostalgia films invading and colonizing even those movies today which have contemporary settings: as though, for some reason, we were unable to focus our own present, as though we have become incapable of achieving aesthetic representations of our own current experience. But if that is so, then it is a terrible indictment of consumer capitalism itself – or, at the very least, an alarming and pathological symptom of a society that has become incapable of dealing with time and history.

So now we come back to the question of why nostalgia film or pastiche is to be considered different from the older historical novel or film. (I should also include in this discussion the major literary example of all this, to my mind: the novels of E.L. Doctorow – *Ragtime*, with its turn-of-the-century atmosphere, and *Loon Lake*, for the most part about our 1930s. But these are, in my opinion, historical novels in appearance only. Doctorow is a serious artist and one of the few genuinely left or radical novelists at work today. It is no disservice to him, however, to suggest that his narratives do not represent our historical past so much as they represent our ideas or cultural stereotypes about that past.) Cultural production has been driven back inside the mind, within the monadic subject: it can no longer look directly out of its eyes at the real world for the referent but must, as in Plato's cave, trace its mental images of the world on its confining walls. If there is any realism left here, it is a 'realism' which springs from the shock of grasping that confinement and of realizing that, for whatever peculiar reasons, we seem condemned to seek the historical past through our own pop images and stereotypes about that past, which itself remains forever out of reach.

Postmodernism and the city

Now, before I try to offer a somewhat more positive conclusion, I want to sketch the analysis of a full-blown postmodern building – a work which is in many ways uncharacteristic of that postmodern architecture whose principal names are Robert Venturi, Charles Moore, Michael Graves, and more recently Frank Gehry, but which to my mind offers some very striking lessons about the originality of postmodernist space. Let me amplify the figure which has run through the preceding remarks, and make it even more explicit: I am proposing the notion that we are here in the presence of something like a mutation in built space itself. My implication is that we ourselves, the human subjects who happen into this new space, have not kept pace with that evolution; there has been a mutation in the object, unaccompanied as yet by any equivalent mutation in the subject; we do not yet possess perceptual equipment to match this new hyperspace, as I will call it, in part because our perceptual habits were formed in that older kind of space I have called the space of high modernism. The newer architecture therefore – like many of the other cultural products I have evoked in the preceding remarks – stands as something like an imperative to grow new organs to expand our sensorium and our body to some new, as yet unimaginable, perhaps ultimately impossible, dimensions.

The Bonaventure Hotel

The building whose features I will very rapidly enumerate in the next few moments is the Bonaventure Hotel, built in the new Los Angeles downtown by the architect and developer John Portman, whose other works include the various Hyatt Regencies, the Peachtree Center in Atlanta, and the Renaissance Center in Detroit. I have mentioned the populist aspect of the rhetorical defence of postmodernism against the élite (and utopian) austerities of the great architectural modernisms: it is generally affirmed, in other words, that these newer building are popular works on the one hand; and that they respect the vernacular of the American city fabric on the other, that is to say, that they no longer attempt, as did the masterworks and monuments of high modernism, to insert a different, a distinct, an elevated, a new utopian language into the tawdry and commercial sign-system of the surrounding city, but rather, on the contrary, seek to speak that very language, using its lexicon and syntax as that has been emblematically 'learned from Las Vegas'.

On the first of these counts, Portman's Bonaventure fully confirms the claim: it is a popular building, visited with enthusiasm by locals and tourists alike (although Portman's other buildings are even more successful in this respect). The populist insertion into the city fabric is, however, another matter, and it is with this that we will begin. There are three entrances to the Bonaventure, one from Figueroa, and the other two by way of elevated gardens on the other side of the hotel, which is built into the remaining slope of the former Beacon Hill. None of these is anything like the old hotel marquee, or the monumental *porte-cochère* with which the sumptuous buildings of yesteryear were wont to stage your passage from city street to the older interior. The entryways of the Bonaventure are as it were lateral and rather backdoor affairs: the gardens in the back admit you to the sixth floor of the towers, and even there you must walk down one flight to find the elevator by which you gain access to the lobby. Meanwhile, what one is still tempted to think of as the front entry, on Figueroa, admits you, baggage and all, onto the second-story balcony, from which you must take an escalator down to the main registration desk. More about these elevators and escalators in a moment. What I first want to suggest about these curiously unmarked ways-in is that they seem to have been imposed by some new category of closure governing the inner space of the hotel itself (and this over and above the material constraints under which Portman had to work). I believe that, with a certain number of other characteristic postmodern buildings, such as the Beaubourg in Paris, or the Eaton Centre in Toronto, the Bonaventure aspires to being a total space, a complete world, a kind of miniature city (and I would want to add that to this new total space corresponds a new collective practice, a new mode in which individuals move and congregate, something like the practice of a new and historically original kind of hyper-crowd). In this sense, then, ideally the mini-city of Portman's Bonaventure ought not to have entrances at all, since the entryway is always the seam that links the building to the rest of the city that surrounds it: for it does not wish to be part of the city, but rather its equivalent and its replacement or substitute. That is, however, obviously not possible or practical, whence the deliberate downplaying and reduction of the entrance function to its bare minimum. But this disjunction from the surrounding city is very different from that of the great monuments of the International Style: there, the act of disjunction was violent, visible, and had a very real symbolic significance – as in Le Corbusier's great *pilotis* whose gesture radically separates the new utopian space of the modern from the degraded and fallen city fabric which it thereby explicitly repudiates (although the gamble of the modern was that this utopian space, in the virulence of its Novum, would fan out and transform that eventually by the power of its new spatial language). The Bonaventure, however, is content to 'let the fallen city fabric continue to be in its being' (to parody Heidegger); no further effects, no larger protopolitical utopian transformation, is either expected or desired.

This diagnosis is to my mind confirmed by the great reflective glass skin of the Bonaventure, whose function I will now interpret rather differently than I did a moment ago when I saw the phenomenon of reflexion generally as developing a thematics of reproductive technology (the two readings are however not incompatible). Now one would want rather to stress the way in which the glass skin repels the city outside; a repulsion for which we have analogies in those reflector sunglasses which make it impossible for your interlocutor to see your own eyes and thereby achieve a certain aggressivity towards and power over the Other. In a similar way, the glass skin achieves a peculiar and placeless dissociation of the Bonaventure from its neighbourhood: it is not even an exterior, inasmuch as when you seek to look at the hotel's outer walls you cannot see the hotel itself, but only the distorted images of everything that surrounds it.

Now I want to say a few words about escalators and elevators: given their very real pleasures in Portman, particularly these last, which the artist has termed 'gigantic kinetic sculptures' and which certainly account for much of the spectacle and the excitement of the hotel interior, particularly in the Hyatts, where like great Japanese lanterns or gondolas they ceaselessly rise and fall – given such a deliberate marking and foregrounding in their own right, I believe one has to see such 'people movers' (Portman's own term, adapted from Disney) as something a little more than mere functions and engineering components. We know in any case that recent architectural theory has begun to borrow from narrative analysis in other fields, and to attempt to see our physical trajectories through such buildings as virtual narratives or stories, as dynamic paths and narrative paradigms which we as visitors are asked to fulfil and to complete with our own bodies and movements. In the Bonaventure, however, we find a dialectical heightening of this process: it seems to me that the escalators and elevators here henceforth replace movement but also and above all designate themselves as new reflexive signs and emblems of movement proper (something which will become evident when we come to the whole question of what remains of older forms of movement in this building, most notably walking itself). Here the narrative stroll has been underscored, symbolized, reified and replaced by a transportation machine which becomes the allegorical signifier of that older promenade we are no longer allowed to conduct on our own: and this is a dialectical intensification of the autoreferentiality of all modern culture, which tends to turn upon itself and designate its own cultural production as its content.

I am more at a loss when it comes to conveying the thing itself, the experience of space you undergo when you step off such allegorical devices into the lobby or atrium, with its great central column, surrounded by a miniature lake, the whole positioned between the four symmetrical residential towers with their elevators, and surrounded by rising balconies capped by a kind of greenhouse roof at the sixth level. I am tempted to say that such space makes it impossible for us to use the language of volume or volumes any longer, since these last are impossible to seize. Hanging streamers indeed suffuse this empty space in such a way as to distract systematically and deliberately from whatever form it might be supposed to have; while a constant busyness gives the feeling that emptiness is here absolutely packed, that it is an element within which you yourself are immersed, without any of that distance that formerly enabled the perception of perspective or volume. You are in this hyperspace up to your eyes and your body; and if it seemed to you before that that suppression of depth I spoke of in postmodern painting or literature would necessarily be difficult to achieve in architecture itself, perhaps you may now be willing to see this bewildering immersion as the formal equivalent in the new medium.

Yet escalator and elevator are also in this context dialectical opposites; and we may suggest that the glorious movement of the elevator gondolas is also a dialectical compensation for this filled space of the atrium – it gives us the chance at a radically different, but complementary, spatial experience, that of rapidly shooting up through the ceiling and outside, along one of the four symmetrical towers, with the referent, Los Angeles itself, spread out breathtakingly and even alarmingly before us. But even this vertical movement is contained: the elevator lifts you to one of those revolving cocktail lounges, in which you, seated, are again passively rotated about and offered a contemplative spectacle of the city itself, now transformed into its own images by the glass windows through which you view it.

Let me quickly conclude all this by returning to the central space of the lobby itself (with the passing observation that the hotel rooms are visibly marginalised: the corridors in the residential sections are low-ceilinged and dark, most depressingly functional indeed: while one understands that the rooms are in the worst of taste). The descent is dramatic enough, plummeting back down through the roof to splash down in the lake; what happens when you get there is something like the vengeance this space takes on those who still seek to walk through it. Given the absolute symmetry of the four towers, it is quite impossible to get your bearings in this lobby; recently, colour coding and directional signals have been added in a pitiful and revealing, rather desperate attempt to restore the coordinates of an older space. I will take as the most dramatic practical result of this spatial mutation the notorious dilemma of the shopkeepers on the various balconies: it has been obvious, since the very opening of the hotel in 1977, that nobody could ever find any of these stores, and even if you located the appropriate boutique, you would be most unlikely to be as fortunate a second time; as a consequence, the commercial tenants are in despair and all the merchandise is marked down to bargain prices. When you recall that Portman is a businessman as well as an architect, and a millionaire developer, an artist who is at one and the same time a capitalist in his own right, you cannot but feel that here too something of a 'return of the repressed' is involved.

So I come finally to my principal point here, that this latest mutation in space – postmodern hyperspace – has finally succeeded in transcending the capacities of the individual human body to locate itself, to organise its immediate surroundings perceptually, and cognitively to map its position in a mappable external world. And I have already suggested that this alarming disjunction point between the body and its built environment – which is to the initial bewilderment of the older modernism as the velocities of spacecraft are to those of the automobile – can itself stand as the symbol and analog of that even sharper dilemma which is the incapacity of our minds, at least at present, to map the great global multinational and decentered communicational network in which we find ourselves caught as individual subjects.

The New Machine

But as I am anxious that Portman's space not be perceived as something either exceptional or seemingly marginalised and leisure-specialised on the order of Disneyland, I would like in passing to juxtapose this complacent and entertaining (although bewildering) leisure-time space with its analog in a very different area, namely the space of postmodern warfare, in particular as Michael Herr evokes it in his great book on the experience of Vietnam, called *Dispatches*. The extraordinary linguistic innovations of this work may still be considered postmodern, in the eclectic way in which its language impersonally fuses a whole range of contemporary collective idiolects, most notably rock language and black language: but the fusion is dictated by problems of content. This first terrible postmodernist war cannot be told in any of the traditional paradigms of the war novel or movie – indeed that breakdown of all previous narrative paradigms is, along with the breakdown of any shared language through which a veteran might convey such experience, among the principal subjects of the book and may be said to open up the place of a whole new reflexivity. Benjamin's account of Baudelaire, and of the emergence of modernism from a new experience of city technology which transcends all the older habits of bodily perception, is both singularly antiquated, in the light of this new and virtually unimaginable quantum leap in the technological alienation:

> He was a moving-target-survivor subscriber, a true child of the war, because except for the rare times when you were pinned or stranded the system was geared to keep you mobile, if that was what you thought you wanted. As a technique for staying alive it seemed to make as much sense as anything, given naturally that you were there to begin with and wanted to see it close; it started out sound and straight but it formed a cone as it progressed, because the more you moved the more you saw, the more you saw the more besides death and mutilation you risked, and the more you risked of that the more you would have to let go of one day as a 'survivor'. Some of us moved around the war like crazy people until we couldn't see which way the run was taking us anymore, only the war all over its surface with occasional, unexpected penetration. As long as we could have choppers like taxis it took real exhaustion or depression near shock or a dozen pipes of opium to keep us even apparently quiet, we'd still be

running around inside our skins like something was after us, ha, ha,
La Vida Loca. In the months after I got back the hundreds of
helicopters I'd flown in began to draw together until they'd formed a
collective meta-chopper and in my mind it was the sexiest thing going:
saver–destroyer, provider–waster, right hand–left hand, nimble fluent,
canny and human; hot steel, grease, jungle-saturated canvas webbing,
sweat cooling and warming up again, cassette rock and roll in one ear
and door-gun fire in the other, fuel, heat, vitality and death, death
itself, hardly an intruder.[1]

In this new machine, which does not, like the older modernist machinery
of the locomotive or the airplane, represent motion, but which can only
be represented *in motion*, something of the mystery of the new
postmodernist space is concentrated.

The aesthetic of consumer society

Now I must try very rapidly in conclusion to characterise the relationship
of cultural production of this kind of social life in this country today. This
will also be the moment to address the principal objection to concepts of
postmodernism of the type I have sketched here: namely that all the
features we have enumerated are not new at all but abundantly
characterised modernism proper or what I call high modernism. Was not
Thomas Mann, after all, interested in the idea of pastiche, and are not
certain chapters of *Ulysses* its most obvious realisation? Can Flaubert,
Mallarmé and Gertrude Stein not be included in an account of
postmodernist temporality? What is so new about all of this? Do we
really need the concept of *post*modernism?

One kind of answer to this question would raise the whole issue of
periodization and of how a historian (literary or other) posits a radical
break between two henceforth distinct periods. I must limit myself to the
suggestion that radical breaks between periods do not generally involve
complete changes of content but rather the restructuring of a certain
number of elements already given: features that in an earlier period or
system were subordinate now become dominant, and features that had
been dominant again become secondary. In this sense, everything we
have described here can be found in earlier periods and most notably
within modernism proper: my point is that until the present day those
things have been secondary or minor features of modernist art, marginal
rather than central, and that we have something new when they become
the central features of cultural production.

But I can argue this more concretely by turning to the relationship between cultural production and social life generally. The older or classical modernism was an oppositional art; it emerged within the business society of the gilded age as scandalous and offensive to the middle class public – ugly, dissonant, bohemian, sexually shocking. It was something to make fun of (when the police were not called in to seize the books or close the exhibitions): an offense to good taste and to common sense, or, as Freud and Marcuse would have put it, a provocative challenge to the reigning reality- and performance-principles or early twentieth-century middle-class society. Modernism in general did not go well with over-stuffed Victorian furniture, with Victorian moral taboos, or with the conventions of polite society. This is to say that whatever the explicit political content of the great high modernisms, the latter were always in some mostly implicit ways dangerous and explosive, subversive within the established order.

If then we suddenly return to the present day, we can measure the immensity of the cultural changes that have taken place. Not only are Joyce and Picasso no longer weird and repulsive, they have become classics and now look rather realistic to us. Meanwhile, there is very little in either the form or the content of contemporary art that contemporary society finds intolerable and scandalous. The most offensive forms of this art – punk rock, say, or what is called sexually explicit material – are all taken in stride by society, and they are commercially successful, unlike the productions of the older high modernism. But this means that even if contemporary art has all the same formal features as the older modernism, it has still shifted its position fundamentally within our culture. For one thing, commodity production and in particular our clothing, furniture, buildings and other artifacts are now intimately tied in with styling changes which derive from artistic experimentation; our advertising, for example, is fed by postmodernism in all the arts and inconceivable without it. For another, the classics of high modernism are now part of the so-called canon and are taught in schools and universities – which at once empties them of any of their older subversive power. Indeed, one way of marking the break between the periods and of dating the emergence of postmodernism is precisely to be found there: in the moment (the early 1960s, one would think) in which the position of high modernism and its dominant aesthetics become established in the academy and are henceforth felt to be academic by a whole new generation of poets, painters and musicians.

But one can also come at the break from the other side, and describe it in terms of periods of recent social life. As I have suggested, non-Marxists and Marxists alike have come around to the general feeling that at some point following World War II a new kind of society began to emerge (variously described as postindustrial society, multinational capitalism, consumer society, media society and so forth). New types of consumption; planned obsolescence; an ever more rapid rhythm of fashion and styling changes; the penetration of advertising, television and the media generally to a hitherto unparalleled degree throughout society; the replacement of the old tension between city and country, center and province, by the suburb and by universal standardization; the growth of the great networks of superhighways and the arrival of automobile culture – these are some of the features which would seem to mark a radical break with that older pre-war society in which high modernism was still an underground force.

I believe that the emergence of postmodernism is closely related to the emergence of this new moment of late, consumer or multinational capitalism. I believe also that its formal features in many ways express the deeper logic of that particular social system. I will only be able, however, to show this for one major theme: namely the disappearance of a sense of history, the way in which our entire contemporary social system has little by little begun to lose its capacity to retain its own past, has begun to live in a perpetual present and in a perpetual change that obliterates traditions of the kind which all earlier social formations have had in one way or another to preserve. Think only of the media exhaustion of news: of how Nixon and, even more so, Kennedy are figures from a now distant past. One is tempted to say that the very function of the news media is to relegate such recent historical experiences as rapidly as possible into the past. The informational function of the media would thus be to help us forget, to serve as the very agents and mechanisms for our historial amnesia.

But in that case the two features of postmodernism on which I have dwelt here – the transformation of reality into images, the fragmentation of time into a series of perpetual presents – are both extraordinarily consonant with this process. My own conclusion here must take the form of a question about the critical value of the newer art. There is some agreement that the older modernism functioned against its society in ways which are variously described as critical, negative, contestatory, subversive, oppositional and the like. Can anything of the sort be affirmed about postmodernism and its social moment? We have seen that there is a way in which postmodernism replicates or reproduces – reinforces – the logic of consumer capitalism; the more significant question is whether there is also a way in which it resists that logic. But that is a question we must leave open.

Note

1. MICHAEL HERR, *Dispatches* (New York: Knopf, 1977), pp. 8–9.

Popular Capitalism and Popular Culture

14 David Harvey, from *The Condition of Postmodernity. An Enquiry into the Origins of Social Change**

As suggested elsewhere in this volume, the debate on postmodernity and postmodernism raises questions about the development of capitalism and of culture. David Harvey, and in the following essay, Iain Chambers, bring a particular rigour and refinement to these topics and are included together for that reason.

The selections from Harvey summarise his sustained analysis in *The Condition of Postmodernity* of a new experience in space – time compression produced under late capitalism, and present his conclusion that this cultural phase is approaching an end. Like Jameson, though with greater precision, Harvey treats postmodernity as an historical condition. Unlike Jameson, he feels it is possible to analyse its levels in such a way as to move outside and beyond it. The mirroring surface of postmodernism is cracked, he concludes, and this allows for new angles and perspectives. As always, the question is who these new perspectives represent. The inspiration for Harvey's hopes for a regrounded ethics in the future lies with the new social movements and changed attitudes towards race, peace and ecology. This gives him confidence that a revised 'historical–geographical materialism' will help fulfil a reoriented Enlightenment project (see headnotes on Habermas and Lyotard).

Harvey's main concerns, as this suggests, are with economic and geo-political themes. Earlier sections in his book discuss the 'post-modernist' films, *Blade Runner* and *Wings of Desire*. Though his description of these works as 'portraying' postmodernism and his final reservations on their inadequate class analysis recall an older, unreconstructed, Marxism, his study as a whole demonstrates the close knowledge and flexible, spatial–temporal analysis this transitional period requires of 'post-Marxism'.

---

* (Oxford: Basil Blackwell, 1989), pp. 327–35, 356–9.

Postmodernity as a historical condition

Aesthetic and cultural practices are peculiarly susceptible to the changing experience of space and time precisely because they entail the construction of spatial representations and artefacts out of the flow of human experience. They always broker between Being and Becoming.

It is possible to write the historical geography of the experience of space and time in social life, and to understand the transformations that both have undergone, by reference to material and social conditions. [Earlier I] proposed an historical sketch of how that might be done with respect to the post-Renaissance Western world. The dimensions of space and time have there been subject to the persistent pressure of capital circulation and accumulation, culminating (particularly during the periodic crises of overaccumulation that have arisen since the mid-nineteeth century) in disconcerting and disruptive bouts of time – space compression.

The aesthetic responses to conditions of time-space compression are important and have been so ever since the eighteenth-century separation of scientific knowledge from moral judgement opened up a distinctive role for them. The confidence of an era can be assessed by the width of the gap between scientific and moral reasoning. In periods of confusion and uncertainty, the turn to aesthetics (of whatever form) becomes more pronounced. Since phases of time – space compression are disruptive, we can expect the turn to aesthetics and to the forces of culture as both explanations and *loci* of active struggle to be particularly acute at such moments. Since crises of overaccumulation typically spark the search for spatial and temporal resolutions, which in turn create an overwhelming sense of time – space compression, we can also expect crises of overaccumulation to be followed by strong aesthetic movements.

The crisis of overaccumulation that began in the late 1960s and which came to a head in 1973 has generated exactly such a result. The experience of time and space has changed, the confidence in the association between scientific and moral judgements has collapsed, aesthetics has triumphed over ethics as a prime focus of social and intellectual concern, images dominate narratives, ephemerality and fragmentation take precedence over eternal truths and unified politics, and explanations have shifted from the realm of material and political – economic groundings towards a consideration of autonomous cultural and political practices.

The historical sketch I have here proposed suggests, however, that shifts of this sort are by no means new, and that the most recent version of it is certainly within the grasp of historical materialist enquiry, even capable of theorization by way of the meta-narrative of capitalist development that Marx proposed.

181

Postmodernism can be regarded, in short, as a historical – geographical condition of a certain sort. But what sort of condition is it and what should we make of it? Is it pathological or portentous of a deeper and even wider revolution in human affairs than those already wrought in the historical geography of capitalism? In this conclusion I sketch in some possible answers to those questions.

Economics with mirrors

'Voodoo economics' and 'economics with mirrors' said George Bush and John Anderson respectively of Ronald Reagan's economic programme to revive a flagging economy in the primary and presidential election campaigns of 1980. A sketch on the back of a napkin by a little-known economist called Laffer purported to show that tax cuts were bound to increase tax yields (at least up to a certain point) because they stimulated growth and, hence, the base upon which taxes were assessed. So was the economic policy of the Reagan years to be justified, a policy that indeed worked wonders with mirrors even if it brought the United States several steps closer to international bankruptcy and fiscal ruin. The strange and puzzling thing is that such a simplistic idea could gain the purchase it did and seem to work so well politically for so long. Even stranger, is the fact that Reagan was re-elected when all the polls showed that the majority of the US electorate (to say nothing of the majority of eligible voters, who did not vote) disagreed fundamentally with him on almost all major issues of social, political, and even foreign policy. Strangest of all is how such a President could leave office riding so high on the wave of public affection, even though more than a dozen senior members of his administration had either been accused or been found guilty of serious infringement of legal procedures and blatant disregard for ethical principles. The triumph of aesthetics over ethics could not be plainer.

Image-building in politics is nothing new. Spectacle, pomp and circumstance, demeanour, charisma, partronage and rhetoric have long been part of the aura of political power. And the degree to which these could be bought, produced, or otherwise acquired has also long been important to the maintenance of that power. But something has changed qualitatively about that in recent times. The mediatization of politics was given a new direction in the Kennedy – Nixon television debate, in which the latter's loss of a presidential election was attributed by many to the untrustworthy look of his five o'clock shadow. The active use of public relations firms to shape and sell a political image quickly followed (the careful imaging of Thatcherism by the now all-powerful firm of Saatchi and Saatchi is a recent example, illustrating how Americanized in this regard European politics is becoming).

The election of an ex-movie actor, Ronald Reagan, to one of the most powerful positions in the world put a new gloss on the possibilities of a mediatized politics shaped by images alone. His image, cultivated over many years of political practice, and then carefully mounted, crafted, and orchestrated with all the artifice that contemporary image production could command, as a tough but warm, avuncular, and well-meaning person who had an abiding faith in the greatness and goodness of America, built an aura of charismatic politics. Carey McWilliams, an experienced political commentator and long-time editor of the *Nation*, described it as 'the friendly face of fascism'. The 'teflon president,' as he came to be known (simply because no accusation thrown at him, however true, ever seemed to stick), could make mistake after mistake but never be called to account. His image could be deployed, unfailingly and instantaneously, to demolish any narrative of criticism that anyone cared to construct. But the image concealed a coherent politics. First, to exorcise the demon of the defeat in Vietnam by taking assertive action in support of any nominally anti-communist struggle anywhere in the world (Nicaragua, Grenada, Angola, Mozambique, Afghanistan, etc.). Second to expand the budget deficit through defence spending and force a recalcitrant Congress (and nation) to cut again and again into the social programmes that the rediscovery of poverty and of racial inequality in the United States in the 1960s had spawned.

This open programme of class aggrandizement was partially successful. Attacks upon union power (led by the Reagan onslaught upon the air traffic controllers), the effects of deindustrialization and regional shifts (encouraged by tax breaks), and of high unemployment (legitimized as proper medicine in the fight against inflation), and all the accumulated impacts of the shift from manufacturing to service employment, weakened traditional working-class institutions sufficiently to render much of the population vulnerable. A rising tide of social inequality engulfed the United States in the Reagan years, reaching a post-war high in 1986; by then the poorest fifth of the population, which had gradually improved its share of national income to a high point of nearly 7 per cent in the early 1970s, found itself with only 4.6 per cent. Between 1979 and 1986, the number of poor families with children increased by 35 per cent, and in some large metropolitan areas, such as New York, Chicago, Baltimore and New Orleans, more than half the children were living in families with incomes below the poverty line. In spite of surging unemployment (cresting at over 10 per cent by official figures in 1982) the percentage of unemployed receiving any federal benefit fell to only 32 per cent, the lowest level in the history of social insurance since its inception in the New Deal. An increase in homelessness signalled a general state of social dislocation, marked by confrontations (many of them with racist or ethnic overtones). The mentally ill were returned to their communities for care, which consisted largely of rejection and violence, the tip of an iceberg of neglect which left nearly 40 million citizens in one of the richest nations of the world with no medical insurance cover whatsoever. While jobs were indeed created during the Reagan years, many of them were low-wage and insecure service jobs, hardly sufficient to offset the 10 per cent decline in the real wage from 1972 to 1986. If family incomes rose, that simply signified that more and more women were entering the workforce.

Yet for the young and the rich and the educated and the privileged things could not have been better. The world of real estate, finance, and business services grew, as did the 'cultural mass' given over to the production of images, knowledge, and cultural and aesthetic forms. The political–economic base and, with it, the whole culture of cities were transformed. New York lost its traditional garment trade and turned to the production of debt and fictitious capital instead. 'In the last seven years', ran a report by Scardino (1987) in the *New York Times*,

> New York has constructed 75 new factories to house the debt production and distribution machine. These towers of granite and glass shine through the night as some of this generation's most talented professionals invent new instruments of debt to fit every imagined need: Perpetual Floating Rate Notes, Yield Curve Notes and Dual Currency Notes, to name a few, now traded as casually as the stock of the Standard Oil Company once was.

The trade is as vigorous as that which once dominated the harbour. But 'today, the telephone lines deliver the world's cash to be remixed as if in a bottling plant, squirted into different containers, capped and shipped back out'. The biggest physical export from New York City is now waste paper. The city's economy in fact rests on the production of fictitious capital to lend to the real estate agents who cut deals for the highly paid professionals who manufacture fictitious capital. Likewise, when the image production machine of Los Angeles came to a grinding halt during the Writers' Guild strike, people suddenly realised 'how much of its economic structure is based on a writer telling a producer a story, and that finally it's the weaving of the tale (into images) that pays the wages of the man who drives the van that delivers the food that's eaten in the restaurant that feeds the family who make the decisions that keep the economy running' (report of Scott Meek in *The Independent*, 14 July 1988).

The emergence of this casino economy, with all of its financial speculation and fictitious capital formation (much of it unbacked by any growth in real production) provided abundant opportunities for personal aggrandizement. Casino capitalism had come to town, and many large cities suddenly found they had command of a new and powerful business. On the back of this boom in business and financial services, a whole new Yuppie culture formed, with its accoutrements of gentrification, close attention to symbolic capital, fashion, design and quality of urban life.

The obverse side of this affluence was the plague of homelessness, disempowerment, and impoverishment that engulfed many of the central cities. 'Otherness' was produced with a vengeance and a vengefulness unparalleled in the post-war era. The forgotten voices and unforgettable dreams of New York's homeless were recorded this way (Coalition For the Homeless, 1987):

I am 37 years old. I look like 52 years old. Some people say that street life is free and easy . . . It's not free and it's not easy. You don't put no money down. Your payment is your health and mental stability.

My country's name is apathy. My land is smeared with shame. My sightscape moves its homeless hordes through welfare's turgid flame. The search goes on for rooms and warmth, some closet hooks, a drawer; a hot place just for one's soup – what liberty is for.

Just before Christmas 1987, the United States Government cut $35 million from the budget for emergency help to the homeless. Meanwhile personal indebtedness continued to accelerate, and presidential candidates began to fight over who could enunciate the pledge of allegiance in more convincing tones. The voices of the homeless sadly went unheard in a world 'cluttered with illusion, fantasy and pretence'.

Cracks in the mirrors, fusions at the edges

'We feel that postmodernism is over', a major United States developer told the architect Moshe Safdie (*New York Times*, 29 May 1988). 'For projects which are going to be ready in five years, we are now considering new architectural appointments.' He said this, reported Safdie, 'with the naturalness of a clothing manufacturer who tells you that he does not want to be stuck with a line of blue coats when red is in'. Perhaps for this very reason, Philip Johnson has put his considerable weight behind the new movement of 'deconstructivism' with all its high-brow appeal to theory. If this is where the developers are heading, can the philosophers and literary theorists be far behind?

On 19 October 1987, someone peeked behind the reflecting mirrors of

US economic policy and, frightened at what they saw there, plunged the world's stock markets into such a fearful crash that nearly a third of the paper value of assets worldwide was written off within a few days. The event provoked ugly memories of 1929, pushed most finance houses to draconian economies, others into hasty mergers. Fortunes made overnight by the young, the aggressive, and the ruthless traders in the hyper-space of instant financial dealing were lost even more speedily than they had been acquired. The economy of New York City and other major financial centres was threatened by the rapid fall in the volume of trading. Yet the rest of the world remained strangely unmoved.

'Different worlds' was the headline in the *Wall Street Journal*, as it compared the 'eerily detached' view from Main Street, USA, with that of Wall Street. 'The crash aftermath is the tale of two cultures – processing different information, operating on different time horizons, dreaming different dreams. . . The financial community – living by the minute and trading by the computer – operates on one set of values', while 'the rest of America – living by the decade, buying and holding – has a different code' which might be called 'the ethic of those who have their hands on shovels'.

Main Street may feel justified in its indifference because the dire predictions in the aftermath of the crash have not as yet materialised. But the mirrors of accelerating indebtedness (personal, corporate, governmental) continue to work overtime. Fictitious capital is even more hegemonic than before in its influence. It creates its own fantastic world of booming paper wealth and assets. Asset inflation takes over where the commodity inflation of the 1970s left off until the mass of funds thrown into the markets to ward off the crash in October 1987 works its way through the economy to produce a resurgence of wage and commodity inflation two years later. Debts get rescheduled and rolled over at ever faster rates, with the aggregate effect of rescheduling the crisis-tendencies of capitalism into the twenty-first century. Yet cracks in the reflecting mirrors of economic performance abound. US banks write off billions of dollars of bad loans, governments default, international currency markets remain in perpetual turmoil.

On the philosophical front, deconstructionism has been put on the defensive by the controversies over the Nazi sympathies of Heidegger and Paul de Man. That Heidegger, the inspiration of deconstruction, should have had such an unrepentant attachment to Nazism, and that Paul de Man, one of deconstructionism's most accomplished practitioners, should have had such a murky past of anti-semitic writing, has proved a major embarrassment. The charge that deconstruction is neo-fascist is not in itself interesting, but the manner of defence against the charge is.

Hillis Miller ('De Man', *Times Literary Supplement* 17 June 1988), for example, appeals to the 'facts' (a positivist argument), to principles of fairness and reasonableness (liberal humanist argument), and to historical context (an historical materialist argument) in his defence of de Man's 'appalling' interventions. The irony, of course, is that these are all ways of arguing that Hillis Miller had pulled apart in the work of others. Rorty, on the other hand, takes his own position to its logical conclusion, declaring that the political opinions of a great philosopher do not have to be taken any more seriously than philosophy itself (which is hardly at all), and that any relationship between ideas and reality, moral positions and philosophical writings is purely contingent. The flagrant irresponsibility of that position is almost as embarrassing as the transgressions that set the whole debate rolling.

The cracks in an intellectual edifice that opens the way to the empowerment of aesthetics over ethics are important. Deconstructionism, like any system of thought and any definition of an overwhelming symbolic order, internalises certain contradictions which at a certain point become more and more self-evident. When Lyotard, for example, seeks to keep his radical hopes alive by appeal to some pristine and unsullied concept of justice, he proposes a truth statement that lies above the mêlée of interest groups and their cacophony of language games. When Hillis Miller is forced to appeal to liberal and positivist values to defend his mentor, Paul de Man, against what he considers the calumny of false accusations, then he, too, invokes universals.

And at the edges of these trends there are all sorts of fusions of the fragments in progress. Jesse Jackson employs charismatic politics in a political campaign which nevertheless begins to fuse some of the social movements in the United States that have long been apathetic to each other. The very possibility of a genuine rainbow coalition defines a unified politics which inevitably speaks the tacit language of class, because this is precisely what defines the common experience within the differences. US trade union leaders finally begin to worry that their support for foreign dictatorships in the name of anti-communism since 1950, has promoted the unfair labour practices and low wages in many countries which now compete for jobs and investment. And when British Ford car workers struck and stopped car production in Belgium and West Germany, they suddenly realised that spatial dispersal in the division of labour is not entirely to the capitalists' advantage and international strategies are feasible as well as desirable. Signs of a new internationalism in the ecological sphere (forced by events for the bourgeoisie, sought out actively by many ecological groups) and in the fight against racism, apartheid, world hunger, uneven geographical development, are everywhere, even if much of it still lies in the realm of pure image-making (like Band Aid) rather than in political organization. The geopolitical stress between East and West also undergoes a notable amelioration (again, no thanks to the ruling classes in the West, but more because of an evolution in the East).

The cracks in the mirror may not be too wide, and the fusions at the edges may not be too striking, but the fact that all are there suggests that the condition of postmodernity is undergoing a subtle evolution, perhaps reaching a point of self-dissolution into something different. But what?

Answers to that cannot be rendered in abstraction from the political – economic forces currently transforming the world of labour, finance, uneven geographical development, and the like. The lines of tension are clear enough. Geopolitics and economic nationalism, localism and the politics of place, are all fighting it out with a new internationalism in the most contradictory of ways. The fusion of the European Economic Community as a commodity trading block takes place in 1992; takeovers and merger manias will sweep the continent; yet Thatcherism still proclaims itself as a distinctive national project resting upon the peculiarities of the British (a proposition which both Left and Right politics tend to accept). International control over finance capital looks inevitable, yet it seems impossible to arrive at that through the collectivity of national interests. In the intellectual and cultural spheres similar oppositions can be identified.

Wenders seems to propose a new romanticism, the exploration of global meanings and the prospects for Becoming through the release of romantic desire out of the stasis of Being. There are dangers in releasing an unknown and perhaps uncontrollable aesthetic power into an unstable situation. Brandon Taylor favours a return to realism as a means to bring cultural practices back into a realm where some kind of explicit ethical content can be expressed. Even some of the deconstructionists seem to be reverting to ethics.

Beyond that there is a renewal of historical materialism and of the Enlightenment project. Through the first we can begin to understand postmodernity as an historical – geographical condition. On that critical basis it becomes possible to launch a counter-attack of narrative against the image, of ethics against aesthetics, of a project of Becoming rather than Being, and to search for unity within difference, albeit in a context where the power of the image and of aesthetics, the problems of time – space compression, and the significance of geopolitics and otherness are clearly understood. A renewal of historical – geographical materialism can indeed promote adherence to a new version of the Enlightenment project. Poggioli(*The Theory of the Avant-Garde* (Cambridge, Mass.: Belknap Press/Harvard University Press, 1968, p. 73) captures the difference thus:

> In the consciousness of the classical epoch, it is not the present that brings the past into culmination, but the past that culminates in the

present, and the present is in turn understood as a new triumph of ancient and eternal values, as a return to the principle of the true and the just, as a restoration or re-birth of those principles. But for the moderns, the present is valid only by virtue of the potentialities of the future, as the matrix of the future, insofar as it is the forge of history in continued metamorphosis, seen as a permanent spiritual revolution.

There are some who would have us return to classicism and others who seek to tread the path of the moderns. From the standpoint of the latter, every age is judged to attain 'the fullness of its time, not by being but by becoming'. I could not agree more.

15 Iain Chambers, 'Contamination, Coincidence and Collusion: Pop Music, Urban Culture and the Avant-Garde*

One of the few firmly agreed effects of postmodernism has been the toppling of hierarchical distinctions between 'high and low' culture. It has therefore brought the assumed separation of art and commerce to an end – to the chagrin of both liberal traditionalist and radical Marxist critics. For when even the uncompromising and anti-bourgeois aesthetics of the avant-garde have been (apparently) neutralised or translated into advertising copy, there seems little hope of cultural or social tranformation through art.

Chambers presents a further option. He argues that pop music, the most highly technologised and commodified of post-war art forms, can retain an avant-gardist edge and democratic potential, precisely in the socially and racially differentiated urban concentrations which generate and sustain it. He therefore eschews the totalising grasp of supporters of the traditional Enlightenment project and avoids both the rhapsodising on pure change or the disdainful camp populism encouraged by Lyotard and Baudrillard. Chambers' view that the historical avant-garde and urban daily life combine in the complexity and 'resignified' meanings of rock music is also a reply to the more familiar, less optimistic, view that the liberationist potential of this music is limited, and that the subordinated voices of white and black youth it expresses are swamped in a homogenised global product.

Chambers' essay was first delivered at the University of Illinois in 1983, before its publication in Nelson and Grossberg with other conference papers and accompanying discussion – where some of the above questions are raised.

See also Chambers, *Popular Culture. The Metropolitan Experience* (1986), especially pp. 214–21; and *Border Dialogues* (1990). For further

* Reprinted from Nelson and Grossberg (eds), *Marxism and the Interpretation of Culture* (London: Macmillan, 1988), pp. 607–11).

discussion of postmodernism and popular culture, see titles by McRobbie, Hebdige and Collins under Further Reading.

It is necessary to take seriously the hypothesis according to which only an excess of imagination seizes the profundity of the real. . .

(Henri Lefebvre)

What might Lefebvre's statement, made in the context of a discussion of Surrealism, mean in the context of the triad pop music, popular culture, and the avant-garde? In seeking an answer, I will be talking about the relationship between an excess of imagination and popular cultural tastes. I want to identify where the project of the historical avant-garde and important tendencies in contemporary urban popular culture meet, as it were, at the periphery of an existing cultural hegemony or cultural block. This involves looking at the struggle for the sense and direction of urban culture that takes place in the 'dailyness' of routines, habits, and the subconsciously exercised expectations of common sense in order to see how an excess of imagination is translated into a practical jolting of common sense, which permits previously mute areas and relations to begin to speak.

To think more concretely about this potentiality, we need to consider the spaces in which diverse social forces are brought together – forces that are gendered, racial, and further differentiated in both major and microscopic fashion. This will render, one hopes, slightly more articulate what is quite clearly a long-standing critical silence in discussions about both pop music and contemporary urban popular culture. While I will be referring here to realities found in advanced capitalist societies, I would also suggest that these tendencies have effects in urban centers throughout the world. The effects are different, but they are, in a very complex way, related to developments within advanced capitalist urban culture.

In *The Art of Noises*, published in 1916, the Italian futurist Luigi Russolo drew attention to the 'voluptuous' sonorities of the new metropolitan environment: an infinite combination of sirens and horns, crowds and trams, engines and machinery. He proposed a new music to be produced by specially constructed machines, considered himself to be a 'noise tuner', and wrote compositions for these instruments bearing such titles as 'A City Wakes Up' and 'A Conference for Cars and Planes'.[1] This futurist provocation usefully serves to isolate a set of significant themes: the machine, mechanical reproduction, and what Antonio Gramsci once called the 'directive function' of the city in national life.

The avant-garde's 'explosion of dissent' (André Breton) in the early decades of the twentieth century signaled a divide between a

191

contemplative attitude toward art (*l'art pour l'art*) and a radical activism
that sought to overcome the 'divorce between action and dream'
(Breton). Futurism's frantic embrace of modernity and the 'machine
epoch,' Dada's direct refusal of 'art' and its proclamation of the victory of
daily life over aesthetics, and the Surrealist project to give free rein to the
unconscious through the liberty of 'automatic writing' profoundly
undermined the traditional demand for artistic 'authenticity.' This had
now become a false request, an irrelevancy; not, as Adorno was fond of
repeating, because the world had grown 'false', but because the
conditions of perception, reception and artistic production had
irreversibly changed. It was now the epoch of the photograph, the
gramophone, the radio, and the cinema: the epoch of mechanical
reproduction.

As though to drive this last point home, several tendencies in the
avant-garde, particularly in the visual arts, borrowed humble objects
from everyday life and simply copied them, or, more provocatively still,
presented them unchanged to the public. Marcel Duchamp takes a
bicycle wheel and signs it as his own 'work'. Half a century later, Andy
Warhol updates this gesture with his silk-screen reproductions of Coca-
Cola bottles and Elvis Presley, Campbell's soup cans and Marilyn
Monroe. In both cases, ironic queries were raised about the status of 'art'
and about the nature of its cultural reproduction in the context of the
contemporary urban world.

Cigarette ends, newspaper clippings, and 'spilt' paint coalesce on a
canvas; Russolo's 'noise machines'; Duchamp's 'ready-mades'; the whole
manifesto of Pop Art: all form part of a twentieth-century collage
suggested and sustained by the metropolis. The mutual 'contamination'
of the ruptural perception of the avant-garde and the expansion of daily
urban culture steadily grows. It touches its logical conclusion when
subway graffiti enters the art gallery and the pop video reactivates the
Surrealist cinema (i.e., David Bowie's 'Ashes to Ashes' video, 1980).
There are no longer any fixed 'sources', no 'pure' sounds, no untainted
'aura' (Walter Benjamin) against which to evaluate the continual
combination, reproduction, and transmission of sounds, images, and
objects that circulate in the heterogeneous flux of the modern city.[2] The
distance between the gestures of the different artistic avant-gardes and
the street blast of a passing portable cassette player balanced on a
T-shirted shoulder is today actually a lot smaller than we might think.

The portable cassette player, like the electric guitar, the programmed
synthesizer, and the drum machine, but, above all, the record,
underscores the importance of mechanical transformation (machines)
and reproduction in the formation of pop music. Pop Music is
'designed for reproducibility' (Walter Benjamin), and one of its possible

histories is a history of the development and effects of its technical reproduction.

Toward the end of 1948, recording tape was introduced; until then, recording music had involved registering the acoustic sound directly onto a lacquer-coated disc. This extremely rigid system – for instance, an error in the musical execution meant discarding the disc and starting again – certainly did not encourage the exploration of the sonorial extensions potentially available in the recording situation. But with the introduction of tape, music could be completely constructed inside the studio. By editing, cutting, and splicing, a final sound could be built up from fragments of recording. A fifty-second demo-tape could be turned into a record lasting more than two minutes: this is how Little Richard's 'Keep A-Knockin' was produced. The result was that 'recording tape shifted the record from the status of a frozen snapshot to that of a musical montage'.[3]

Recording tape represented the first major innovation in post-war recording procedures. The second, occurring in the late 1960s, involved the introduction of multi-track recording facilities. The use of echo and double-tracking in the 1950s and early 1960s in order to 'beef up' the sound had already pointed in this direction. But with the introduction of stereo records and then, in rapid succession, four-, eight-, sixteen-, twenty-four-, and thirty-two-track recording, the sonorial framework was vastly extended. Adding recorded track to track, piling up diverse sounds, a four-person group, for example, could produce eight or sixteen 'voices' to be simultaneously mixed in the final recorded form.

Multi-track recording permits many musical directions, some seemingly diametrically opposed. While the 'artistic' aspiration of parts of 'progressive music' now found the space for their rock operas and suites, in the very different reality of reggae, 'dub' was able to phase instruments and voices in and out, suspend the pulse and then intensify it, chop up the sound and then enrich it with further effects, while stretching the whole swirling pattern across a stuttering 'roots' bass-drum 'ridim.'

Technology has been central to pop from its beginnings. It is impossible to discuss the music without referring to it: whether it is Elvis working on his sound in the tiny Sun studio in the early 1950s, or the mesmerising dance floor success of disco twenty years later. Pop music has never existed apart from technological intervention; this only draws further attention to the daily tensions involved at the technological 'interface where the economies of capital and libido interlock'.[4]

The fact that the recording studio, with its technology and accompanying financial requirements, is the central site of pop's sonorial production by no means implies a simple technological determinism. The history of pop reveals other, often unsuspected tendencies, among them the story of a continual appropriation of pop's technology and reproductive capacities. This has resulted in diversified cultural investments, involving different fractions of white metropolitan youth taking up guitars and synthesizers and adopting various imported sounds, as well as black youth 'resignifying' the use of the microphone and the turntable (the deejay's 'toast' and 'rap') and studio console ('dub'). Both maintain the fruitful paradox of subordinated, frequently oral-centered cultures mastering and extending the electronic medium of pop and, in the process, re-presenting their 'selves' in the heartlands of contemporary urban life.

In the exclusive reality of the historical avant-garde, the attempt was undertaken to produce new languages that subtracted themselves from the dulled continuity of past acceptance and present expectation. An analogous case might be made for pop: rock 'n' roll and punk are both obvious occasions when particular musical proposals tore apart an earlier syntax and associated cultural attitudes.

I want to add to these stark examples the suggestion that what such eruptive symptoms expose has its daily currency in mechanical reproduction, in its ingression into the web of sonorial reality where records, borrowing an expression from Susan Sontag, 'democratise all experiences by translating them' into sounds.[5] Today, we no longer confront 'organic' expressions but a cultural 'cut-up', a series of fragments – New York rap, London punk, Nigerian 'juju', soul, country-and-western ballads, white funk. We subsequently select from these sounds a meaningful bricolage, an environment of sense. The fragmentation of the eye and ear, so self-consciously pursued by the avant-garde in its desire to liberate new experiences, new horizons, is overtaken by the permissive circulation of possibilities permitted by radio, film, television, records, cassettes, video.

This situation both augments and, in an important sense, disrupts the more obvious connections between pop and the recent musical avant-garde. From the late 1960s onward, the music of Frank Zappa, of such German groups as Can, Amon Duul II, and Tangerine Dream, and in England Henry Cow, Brian Eno, and even David Bowie, can be linked to the experiments in serial composition, repetition, and incidental 'noise' found in the work of Varèse, Stockhausen, Cage, Riley, LaMonte Young, Glass, and others. But the 1970s were also characterised by an increasing attention to pop's own internal languages and the subsequent basis for a self-generated pop avant-gardism. The elements of this second tendency can be found in the whimsical musical bric-a-brac of Roxy Music, the neurotic funk experiments of David Bowie, and the studied ruptural aesthetics of such postpunk groups as Public Image Ltd and the Gang of Four. In particular, it was punk and its aftermath that clarified the possibility of reassessing pop's existing musical languages and suggested a sonorial collage in which the joins were left exposed as the signifiers of 'noise' and 'sound' or 'din' and 'music', were shifted back and forth along the cultural reception of the acoustic spectrum.

The most interesting reflection to be made here is the one I hinted at above – of how mechanical reproduction sweeps away the separate status of the historical avant-garde (which also explains my use of the adjective 'historical' up to this point). The previous distance between the avant-garde and daily urban culture is overcome as the former becomes enveloped by the visual and sonorial languages of the latter. Inside the metropolitan plasma of today, the concentrated moment of attention that once accompanied the response to both traditional and subversive art is replaced by Benjamin's concept of 'distracted reception'. The fabric of tradition is absentmindedly unstitched and a deritualised culture, invaded by the profanity of diverse tastes; it is gradually mastered 'by habit under the guidance of tactile appropriation'.[6]

In the case of pop music, tactile appropriation – the physical reception of the tangible – is concentrated in the differentiated presence and signification of the body. Let me explain. While the apparently nebulous zone of romance is the privileged domain in pop's emotional empire – and I am referring not only to that usually associated with juvenile girls building fantasies around the pin-ups and records of male stars but, in particular, to the dominant male romanticism of an imaginary street life – it is the body that is its principal focus and carrier.

The musical languages of pop – the wrenched sentiments of soul, the exuberance of rock 'n' roll, the verbal contortions of rap, the screeched angst of punk – all tend to propel the body through the sensorial 'grain' (Roland Barthes) of the music to the center of the stage. There, in dancing and the immediacy of performance, it is this physical sense of the musical 'now' that is pivotal, for it 'is the body that ultimately makes, receives and responds to music; and it is the body that connects sounds, dance, fashion and style to the subconscious anchorage of sexuality and eroticism'.[7] It being here, where romance and 'reality' are fused together, that common sense is often taunted, twisted and torn apart.

So, my concluding suggestion is that the avant-garde project of purposefully mismatching perception and the taken-for-granted in order to release perspectives from the fetish of common sense tends to find a contemporary realisation in the daily culture of the metropolis. Here, the once-researched shock of the historical avant-garde, the transitory immediacy of perpetual sonorial and visual reproduction, and the 'dense and concrete life' of subordinated cultures – 'a life whose main stress is on the intimate, the sensory, the detailed and the personal' – are indiscriminately mixed together.[8]

Further, this urban complexity forces into an extensive, if still frequently unsuspected, dialogue the once-separated episodes of the avant-garde, of popular culture, and a politics based on the detailed possibilities of the everyday: on its class, racial, sexual, local and national construction, variation, peculiarity. As these trajectories cross each other's path and dissolve in the fervent flux of metropolitan life, they increasingly gesture toward a new project. Whatever its eventual shape, that project will need to interrogate existing cultural hegemony and subtract itself from the tired logic of the predictable if it is to challenge successfully existing definitions of daily life. But to do this it will have to be constructed *inside* this present complexity.

Notes

1. LUIGI RUSSOLO *L'arte dei rumori* (Milan: Edizioni Futuriste di 'Poesia', 1916). Republished as a supplement in *Alfabeta*, **43**, Milan (December 1982).

2. WALTER BENJAMIN 'The Work of Art in the Age of Mechanical Reproduction', *Illuminations*, trans. Harry Zohn (London: Fontana, 1973). All references to the essay are to this edition.

3. IAIN CHAMBERS, *Urban Rhythms* (London: Macmillan, 1984), p. 14.

4. PETER WOLLEN, *Readings and Writings* (London: Verso, 1982), p. 176. It is worthwhile recalling a note of Benjamin's on the relation between film and technology: 'In the case of films, mechanical reproduction is not, as with literature and painting, an external condition for mass distribution. Mechanical reproduction is inherent in the very technique of film production. This technique not only permits in the most direct way but virtually causes mass distribution' (Benjamin, p. 246). The same can be said for the contemporary production of pop music.

5. The context of this quotation is, 'The subsequent industrialisation of camera technology only carried out a promise inherent in photography from its very beginnings: to democratise all experiences by translating them into images' (Susan Sontag. *On Photography* (Harmondsworth: Penguin, 1979), p. 7). The history of recorded music, where we all have the possibility of indulging our tastes and becoming 'experts', leads toward similar conclusions.

6. BENJAMIN, p. 242.

7. CHAMBERS, p. 210.

8. RICHARD HOGGART, *The Uses of Literacy* (Harmondsworth: Penguin, 1958), p. 81.

A Feminist Postmodernism?

16 Julia Kristeva, 'Postmodernism?'*

The use of the term 'postmodernism' has been surprisingly rare in French debates (see Introduction, p. 15). Hence, perhaps, one reason for the question mark accompanying its use as the title to Kristeva's essay, a piece written, significantly, for an American publication.

To add to this, the use of the concept 'postmodernism' in relation to feminism has often been problematic. Craig Owens observed in 1983 that 'the absence of discussions of sexual difference' and 'the fact that few women had engaged in the modernism/postmodernism debate suggest that postmodernism may be another masculine invention engineered to exclude women' (Foster (ed.), 1985, p. 61). With some justification, Meaghan Morris saw this and later similar comments by Huyssen (1986) and Jonathan Arac (1986) as just such an invention. Her reply, in *The Pirate's Fiancée* (1988) was a six-page bibliography of relevant works by women, including Julia Kristeva and other French feminists.

But the reasons for Kristeva's inclusion in such a list are not self-evident. Her reference, first of all, to modernist writers (Pound, Céline, Mayakovksy, Mallarmé) in the present essay and elsewhere, along with her admiration for the 'individuating' explorations of modern writing against the degraded 'collectivising' effects of the mass media suggest a negative attitude towards postmodernism. Secondly, her reference to male writers and her distance from forms of political activism have brought many to query her contribution to feminism. (see Kipnis below, and Joanna Hodge in A. Benjamin (ed.), (1989), pp. 86–111.)

---

* Reprinted from Harry Garvin (ed.), *Romanticism, Modernism, Postmodernism* (Pennsylvania: Bucknell Review, 1980), pp. 136 – 41.

The explanation for Kristeva's position could be said to lie in a thorough-going scepticism towards monolithic systems and categories, and her deconstructive, psycho-semiotic theory of language and identity. It is these that she brings to postmodernism. Her answer to the query of her title is accordingly the speculation that postmodernist writing expands 'the limits of the signifiable', that this 'writiing-as-experience-of-limits' (in Artaud, Burroughs, and the art of Robert Wilson, John Cage) explores forms of expression in the 'imaginary', pre-symbolic (and pre-gendered) realm of an infant's relation to its mother. Postmodernist writing proceeds therefore without the safety net of religious or political justification supporting earlier writing. The fact that Kristeva assigns the exploration of the 'unpresentable' to art means that she avoids positioning women as this 'unpresentable' – as the fixed other and quintessence of postmodernism implied by other accounts. Eventually, therefore, her argument connects critically, if obliquely, with themes developed elsewhere in the debate on postmodernism: with the growth of economic rationalisation and media saturation, the loss of confidence in grand narratives and the aesthetic exploration of the unnameable and unthinkable.

On feminism and postmodernism see, in addition to the above references, Alice Jardine, *Gynesis: Configurations of Woman and Modernity* (1985); Linda J. Nicholson (ed.), *Feminism/Postmodernism* (1990); Sarah Lovibond, 'Feminism and Postmodernism' in *Postmodernism and Society*, ed. Roy Boyne and Ali Rattansi (1990). Fred Pfeil's 'Postmodernism as a "Structure of Feeling"' in Nelson and Grossberg (eds), (1988), pp. 381–403, relates interestingly to the present essay by Kristeva. Using Lacan and Marx, Pfeil examines a de-Oedipalisation' in American middle-class life and the consequently changed subjectivities expressed in examples from contemporary popular and avant-garde culture.

This question could be reformulated to read: first, in what way can anything be written in the twentieth century, and second, in what way can we talk about this writing? This formulation of the problem demands that we first elucidate those particularities of the twentieth century having a bearing on literary activity. With this foundation any literary inquiry transforms itself into first an epistemological, and then into a sociohistorical investigation. I shall emphasise these two aspects of the inquiry.

First, those sciences dealing with symbolic capabilities (linguistics, semiology, psychoanalysis and anthropology), as well as bioneurological research, have clearly demonstrated that the position of language within human experience is determinant but fragile.

Language is *determinant* because all social phenomena are symbolic. The discovery of the unconscious scandalises us not because it postulates sexual determinism, but rather because it reveals that sex is an unconscious and, consequently, a symbolic arrangement structured like language. The continuing elucidation of social mechanisms by structural anthropology is significant not because of its assertion, annoying from a feminist perspective, that women are objects of exchange, but rather by virtue of its revelation, offensive from the perspective of all anthropological narcissism, that individuals are no more than ephemeral variables in an eternally repeating machine of identification and rejection, of yes and no, of mimesis and aggression, that clearly presides over the phonological structure of language.

Language is *fragile* because any *particular* language as the object of linguistic scrutiny, along with the variations of discourse particular to linguistic communication in that language, is merely an infinitesimal yet minimal part of the totality of symbolic experience. The biological reservoir, both instinctual and emotional, threatens not only the thin film of language but also the phenomenon of symbolism itself. It produces somatic symptoms, inhibition, and anguish in which what is incapable of being symbolised takes shape as a writing with a changed basis that no longer inscribes itself in its own space, that is, within the sign. Hence, it no longer inscribes itself at all but either cries out or suffocates.

Language is additionally fragile in its status as an objectively real medium of communication, posited as an object of study by those sciences which inherited the rationale of the nineteenth century. When the biological reservoir threatens the symbolic system, the speaking being reveals itself capable of unimaginable restructuring in language or discourse of its crises or breakdowns. Are we not then caught up in a vertiginous creation of languages, semiotic systems, and innumerable idiolects that radically and dramatically attempt not merely to survive, but even more ambitiously attempt to provide us with an aesthetic corpus?

If it is true that the sciences of Man have used language as a lever to breach the protective shield and the neuralgic locus of rationality, it is also true that this epistemological reinvestigation, the hallmark of our century, is accompanied by one of the most formidable attempts to *expand the limits of the signifiable* that is, to expand the boundaries of human experience through the realignment of its most characteristic element, language.

Let us say that postmodernism is that literature which writes itself with the more or less conscious intention of expanding the signifiable and thus human realm. With this in mind, I should call this practice of writing an 'experience of limits', to use Georges Bataille's formulation: limits of language as communicative system, limits of the subjective and naturally the sexual identity, limits of sociality. Compared to the media, whose function it is to collectivise all systems of signs, even those which are unconscious, writing-as-experience-of-limits *individuates*. This individuation extends deep within the constituent mechanisms of human experience as an experience of meaning; it extends as far as the very obscure and primary narcissism wherein the subject constitutes itself in order to oppose itself to another, and to the extent that it does so. Insofar as the return to this particular mechanism of individuation characterises psychosis, writing-as-experience-of-limits is its replacement. For precisely this reason it is the most fascinating and bizarre rival of psychoanalysis. Since Freud and the *Gradiva*, it has appeared that psychoanalysis has taken the place of that particular literature which relies on, or reduces itself to, fantasy. And yet, psychoanalysis has just barely and with great difficulty begun to perceive that this literature-as-experience-of-limits has, by virtue of its proposed elaboration of the mechanisms of primary narcissism, robbed psychoanalysis of psychosis and everything that entails.

The second point that this inquiry emphasises is that the history of the twentieth century entails a series of eruptions within the ambivalence between state and morality or religion. Since the eighteenth-century split between the political and the sacred (religious as well as secular morality), two consequences have been experienced in two different spheres. First, in the sphere of politics there has been an overcoding of economic rationalism whose apogee is technocratic centralism. Second, in the sphere of morality, a gap has opened up due not only to the flagrant lack of institutions (may the Lord preserve us from them), but above all to the lack of languages with which to speak of the impossibility and risk involved. There are two possible responses to these consequences: either the state recognises its moral prerogatives and integrates them into its economic rationalism – which would result in a fascist or Stalinist totalitarianism – or the state abandons this role and plays its part indirectly through technocratic liberalism – a course that entails a proliferation of aesthetic practices on the level that concerns us.

In Europe, for example, literature used to occupy its once traditional position as political counselor or critic, but in the twentieth century it has found itself in the wake of totalitarianism – here I am thinking of Pound, Céline, or Mayakovsky. In the formal craftsmanship of their work these writers touch upon the borderline states of meaning and subjectivity in order to elaborate and sublimate them and to make them livable. Consequently, in other aspects of their work they run up against what I call the 'positive trap', the necessarily phantasmagorical desire to see a particular spirit – that affirmative, positive, unifying, convocational, phallic spirit which presides at any undertaking – incorporated into an ideology or even an institution like a state or party. Hence they counterinvest this desire, and this counterbalance to the experience of death and resurrection that is writing, or more specifically a writing-as-experience-of-limits, becomes a crushing weight on them. When contemporary writers of genius who are conscious of this lesson of history reject political temptation, it is often religion that fills the role of offering caution, rationality, reassurance, or justification of their frankly gratuitous and risky activity; thus, Solzhenitsyn stands in contrast to Céline.

The question is whether or not this borderline writing has changed in aspect and economy since Mallarmé and Joyce, who together reflect that contemporary radical quality of borderline writing which in other civilisations and times had analogies in the mystical tradition. If we take Artaud and Burroughs as examples, it becomes clear that this writing confronts more directly than did its predecessors the *asymbolicity* peculiar to psychosis or the logical and phonetic drifting that pulverises and multiplies meaning while pretending to play with it or flee from it. All the better does it thereby both experience its discomfiture and put up with it, founding its meaning upon Artaud's semiotic glossolalias and Burroughs's cut-up style unfolding and suspending discursive logic and the speaking subject. If we focus on Bataille or on his more abject but more modest opposite, Céline, we find that this writing-as-experience-of-limits is first slandered, then it revolts and assumes once more the cutting edge of that 'comedy' which Hegel perceived as the basis of the relationship between the Self and the anterior objective or common Spirit, expressing their indissoluble contradiction before the appearance of revealed religion. The abjectness of Bataille and Céline is discharged into black humor, and it seems that no transcendence can possibly occur except through derisive 'bailing-out' plays on language, which themselves are effective only by an arbitrary gratuitousness.

All these tendencies, to which could be added postfuturist or postsurrealist writings, demonstrate a basic realignment in style that can be interpreted as an exploration of the typical imaginary relationship, that to the mother, through the most radical and problematic aspect of this relationship, language. This relationship returns to the presymbolic, to an arrangement of rhythms and alliterations that either stands up against meaning or shapes it. Isn't this what we are listening to on stage, all the way up to Robert Wilson and John Cage? The emptying and circumventing of language and the theatricalisation of gestures, sounds, and color are the supports against which this body-to-body struggle with psychosis has come to rest. It is not surprising that certain 'feminine' attempts at writing claim their feminine specificity by virtue of these gaps in meaning, brushing up against either enigma or void. These feminine attempts, propelled toward the experiments of Mallarmé and Joyce, have no stylistic and thus no literary novelty; yet they do advantageously demonstrate that women, too, can attempt to articulate their own body-to-body discourse with the mother.

In addition, postmodern writing as it appears, for example, in *Tel Quel* and in the writings of Sollers in particular, provokes renewed, growing, and overflowing interest in *significance,* as opposed to the particular nineteenth-century avant-garde notion of meaning. And in a kind of Dantesque project incorporating the formal experience of its predecessors, postmodern writing rediscovers *lyricism* (an admission of the subject's ecstasy – *jouissance*) as well as *epic breadth* (a rhetorical procedure of historical totalisation). Through its permanent debate with the event, with politics, with political, sexual and paranoid dilemmas, this writing is the antidote to (a polar opposite of?) the Ptolemaic universe and its measure. Compare, for example, Solzhenitsyn's *Gulag* with Sollers's *Paradise.*

Writing is clearly practical knowledge within the imaginary, a technique of fantasy. As such it is always simulated and mimicked. Within fantasy, this can be a communal experience; writing participates in the constitution of a community as a subtle and somewhat anarchical agent, but an agent of a larger group just the same.

Confronted with borderline writing, however, the imaginary is brought to the point where it leaves the community. This writing expresses into signs what in the imaginary is irreducible to others' experience – the most singular of products, even though no one escapes from this singularity. Consider *aggressivity* and its ultimate objects, words. If aggressivity is both anterior and posterior to language, the only thing we can say about it with any assurance at all concerns that part of aggressivity (or the death drive) which isolates objects in order to name them, which in other words founds signs. Thus post-modern writing explores this almost imperceptible exchange between signs and death by its contents or rhetoric, by its fantasies or language-defying style, by its political involvement engulfed in abjectness and laughter, by its silences punctuated by a rhythm that 'composes' a logic out of our fiber', to quote Mallarmé.

At this degree of singularity, we are faced with idiolects, proliferating uncontrollably with the enormous risk of becoming solitary monuments, gigantic but invisible, within a society whose general tendency, on the contrary, is toward uniformity. Obviously, we shall never have another Cosette, Père Goriot, or Julian Sorel from writing; the obscure fantasy backroom has become the brilliant TV screen. As far as writing is concerned, it has since set out to blaze a trail amidst the unnamable: Beckett is the best example with his derisory and infernal testimony.

Suspicious of the mass-produced unconscious and of everyone's favourite fantasy, warned by the twentieth-century's experience that generalising fantasies only leads more quickly to even more massive ones, writing is not hiding itself away. Despite its phobias, writing is nonetheless definitely venturing into the darkest regions where fear, anguish and a defiance of verbal clarity originate. Never before in the history of humanity has this exploration of the limits of meaning taken place in such an unprotected manner, and by this I mean without religious, mystical, or any other justification.

Will one of these idiolects dominate? Which one?

I would bet on the closest, most varied, multiple, heteroclitic, and unrepresentable idiolect. What is unrepresentability? That which, through language, is part of no particular language: rhythm, music, instinctual balm. That which, through meaning, is intolerable, unthinkable: the horrible, the abject. Modern writing knows how to 'musicate' best (to use Diderot's term) that which for our mascara and soap-opera age is the most horrible and abject. Abject music in which we can survive without stopping up our eyes and ears. This is the modern, and I mean nontranscendent, variation of the truth.

17 Laura Kipnis from 'Feminism: the Political Conscience of Postmodernism?'*

A recent central concern for feminists has been whether feminism's double commitment to the deconstruction of structures of domination and to freedom, equality and justice for women has meant that it is to be aligned with postmodernism or the political project of the Enlightenment (see Lovibond in Boyne and Rattansi, 1990; and essays in Nicholson (ed.), 1990). In addition, there are those who would wish to work outside and against the theoretical sources and ethnocentricism of both of these traditions (see Nancy Hartstock, 'Rethinking Modernism: Minority versus Majority Theories', *Cultural Critique*, 7 (Fall 1987): 187–206).

In her essay, Laura Kipnis usefully summarises the differences between French and American feminisms in terms which broadly parallel this first distinction. In her view French feminism is postmodernist but has failed to fulfil its political potential, turning away from the 'popular' in much the same way a defeated Western Marxism has turned away from the 'masses'. Having produced a crisis in modernism it has vacated the field of popular forms and attitudes to the New Right, while itself regressing to the élitism of a modernist avantgarde. Whereas other commentators (Callinicos, Pfeil) have seen postmodernism as the cultural expression of a new middle class and new conservatism, Kipnis argues that Left feminist, deconstructive postmodernism, can and should rival this new populism. This means stepping outside the luxury of theoretical and textual concerns which only further secure First World hegemony and privilege. An expressly 'political decentring' would fulfil the postmodernist feminist project and help close this particular epoch.

---

* Reprinted from Andrew Ross (ed.), *Universal Abandon? The Politics of Postmodernism* (Edinburgh University Press, 1989), pp. 157 – 66).

It is clear that the question of subjectivity lies at the epicenter of the current reformulation of modernism. Within what can broadly be called current left theory – Marxism, feminism, left poststructuralism – 'the subject' is a rubric that now seems to determine just what political questions we may ask. This 'subject' we know by its traits: it is split; it speaks; it is gendered; it is social, or it is a linguistic effect; it is castrated, and it thinks it knows so much. Alternatively, we have its obituary, as narrated by Baudrillard among others: it is occultated, disappears, and dies. Given that discourse is also productive, it is hard not to see this theoretical proliferation of the subject – its production as a site of attention, investigation, and speculation – as symptomatic of some kind of necessity. Its insistent visibility, which provides a certain bolstering of the category itself, provokes the question of what exactly it is that the subject needs bolstering against – its fragmentation in the chop shop of late capitalism, or perhaps some glimmer of self-knowledge that the necessary historical precondition for a critique of the subject is the loss of its legitimating function? What other political determinations can account for such excessive visibility of a category that operated precisely from a blindness to its own determinations, whose greatest desire was to turn itself into an effect of nature? This subject that drops its veils one by one to reveal its naked status as construction, rather than nature, bares everything *except* the answer to its insistent appearance: if everywhere we look the subject is all that is visible, what is it that is hidden?

Inasmuch as the subject is itself an ideological category, the question of its current hypervisibility must be profoundly political; notwithstanding that the field of the visual, as Lacan makes clear, is itself bound up with the constitution of subjectivity. Visibility is a complex system of permission and prohibition, of presence and absence, punctuated alternately by apparitions and hysterical blindness. Let us suppose, initially, that this visibility of the subject, so necessarily tied to the loss of its legitimating function, is another dynamic of the closing off of the political space of modernity, in which consolidation of political power took place under the banner of Enlightenment rationality and reason. In the 'centered subject', with its synecdochical relation to the political centrality of the West, lay a mandate to make the rest of the world its object: of conquest, knowledge, surplus-value. Then, in the recent appearance of the category of the 'decentered subject', lurks the synecdoche of the decline of the great imperial powers of modernity, the traumatic loss of hegemony of the West, which here in the psychic economy of the United States, we have continually reflected back to us in compensatory fantasies like *Rambo, Red Dawn,* and Ronald Reagan.

What is interesting about this waning modernity is the theoretical crisis it engenders, in which the traditional narratives of liberation fall under suspicion, opening a theoretical void that these various modernisms attempt, but are unable, to fill. What is crucially lacking is a postmodern political discourse. I want to attempt to trace this symptomatic gap as it is manifested in First-World feminist theory, which seems to be suspended between an emergent postmodern political logic and a residual modernism.

It is now common, in feminist theory, to distinguish broadly between Anglo-American feminism on the one hand and continental feminism on the other. This is clearly an inadequate formulation, yet the distinction that emerges in this bifurcation is one I want to momentarily maintain for heuristic purposes: it is a distinction between competing theories of representation, derived from a posture toward the signifier. Terry Eagleton has observed that the history of Marxism itself follows the Saussurean trajectory of the linguistic sign: 'First we had a referent, then we had a sign, now we just have a signifier', and according to Eagleton's schema, this final moment, the autonomy of the signifier, is identified with Althusserian Marxism.[1] These successive moments of the sign seem to occur simultaneously within current feminist theory, with the divisions drawn nominally according to *nation* rather than *chronos*, and with the culminating moment of the autonomy of the signifier associated, for feminism, with Lacan, rather than Althusser.

What is generally called American feminism generally relies on a theory of language as transparency. This entails a belief in a recoverable history, in authored productions, in the focus on speech over language, in the conscious over the unconscious, and in the phallus as a biological, rather than a symbolic, entity. In this camp, it is a short trip from a sign to a referent, and this produces, as sites of political engagement, the struggle for the terrain of the realist novel, the demand for access to the discourse of subjectivity, the possibility of an isolated sign or image as a potential site for political action, and in general, a politics of reformism.

Continental, or poststructural, feminism, in contrast to American feminism, follows the Saussurean division of the sign; emphasises the materiality of the signifier; privileges the synchronic over diachronic, structure over subject, and signification over meaning; and asserts that women have no position from which to speak. Its focus on the priority of system marks the unconscious as the privileged area of exploration and modernist rupture as the privileged aesthetic practice. From this vantage point, the priority of both psychoanalytic theory and modernist aesthetics in poststructural feminism can be seen as a by-product of the Saussurean legacy of the synchronic, which runs through Lévi-Strauss to Lacan.

The contention of poststructural feminists is that naming the political subject of feminism *the female sex* reproduces the biological essentialism and the binary logic that have relegated women to an inferior role. (Kristeva: 'the belief that "one is a woman" is almost as absurd and obscurantist as the belief that "one is a man".')[2] This contention produces, as a site of political attention and engagement, a 'space' rather than a sex: the margin, the repressed, the absence, the unconscious, the irrational, the feminine – in all cases the negative or powerless instance. Whereas 'American feminism' is a discourse whose political subject is biological women, 'continental feminism' is a political discourse whose subject is a structural position – variously occupied by the feminine, the body, the Other.

From these radical insights of continental feminism we move to the practice of *écriture féminine*, which in posing a counterlanguage against the binary patriarchal logic of phallogocentrism, is an attempt to construct a language that enacts liberation rather than merely theorising it. For Cixous, it is the imaginary construction of the female body as the privileged site of writing; for Irigaray, a language of women's laughter in the face of phallocratic discourse; for both, private, precious languages that rely on imaginary spaces held to be outside the reign of the phallus: the pre-Oedipal, the female body, the mystical, women's relation to the voice, fluids.[3]

Here we have, once again, the assertion of a political praxis through essentially modernist textual practices, which relegates the analysis of the symbolic construction of alterity into an aestheticism that closes off referentiality like blinders on a horse: in this notion of literary 'productivity', the text itself comes to operate as a transcendental signified, as an ultimate meaning.[4] The attempt to straitjacket these designated spaces into the text seems an essentially defensive maneuver, safeguarding against their escape beyond the confines of *écriture* into wider social praxis by limiting the dissemination of these forms of knowledge to the consumers of avant-garde culture.

What would it mean to find these operations now in literary ccnfinement, these procedures held to deconstruct binarisms, dismantle phallocentrism, and decenter subjects, *outside* writing, to suspend the current orthodoxy that reality and history are simply texts, while retaining the radical insights of feminist deconstruction? It is worth noting that another theoretical discourse, dependency theory in economics (a theory closely linked in time frame to poststructuralism), in which the object of attention is not textual but is, rather, the connection between economic development and underdevelopment in the unequal exchange relations of First to Third World, tells a story very similar to that of poststructural feminism, in its account of the mechanisms by which a dominant term comes to repress a secondary term. And in *this* telling, the deconstruction of these binarisms is anything but a symbolic practice.[5]

A narrative has emerged in postmodernist theory that reads something like this. Feminism is the paradigmatic political discourse of postmodernism.[6] Its affirmation of the absence, the periphery, the Other – spaces in which the position of women is structrually and politically inscribed – has more current political credibility than Marxism, a patriarchal discourse of 'mastery/transparency/rationalism,' a master code issuing from a transcendent point of view, the path that leads from 'totality to totalitarianism, from Hegel to the gulag'.

A slightly different narrative can be pieced together from these elements. If Marxism is viewed as the radical political discourse of modernity, and feminism as the radical political discourse of postmodernity, it can be seen that each functions as a dominant articulating principle through which other, disparate political struggles enunciate the possibility of political transformation. According to the crisis-in-Marxism theorists, Marxism's primary and vestigial ambition to unify isolated working-class struggles into a mass movement of the proletariat has hampered its ability today to provide articulations for new and emerging political positions – given transformations in the nature of labor and in the types of world geopolitical struggles of postcolonialism – in addition to its perceived inability to seriously theorise the subalternity of women.

The emergence in feminist theory of the periphery, the absence, and the margin implies a theory of women not as class or caste, but as colony – and this was in fact an analysis made early on in American feminism (and earlier still in Simone de Beauvoir's depiction of woman as Other) by women in SDS casting their controversial break with the male-dominated Left in the political rhetoric of the day: 'As we analyze the position of women in capitalist society and especially in the United States we find that women are in a colonial relationship to men and we recognise ourselves as part of the Third World' (1967).[7] What this analogy (whose genealogy can be traced back through the New Left to the black-power movement, and the crucial influence on black power by African decolonisation movements) suggests is that the theoretical emergence of these political spaces now being described by continental feminists parallels the narrative of the decline of the great imperial powers of modernity, the liquidation of the European empires and the postcolonial rearrangements of the traditional centers on a world scale. It is France, after all, that has produced an influential body of theory based on the centrality of castration in the construction of human subjectivity. Perhaps this is why the American reception of Lacan has been primarily as a literary theory: to confine this disturbing knowledge to the text and recycle it through the recuperative apparatus of literary humanism, rather than allowing the emergence of France as the world capital of theory to perhaps be read as the sequel of its own political decentering and loss of mastery – in the war, in Indo-China, in North Africa.

Yet, much of European postwar decolonisation took place out of practical and economic necessity more so than out of ideological conviction: the colonial mind persists long after its political and economic structures have been dismantled. Continental feminism offers a radical structural analysis of operations it prefers to call phallogocentrism, but then retreats from the implications of its own analysis into the autonomy of the text, seizing on a modernist refusal of reference to enact its ambivalence. Continental feminism would seem to be the most potentially radical current in contemporary political theory, freeing itself from the essentialism and the liberal tradition of American feminism. Yet, it also seems beset by the same conjunctural elements associated with the depoliticisation of Western Marxism, prone to aestheticisation, theoretical autonomy, and a deliberate distance from political praxis. It identifies the structural position of a new political subject, inscribing itself into that moment, and is then paralyzed by this knowledge and by its own First-World status, hysterically blind to the geopolitical implications of its own program. And legitimately so, because the knowledge offered here is not benign. It is that real shifts in world power and economic distribution have little to do with *jouissance*, the pre-Oedipal, or fluids, and that the luxury of First-World feminism to dwell on such issues depends on the preservation of First-World abundance guaranteed by systematic underdevelopment elsewhere and by the postponement, by whatever means, of the political decentering that will mean the close of that historical epoch.

This paper was first written during the week of the US bombing of Libya, so euphemistically presented to us by our ruling powers as a 'surgical strike'. This phrase, along with Reagan's memorable diagnosis of Qaddafi as 'flaky', brings to mind another form of surgical strike, the lobotomy, so often performed with ice-picks and on women, following the diagnosis of irrationality. Here we have Qaddafi, cast in the role of Frances Farmer, with the US in the role of psychiatric surgeon. ('That the colonial is coded female has been clear enough even without the *New York Post*'s artist's rendering of Qaddafi as a woman.) Our network news these days is full of irrational Libyans and irrational Palestinians, needing a little frontal-lobe job, and its own ideological mission is now admitted so freely that CBS's latest slogan for its news is 'We keep America on top of the world.' The diagnosis of national aspirations that don't coincide with the master plan of the West is 'psychopathology', which demands a 'cure' – the full array of state-repressive apparatuses: for Libyans, bombs; in the case of women, rape, battery, confinement, and medical and psychiatric abuse – repressive apparatuses in a familial guise.

As is shown in the current hysteria over 'international terrorism' – the ultimate conspiracy theory into which our government has managed to fuse the Soviet Union, Islamic fundamentalism, the Sandinistas, and Palestinian nationalism – the reaction to any decentering *telos* is symptomatic blindness rather than insight: there is an unwillingness and inability to fully comprehend this phenomenon of shifts in power and spheres of influence, and of new forms of political struggle in which civilian tourists are held responsible for the actions of their governments. When retaliation is taken, as has been announced, for 'American arrogance', *this* is the postmodern critique of the Enlightenment; it is, in fact, a decentering; it is the margin, the absence, the periphery, rewriting the rules from its own interest.

By associating feminism with these other political struggles and with a particular historical space, I do not mean to efface gendered oppression or actual historical women in the name of some putatively great oppression. The rise of the current women's movement paralleled (and, according to some more unreconstructed elements, caused) the decline of the black-power movement in the United States, suggesting a metonymy of struggle within this historical space. If feminism *is* read as a decolonising movement, allied with other decolonising movements, this is, in a sense, to say that the Right is right when it identifies feminism as a threat to the 'American way of life'. Yet, this latent knowledge of the political stakes produces the impasse that I think we currently see in feminist theory: after the critique of liberal reformism, after the dismantling of the biologistic, but uplifting, fable that women will, given the chance, construct a nonhierarchical political utopia, the political options are indeed narrower. It is either 'out of the mainstream and into the revolution', or out of the revolution and into the text. On the local level, the decline of the narratives of liberation of modernity and the retreat from the political implications of postmodernity have left the field wide open for the Right, which has successfully fought on the terrain of popular interpellation: controlling the terms of popular discourse, arrogating the terrain of nature, family, community, and the fetus; not hesitating to appropriate and rearticulate a traditionally left rhetoric of liberation and empowerment. It is striking that Phyllis Schlafly's antifeminist manifesto, *The Power of the Positive Woman* (1977), opens with the question, 'How are women to acquire power in the world?'[8] and in fact, Schlafly modeled herself into one of the most effective political figures outside electoral politics in the United States by using the rhetoric of disenfranchisement to mobilise radical feminism's Other – suburban housewives – into an effective political force. By manipulating the exclusions admittedly operating in feminist discourse of the seventies to marshal fear and *ressentiment* among women who saw feminism as élitist and classist and the ERA (Equal Rights Amendment) as a threat to their tenuous hold on any corner of empowerment in the world, Schlafly created a grass-roots movement that turned the expected ratification of the ERA by liberal feminists into a crashing defeat.

What this suggests is that the insights of a left postmodernism's renegotiation of the popular are relevant to a feminist theory that is increasingly unable to interpellate a popular audience or capture a popular imagination. Instead, avant-gardist strategies of negation – proffered as a counterforce to the technics of a popular culture dedicated to the production of the spuriously self-identified subject – end up producing their own Other: the 'mass' of mass culture that resides outside the vanguard élite, outside the intelligentsia, and outside the university. If the popular is seen as an access to hegemony rather than an instrument of domination, what follows is a postmodern strategy of struggle over the terrain of popular interpellation, an acknowledgment that hegemony is won rather than imposed.

But this again presumes that we are only the subject of political transformation, rather than the object. The hypervisibility of the subject, the symptom that introduced this etiology of current theory, parallels its deconstruction on the world stage. The neomodernist desire to locate the space of the margin and the absence within the text – to hold that theory has autonomously arrived at the point at which it achieves recognition of the periphery – is simply to theorise again from first-world interest, to display a hysterical blindness to the fact that the periphery has forced itself upon the attention of the center. To the extent that any deconstructive theory prioritises the autonomous text, it maintains this blindness; it reinvents and reinvests in the centrality of that center. To the extent that a feminist theory discovers these crucial spaces in textual rather than in political practice, it indicates the resistance of First-World feminists to the dangerous knowledge that in a *world* system of patriarchy, upheld by an international division of labor, unequal exchange and the International Monetary Fund, we First-World feminists are also the beneficiaries.

Notes

1. TERRY EAGLETON, 'The End of English' (Paper delivered at the School of the Art Institute of Chicago, April 1986).

2. JULIA KRISTEVA, 'Women Can Never Be Defined', in *New French Feminisms*, ed. Elaine Marks and Isabelle de Courtivron (New York: Shocken Books, 1981), p. 137.

3. See TORIL MOI's *Sexual/Textual Politics* (New York: Methuen, 1985) for a comparison of the Anglo-American and continental traditions and a critique of the politics of écriture féminine.

4. FREDRIC JAMESON, *The Prison House of Language* (Princeton: Princeton University Press, 1972), p. 182. Jameson is writing about *Tel Quel* here (including

Kristeva), and about Derrida, who has invented a new transcendental signified, 'namely that of script itself'.

5. On dependency theory see ANDRÉ GUNDER FRANK, *Capitalism and Underdevelopment in Latin America* (New York: Monthly Review Press, 1969).

6. Two recent examples in aesthetic theory are Craig Owen's 'The Discourse of Others: Feminists and Postmodernism', in *The Anti-Aesthetic: Essays on Postmodern Culture*, ed. Hal Foster (Port Townsend, Wash.: Bay Press, 1983), and Huyssen's 'Mass Culture as Woman'.

7. Quoted in ALICE ECHOLS, *The Radical Feminist Movement in the United States, 1967 – 75* (unpublished doctoral dissertation, University of Michigan, 1986), p. 32.

8. PHYLLIS SCHLAFLY, *The Power of the Positive Woman* (New York: Jove, 1977).

Black Culture and Postmodernism

18 Cornel West, From 'An Interview with Cornel West' *Anders Stephanson**

The decentring processes of postmodernism have questioned ethno-centric, epistemological and cultural models, foregrounding subordi-nated or marginalised discourses and traditions. The perspective of Afro-American intellectuals and artists inhabiting combined white and black histories is therefore of particular theoretical and practical interest.

The Black American novelist Toni Morrison has commented that for blacks the alienated psychological and social condition associated with modernism and postmodernism coincided with slavery: 'modern life begins with slavery. From a woman's point of view, in terms of confronting the problems of where the world is now, black women had to deal with 'postmodern' problems in the nineteenth century and earlier . . . certain kinds of dissolution, the loss of and the need to reconstruct certain kinds of stability' (*City Limits*, 31 March–7 April, 1988). In the following extract Cornel West similarly identifies a distinctively black cultural postmodernism (both West and Toni Morrison point to the inspiration of blues and jazz; see also the selection and headnote to Houston A. Baker above, (chapter 8); a double counter to the postmodernism which spells 'the Americanisa-tion of the world' and to the less progressive European models. The series of differences and divisions, in culture, class, institution, race and rhetoric, which West identifies here, provide the experiential source for a sophisticated neo-Gramscian politics in his work. He describes this elsewhere as precluding 'the logocentric economism of pre-Gramscian Marxisms and the labyrinthine abyss of poststructur-alisms'. It means staying alert to 'the conjunctural opportunities' presented within the economic, cultural and ideological constraints comprising 'the multileveled oppression of Africans in the United

* Reprinted from Andrew Ross (ed.), *Universal Abandon? The Politics of Postmodernism* (Edinburgh: Edinburgh University Press, 1989), pp. 272–82.

States of America and elsewhere'. ('Marxist Theory and the Specificity of Afro-American Oppression' in Nelson and Grossberg, *Marxism and the Interpretation of Culture* (1988), pp. 24, 25).

Of related interest are Timothy Maliqalim Simone's *About Face. Race in Postmodern America* (1989), and bell hooks, *Yearning. Race Gender and Cultural Politics* (New York and London: Turnaround, 1991).

Anders Stephanson: The poststructuralist problematic seems now to have been engulfed by the general debate on postmodernism. A certain confusion of terminology marks this debate. Conceptual pairs like modernity/postmodernity and modernism/postmodernism mean very different things depending on country and cultural practice.

West: Three things are crucial in clearing that up: historical periodisation, demarcation of cultural archives and practices, and politics/ideology. Take history and demarcation for example. It is clear that 'modern' philosophy begins in the seventeenth century, well before the Enlightenment, with the turn toward the subject and the new authority, the institutionalisation, of scientific reason. What we call postmodern philosophy today is precisely about questioning the foundational authority of science. This trajectory is very different from that of modern*ist* literary practices, which in turn is quite different from that of architecture: the former, to simplify, attacks reason in the name of myth, whereas the latter valorises it together with technique and form. These problems of periodisation and demarcation are often ignored. For instance, Portoghesi's work on postmodern architecture seems to assume that his historical framework is an uncontroversial given.

Stephanson: In this sense, Lyotard's initial theorisation of the postmodern condition is profoundly marked by its French provenance.

West: Yes. His book, in many ways an overcelebrated one, is really a French reflection on the transgressions of *modernism* that has little to do with *postmodernism* in the American context. In France, modernism still appears to be the *centering* phenomenon. Figures like Mallarmé, Artaud, Joyce, and Bataille continue to play a fundamental role. In the United States, as Andreas Huyssen has emphasised, postmodernism is an avant-garde – like rebellion against the modernism of the museum, against the modernism of the literary and academic establishment. Note, too, the disjunction here between cultural postmodernism and postmodern politics. For Americans are politically always already in a condition of postmodern fragmentation and heterogeneity in a way that Europeans have not been; and the revolt against the center by those constituted as marginals is an *oppositional* difference in a way that poststructuralist notions of difference are not. These American attacks on universality in the name of difference, these 'postmodern' issues of Otherness (Afro-Americans, Native Americans, women, gays) are in fact an implicit critique of certain French postmodern discourses about Otherness that really serve to hide and conceal the power of the voices and movements of Others.

Stephanson: From an American viewpoint, the debate between Lyotard and Habermas is thus rather off-the-mark.

West: Interesting *philosophical* things are at stake there, but the politics is a family affair, a very narrow family affair at that. Habermas stands for the grand old tradition of the Enlightenment project of *Vernunft*. I have some affinities with that tradition, but there is nothing new about what he has to say. Lyotard's attack on Habermas comes out of valorisation of the transgression of modernism *vis-à-vis* an old highbrow, Enlightenment perspective. All this is very distant from the kind of debates about postmodernism we have in the States, though of course one has to read it, be acquainted with it.

Stephanson: Agreed, but the debate has not been without effect here either. For instance, it is now often felt necessary in architectural discussions to make references to Lyotard.

West: It has become fashionable to do so because he is now a major figure, but I am talking about *serious* readings of him. Anyone who knows anything about Kant and Wittgenstein also knows that Lyotard's readings of them are very questionable and wrenched out of context. When these readings then travel to the United States, they often assume an authority that remains *uninterrogated*.

Stephanson: A case in point is the concept of 'life-world', now freely bandied about and most immediately originating in Husserl. In the later Habermas it fulfills an important function as the site of colonisation for the 'systems-world'. This, roughly, seems to combine Weber with Husserl, but the result is in fact nothing so much as classic American sociology.

West: When Habermas juxtaposes the life-world with the colonising systems, it strikes me as a rather clumsy Parsonian way of thinking about the incorporation of culture into advanced capitalist cycles of production and consumption. On the one hand, Habermas has in mind the fundamental role that culture has come to play, now that the commodification process has penetrated cultural practices which were previously relatively autonomous; on the other hand, he is thinking of how oppositional forces and resistance to the system (what I call the process of commodification) are on the wane. This is simply a less

215

effective way of talking about something that Marxists have been talking about for years.

Stephanson: Yet, it is obvious that both Lyotard and Habermas must have done something to fill a kind of lack somewhere: otherwise their reception here would be inexplicable.

West:True. These remarks do not explain why Habermas and Lyotard have gained the attention they have. Habermas, of course, speaks with the status of a second-generation Frankfurt school theorist; and he has become such a celebrity that he can drop a number of terms from a number of different traditions and they take on a salience they often do not deserve. More fundamentally, his encyclopedic knowledge and his obsession with the philosophical foundations of democratic norms also satisfy a pervasive need for left-academic intellectuals – a need for the professional respectability and rigor that displace political engagement and this-worldly involvement. At the same time, his well-known, but really tenuous, relation to Marxism provides them with an innocuous badge of radicalism. All of this takes place at the expense of an encounter with the Marxist tradition, especially with Gramsci and the later Lukács of the Ontology works. In this sense, Habermas unwittingly serves as a kind of opium for some of the American left-academic intelligentsia. The impact of Lyotard, on the other hand, is probably the result of the fact that he was the first serious European thinker to address the important question of postmodernism in a comprehensive way. Deleuze, to take a related philosopher, never did; though he is ultimately a more profound poststructuralist who should get more attention than he does in the United States. His early book on Nietzsche is actually an originary text.

Stephanson: Why?

West: Because Deleuze was the first to think through the notion of difference independent of Hegelian ideas of opposition, and that was the start of the radical anti-Hegelianism which has characterised French intellectual life in the last decades. This position – the trashing of totality, the trashing of mediation, the valorisation of difference outside the subject – object opposition, the decentering of the subject – all these features we now associate with postmodernism and poststructualism go back to Deleuze's resurrection of Nietzsche against Hegel. Foucault, already assuming this Deleuzian critique, was the first important French intellectual who could *circumvent*, rather than confront, Hegel, which is why he says that we live in a 'Deleuzian age'. To live in a Deleuzian age is to live in an anti-Hegelian age so that one does not have to come to terms with Lukács, Adorno or any other Hegelian Marxists.

Stephanson: Nietzsche's ascendancy was not without maleficent effects when French theory was imported into the United States.

West: It was unfortunate for American intellectual life, because we never had the Marxist culture against which the French were reacting. Nor was it a culture that took Hegel seriously: the early John Dewey was the only left Hegelian we ever had. Nietzsche was received, therefore, in the context of analytic philosophy, and you can imagine the gaps and hiatuses, the blindness that resulted when Nietzsche entered narrow Anglo-American positivism. In literary criticism, on the other hand, Nietzsche was part of the Derridean baggage that the 'New Critics' were able easily (and often uncritically) to assimilate into their close readings. As a result, we now have a 'Tower of Babel' in American literary criticism.

Stephanson: The current, however, does not run in only one direction. Is the present French interest in 'postanalytic' philosophy an indication that intellectual life is being reorientated toward the United States, at least in terms of objects of inquiry?

West:No doubt. French society has clearly come under the influence of Americanisation, and West Germany, always somewhat of a fifty-first state, has moved in this direction as well. More immediately, now that the university systems in Europe no longer have the status or financial support they once had, American universities are pulling in the European intellectuals, offering money and celebrity status but also a fairly high level of conversation.

Stephanson: Features of what we associate with the concept of postmodernism have been part of American life for a long time: fragmentation, heterogeneity, surfaces without history. Is postmodernism in some sense really the codification of life in Los Angeles?

West: Only in one form and specifically at the level of middlebrow culture. The other side is the potentially oppositional aspect of the notion. Postmodernism ought never to be viewed as a homogenous phenomenon, but rather as one in which political contestation is central. Even if we look at it principally as a form of Americanisation of the world, it is clear that within the US there are various forms of ideological and political conflict going on.

Stephanson: The black community, for example is more 'contestational' than average America.

West: The black political constituency still has some sense of the reality of the world, some sense of what is going on in the third world. Look at the issues Jesse Jackson pressed in 1984 and now in 1988, and you find that they were issues normally reserved for the salons of leftist intellectuals. Bringing that on television had a great impact.

Stephanson: Yet, the black American condition, so to speak, is not an uplifting sight at the moment.

West: Not at all. There is increasing class division and differentiation, creating on the one hand a significant black middle class, highly anxiety-ridden, insecure, willing to be co-opted and incorporated into the powers that be, concerned with racism to the degree that it poses constraints on upward social mobility; and, on the other, a vast and growing black underclass, an underclass that embodies a kind of *walking nihilism* of pervasive drug addiction, pervasive alcoholism, pervasive homicide, and an exponential rise in suicide. Now, because of the deindustrialisation, we also have a devastated black industrial working class. We are talking here about tremendous hopelessness.

Stephanson: Suicide has increased enormously?

West: It has increased six times in the last decades for black males like myself who are between eighteen and thirty-five. This is unprecedented. Afro-Americans have always killed themselves less than other Americans, but this is no longer true.

Stephanson: What does a black oppositional intellectual do in these generally dire circumstances?

West: One falls back on those black institutions that have attempted to serve as resources for sustenance and survival, the black churches being one such institution, especially their progressive and prophetic wing. One tries to root oneself organically in these institutions so that one can speak to a black constituency, while maintaining a conversation with the most engaging political and postmodernist debates on the outside so that the insights they provide can be brought in.

Stephanson: That explains why you are, among other things, a kind of lay preacher. It does not explain why you are a Christian.

West: My own left Christianity is not simply instrumentalist. It is in part a response to those dimensions of life that have been flattened out, to the surfacelike character of a postmodern culture that refuses to speak to issues of despair, that refuses to speak to issues of the absurd. To that extent I still find Christian narratives and stories *empowering and enabling*.

Stephanson: What does it mean to a black American to hear that, in Baudrillard's language, we are in a simulated space of hyperreality, that we have lost the real?

West: I read that symptomatically. Baudrillard seems to be articulating a sense of what it is to be a French, middle-class intellectual, or perhaps what it is to be middle class generally. Let me put it in terms of a formulation from Henry James that Fredric Jameson has appropriated: there is a reality *that one cannot not know*. The ragged edges of the Real, of *Necessity*, not being able to eat, not having shelter, not having health care, all this is something that one cannot not know. The black condition acknowledges that. It is so much more acutely felt because this is a society where a lot of people live a Teflon existence, where a lot of people have no sense of the ragged edges of necessity, of what it means to be impinged upon by structures of oppression. To be an upper-middle-class American is actually to live a life of unimaginable comfort, convenience, and luxury. Half of the black population is denied this, which is why they have a strong sense of reality.

Stephanson: Does that make notions of postmodernism meaningless from a black perspective?

West: It must be conceived very differently at least. Take Ishmael Reed, an exemplary postmodern writer. Despite his conservative politics, he cannot deny the black acknowledgment of the reality one cannot not know. In writing about black American history, for instance, he has to come to terms with the state-sponsored terrorism of lynching blacks and so on. This is inescapable in black postmodernist practices.

Stephanson: How is one in fact to understand black postmodernist practices?

West: To talk about black postmodernist practices is to go back to bebop music and see how it relates to literary expressions like Reed's and Charles Wright's. It is to go back, in other words, to the genius of Charlie Parker, John Coltrane and Miles Davis. Bebop was, after all, a revolt against the middle-class 'jazz of the museum', against swing and white musicians like Benny Goodman, who had become hegemonic by colonising a black art form. What Parker did, of course, was to Africanise jazz radically: to accept the polyrhythms, to combine these rhythms with unprecedented virtuousity on the sax. He said explicitly that his music was not produced to be accepted by white Americans. He would be suspicious if it were. This sense of revolt was to be part and parcel of the postmodern rebellion against the modernism of the museum.

Stephanson: To me, bebop seems like a black cultural avant-garde that corresponds historically to abstract expressionism in painting – the last gasp of modernism – on which indeed it had some considerable influence.

West: Certainly they emerge together, and people do tend to parallel them as though they were the same; but abstract expressionism was not a revolt in the way bebop was. In fact, it was an instance of modernism itself. Bebop also had much to do with fragmentation, with heterogeneity, with the articulation of difference and marginality, aspects of what we associate with postmodernism today.

Stephanson: Aspects of the cultural dominant, yes; but these elements are also part of modernism. Surely one can still talk about Charlie Parker as a unified subject expressing inner *angst* or whatever, an archetypal characteristic of modernism.

West: True, but think too of another basic feature of postmodernism, the breakdown of highbrow and pop culture. Parker would use whistling off the streets of common black life: 'Cherokee', for instance, was actually a song that black children used to sing when jumping rope or, as I did, playing marbles. Parker took that melody of the black masses and filtered it through his polyrhythms and technical virtuosity, turning it into a highbrow jazz feature that was not quite highbrow anymore. He was already calling into question the distinction between high and low culture, pulling from a bricolage, as it were, what was seemingly popular and relating it to what was then high. Yet, I would not deny the modernist impulse, nor would I deny that they were resisting jazz as commodity, very much like Joyce and Kafka resisted literary production as commodity. In that sense bebop straddles the fence.

Stephanson: The ultimate problem, however, is whether it is actually useful to talk about someone like Charlie Parker in these terms.

West: It is useful to the degree that it contests the prevailing image of him as a modernist. As you imply, on the other hand, there is a much deeper question as to whether these terms *modernism/postmodernism* relate to Afro-American cultural practices in any illuminating way at all. We are only at the beginning of that inquiry.

Stephanson: Was there ever actually a mass black audience for bebop?

West: Yes, Parker's was the sort of music black people danced to in the 1940s. Miles's 'cool' stage was also big in the 1950s with albums like 'Kinda Blue', though it went hand in hand with the popularity of Nat King Cole and Dinah Washington.

Stephanson: What happened to this avant-garde black music when Motown and Aretha Franklin came along?

West: It was made a fetish for the educated middle-class, principally, but not solely, the white middle class. In absolute terms, its domain actually expanded because the black audience of middle-class origin also expanded. But the great dilemma of black musicians who try to preserve a tradition from mainstream domestication and dilution is in fact that they lose contact with the black masses. In this case, there was eventually a move toward 'fusion', jazz artists attempting to produce objects intended for broader black-and-white consumption.

Stephanson: Miles Davis is the central figure of that avant-garde story.

West: And he crossed over with the seminal record *Bitches Brew* in 1970, accenting his jazz origins while borrowing from James Brown's polyrhythms and Sly Stone's syncopation. *Bitches Brew* brought him a black mass audience that he had lost in the 1960s – certainly one that Coltrane had lost completely.

Stephanson: Crossover artists, in the sense of having a racially mixed mass audience, are not very numerous today.

West: No, but there are more than ever: Whitney Houston, Dionne Warwick, Lionel Richie, Diana Ross and Anita Baker. Baker is a very different crossover artist because she is still deeply rooted in the black context. Michael Jackson and Prince are crossover in another sense: their music is less rooted in black musical traditions and much more open to white rock and so forth.

Stephanson: In Prince's case it has to do with the fact that he is not entirely from a black background.

West: Still, he grew up in a black foster home and a black Seventh Day Adventist church, but in Minneapolis, which is very different from growing up like Michael Jackson in a black part of Gary, Indiana. Minneapolis has always been a place of cultural cross-fertilisation, of interracial marriages and relationships. The early Jackson Five, on the other hand, were thoroughly ensconced in a black tradition, and Michael began his career dancing like James Brown. Now, he is at the center of the black-white interface.

Stephanson: Prince never really played 'black' music as one thinks of it. His music is 'fused' from the start.

West: To be in a black context in Minneapolis is already to be in a situation of fusion, because the blacks themselves have much broader access to mainstream white culture in general. You get the same thing with other black stars who have come out of that place.

Stephanson: Michael Jackson, by contrast, is now a packaged middle-American product.

West: A nonoppositional instance of commodification in black skin that is becoming more and more like candy, more radical than McDonald's, but not by much. It is watered-down black music, but still with a lot of the aggressiveness and power of that tradition.

Stephanson:Music is *the* black means of cultural expression, is it not?

West: Music and preaching. Here, rap is unique because it combines the black preacher and the black music tradition, replacing the liturgical – ecclesiastical setting with the African polyrhythms of the street. A tremendous *articulateness* is syncopated with the African drumbeat, the African funk, into an American postmodernist product: there is no subject expressing originary anguish here but a fragmented subject, pulling from past and present, innovatively producing a heterogeneous product. The stylistic combination of the oral, the literate, and the musical is exemplary as well. Otherwise, it is part and parcel of the subversive energies of black underclass youth, energies that are forced to take a cultural mode of articulation because of the political lethargy of American society. The music of Grandmaster Flash and the Furious Five, Kurtis Blow and Sugar Hill Gang has to take on a deeply political character because, again, they are in the reality that the black underclass *cannot not know*: the brutal side of the American capital, the brutal side of American racism, the brutal side of sexism against black women.

Stephanson: I always thought rap was too indigenous a black form of expression to make it in the general marketplace. Run/DMC has proven me wrong on this.

West: Indeed. Run/DMC is as indigenous as you can get. Upper-middle-class white students at Yale consume a lot of Run/DMC.

Stephanson: Yet, the constitutive elements of rap seemed to me too fixed for it to become a permanent presence on the crossover scene: more anonymous and less easily assimilated into existing white concepts of melody and structure. This, too, is probably wrong.

West: People said the same thing about Motown in 1961, the same thing about Aretha Franklin, who is about as organic as you can get. She is not as accepted by mainstream white society as the smoother and more diluted Warwick and Ross, but she *is* accepted. That, from the perspective of 1964-65, is unbelievable. The same thing could happen with rap music, since the boundaries are actually rather fluid. But it won't remain the same.

Stephanson: Where will rap end up?

West: Where most American postmodern products end up: highly packaged, regulated, distributed, circulated and consumed.

222

Stephanson: Preaching, as you said, is obviously a cultural form of expression; but is it a specifically *artistic* form?

West: Sure. The best preachers are outstanding oral artists, performance artists. Martin Luther King, Jr gave white America just a small taste of what it is to be an artistic rhetorician in the black churches. Tremendous gravity and weight are given to these artistic performances because people's *lives* hang on them. They provide some hope from week to week so that these folk won't fall into hopelessness and meaninglessness, so that they won't kill themselves. The responsibility of the black preacher – artist is, in that sense, deeply functional, but at the same time it entails *a refinement of a form* bequeathed to him by those who came before. Black preaching is inseparable here from black singing. Most secular black singers come out of the choir, and the lives of the congregation hang on how they sing the song, what they put into the song, how passionate, how self-invested they are. Preaching is just less visible to the outside as an art form because words uttered once don't have the same status as cultural products; but the black preachers are artists with a very long tradition.

Stephanson: Since it does not lend itself to mechanical reproduction, preaching is also hard to destroy by turning it into a business. How is this artistic form of expression actually evaluated?

West: In terms of the impact the preacher has on the congregation. This impact can take the form of contankerous response, or the form of existential empowerment, the convincing of people to keep on keeping on, to keep on, struggling, contesting and resisting.

Stephanson: It is Kant's acrobat who intervenes constantly to transform an otherwise unstable equilibrium into another equilibrium.

West: Well put. Black sermonic practices have not received the attention they deserve. As a matter of fact, black linguistic practices as such need to be examined better because they add a lot to the American language.

Stephanson: Black language creates a wealth of new words, which are then quickly picked up by the mainstream.

West: Usually with significant semantic changes. Stevie Wonder's 'Everything is alright, uptight, out of sight' is a string of synonyms. *Uptight*, when I was growing up, meant smooth, cool, everything is fine. By the time it got to middle America, *uptight* meant anxiety-ridden, the inability of everything to be fine. Similar semantic shifts, though perhaps less drastic, take place with *chilling out, mellowing out*, and other black expressions. *Chilling out* meant letting things be, a sort of Heideggerian notion of *aletheia*, letting the truth reveal itself, letting it shine, letting it come forth.

Stephanson: Given the social circumstances of which it is a product, black American language seems to me, on the outside, not to allow very easily for prevalent white orders of theoretical reflection.

West: It is a hustling culture, and a hustling culture tends to be *radically* 'practicalist', deeply pragmatic, because the issue is always one of surviving, getting over.

Stephanson: This, I imagine, demands some sharp linguistic twists for you.

West: I am continually caught in a kind of 'heteroglossia', speaking a number of English languages in radically different contexts. When it comes to abstract theoretical reflection, I employ Marx, Weber, Frankfurt theorists, Foucault, and so on. When it comes to speaking with the black masses, I use Christian narratives and stories, a language meaningful to them but filtered through and informed by intellectual developments from de Tocqueville to Derrida. When it comes to the academy itself there is yet another kind of language, abstract but often atheoretical, since social theorising is mostly shunned. Philosophers are simply ill-equipped to talk about social theory: they know Wittgenstein but not Weber, they know J.L. Austin but not Marx.

Postmodernist Fiction

19 Umberto Eco, 'Postmodernism, Irony, the Enjoyable'*

Umberto Eco's writings, in semiotic theory, fiction and occasional journalism, show a breadth and mobility (his essays discuss fashion, sport, film, fine art, popular fiction, high modernism, the medieval world, and contemporary politics) which make him a living example of the multi-accented simultaneity characterising postmodernism. His *The Name of the Rose* (1981) was a best-selling example of this inter-animation of previously separated categories of fiction and non-fiction: a detective thriller (in its classic form, the most conventional-ised and closed of popular narratives) which combines gothic sus-pense with chronicle and scholarship, which knits the medieval with the modern, and boxes narrative within narrative to produce a comic mystery 'about' the suppression and rescue of the subversive power of the comic itself.

The present essay is taken from Eco's supplementary reflections on the novel. Not the least interesting aspect of this is his reference to the authority of American examples (the present Introduction argues that postmodernism is in the first instance an American phenom-enon). Postmodernism, Eco defines by its intertextuality and know-ingness and by its relation to the past. Whereas modernism wished but failed to abolish the past, postmodernism revisits it, at any historical time, with irony – a perspective worth comparing with the apocalyptic tones and soulful nihilism found in other accounts.

See also, in particular, Echo's volume *Faith in Fakes* (1986), pub-

---

* Reprinted from *Reflections on 'The Name of the Rose'*, trans. William Weaver (London: Secker and Warburg, 1985), pp. 65–72.

lished in the United States and in paperback in Great Britain as *Travels in Hyperreality* (1987). For some discussion of *The Name of the Rose* in the present context, see Jim Collins, *Uncommon Cultures. Popular Culture and Postmodernism* (1989), pp. 60–4.

Between 1965 and today, two ideas have been definitively clarified: that plot could be found also in the form of quotation of other plots, and that the quotation could be less escapist than the plot quoted. In 1972 I edited the *Almanacco Bompiani*, celebrating 'The Return to the Plot', though this return was via an ironic re-examination (not without admiration) of Ponson de Terrail and Eugène Sue, and admiration (with very little irony) of some of the great pages of Dumas. The real problem at stake then was, could there be a novel that was not escapist and, nevertheless, still enjoyable?

This link, and the rediscovery not only of plot but also of enjoyability, was to be realised by the American theorists of postmodernism.

Unfortunately, 'postmodern' is a term *bon à tout faire*. I have the impression that it is applied today to anything the user of the term happens to like. Further, there seems to be an attempt to make it increasingly retroactive: first it was apparently applied to certain writers or artists active in the last twenty years, then gradually it reached the beginning of the century, then still further back. And this reverse procedure continues; soon the postmodern category will include Homer.

Actually, I believe that postmodernism is not a trend to be chronologically defined, but, rather, an ideal category – or, better still, a *Kunstwollen*, a way of operating. We could say that every period has its own postmodernism, just as every period would have its own mannerism (and, in fact, I wonder if postmodernism is not the modern name for mannerism as metahistorical category). I believe that in every period there are moments of crisis like those described by Nietzsche in his *Thoughts Out of Season*, in which he wrote about the harm done by historical studies. The past conditions us, harries us, blackmails us. The historic avant-garde (but here I would also consider avant-garde a metahistorical category) tries to settle scores with the past. 'Down with moonlight' – a futurist slogan – is a platform typical of every avant-garde; you have only to replace 'moonlight' with whatever noun is suitable. The avant-garde destroys, defaces the past: *Les Demoiselles d'Avignon* is a typical avant-garde act. Then the avant-garde goes further, destroys the figure, cancels it, arrives at the abstract, the informal, the white canvas, the slashed canvas, the charred canvas. In architecture and the visual arts, it will be the curtain wall, the building as stele, pure parallelepiped, minimal art; in literature, the destruction of the flow of discourse, the

Burroughs-like collage, silence, the white page; in music, the passage from atonality to noise to absolute silence (in this sense, the early Cage is modern).

But the moment comes when the avant-garde (the modern) can go no further, because it has produced a metalanguage that speaks of its impossible texts (conceptual art). The postmodern reply to the modern consists of recognising that the past, since it cannot really be destroyed, because its destruction leads to silence, must be revisited: but with irony, not innocently. I think of the postmodern attitude as that of a man who loves a very cultivated woman and knows he cannot say to her, 'I love you madly', because he knows that she knows (and that she knows that he knows) that these words have already been written by Barbara Cartland. Still, there is a solution. He can say, 'As Barbara Cartland would put it, I love you madly.' At this point, having avoided false innocence, having said clearly that it is no longer possible to speak innocently, he will nevertheless have said what he wanted to say to the woman: that he loves her, but he loves her in an age of lost innocence. If the woman goes along with this, she will have received a declaration of love all the same. Neither of the two speakers will feel innocent, both will have accepted the challenge of the past, of the already said, which cannot be eliminated; both will consciously and with pleasure play the game of irony . . . But both will have succeeded, once again, in speaking of love.

Irony, metalinguistic play, enunciation squared. Thus, with the modern, anyone who does not understand the game can only reject it, but with the postmodern, it is possible not to understand the game and yet to take it seriously. Which is, after all, the quality (the risk) of irony. There is always someone who takes ironic discourse seriously. I think that the collages of Picasso, Juan Gris and Braque were modern: this is why normal people would not accept them. On the other hand, the collages of Max Ernst, who pasted together bits of nineteenth-century engravings, were postmodern: they can be read as fantastic stories, as the telling of dreams, without any awareness that they amount to a discussion of the nature of engraving, and perhaps even of collage. If 'postmodern' means this, it is clear why Sterne and Rabelais were postmodern, why Borges surely is, and why in the same artist the modern moment and the postmodern moment can coexist, or alternate, or follow each other closely. Look at Joyce. The *Portrait* is the story of an attempt at the modern. *Dubliners*, even if it comes before, is more modern than *Portrait*. *Ulysses* is on the borderline. *Finnegans Wake* is already postmodern, or at least it initiates the postmodern discourse: it demands, in order to be understood, not the negation of the already said, but its ironic rethinking.

On the subject of the postmodern nearly everything has been said, from the very beginning (namely, in essays like 'The Literature of Exhaustion' by John Barth, which dates from 1967). Not that I am entirely in agreement with the grades that the theoreticians of postmodernism (Barth included) give to writers and artists, establishing who is postmodern and who has not yet made it. But I am interested in the theorem that the trend's theoreticians derive from their premises:

> My ideal postmodernist author neither merely repudiates nor merely imitates either his twentieth-century modernist parents or his nineteenth-century premodernist grandparents. He has the first half of our century under his belt, but not on his back . . . He may not hope to reach and move the devotees of James Michener and Irving Wallace – not to mention the lobotomised mass-media illiterates. But he *should* hope to reach and delight, at least part of the time, beyond the circle of what Mann used to call the Early Christians: professional devotees of high art . . . The ideal postmodernist novel will somehow rise above the quarrel between realism and irrealism, formalism and 'contentism', pure and committed literature, coterie fiction and junk fiction . . . My own analogy would be with good jazz or classical music: one finds much on successive listenings or close examination of the score that one didn't catch the first time through; but the first time through should be so ravishing – and not just to specialists – that one delights in the replay.

This is what Barth wrote in 1980, resuming the discussion, but this time under the title 'The Literature of Replenishment: Postmodernist Fiction'. Naturally, the subject can be discussed further, with a greater taste for paradox; and this is what Leslie Fiedler does. In 1980 *Salmagundi* (no. 50–1) published a debate between Fiedler and other American authors. Fiedler, obviously, is out to provoke. He praises *The Last of the Mohicans*, adventure stories, Gothic novels, junk scorned by critics that was nevertheless able to create myths and capture the imagination of more than one generation. He wonders if something like *Uncle Tom's Cabin* will ever appear again, a book that can be read with equal passion in the kitchen, the living room, and the nursery. He includes Shakespeare among those who knew how to amuse, along with *Gone with the Wind*. We all know he is too keen a critic to believe these things. He simply wants to break down the barrier that has been erected between art and enjoyability. He feels that today reaching a vast public and capturing its dreams perhaps means acting as the avant-garde, and he still leaves us free to say that capturing readers' dreams does not necessarily mean encouraging escape: it can also mean haunting them.

20 Linda Hutcheon, 'Telling Stories: Fiction and History'*

For Umberto Eco (see above), postmodernism is chiefly a matter of technique and tone; its main effect the thrill which simultaneously disturbs and delights. For Linda Hutcheon postmodernism is more interrogative and instructive. In a series of related studies – of 'narcissistic' narrative, parody, and the poetics of postmodernism – she has come to identify postmodernist fiction pre-eminently with what she describes as 'historiographic metafiction'; a mode (including a novel such as Eco's *The Name of the Rose*) which self-consciously problematises the making of fiction and history. Postmodernist inter-textuality neither repudiates nor simply ironises the past; nor does it merely reproduce the past as nostalgia, as Hutcheon believes Fredric Jameson and Terry Eagleton argue it does. Instead, postmodernist fiction reveals the past, she says, as always ideologically and discur-sively constructed. Its irony and use of paradox signal a critical distance within this world of representations, prompting questions not about 'the' truth, but 'whose' truth prevails. The political effect of this fiction therefore lies in the double action by which it inscribes and intervenes in a given discursive order. In the following selection, Hutcheon replies to Eagleton, ironically, by way of the evidence of his own historical fiction, *Saints and Scholars*.

See Terry Eagleton's 'Capitalism, Modernism and Postmodernism' in *Against the Grain* (1986), pp. 138–47. On postmodernist fiction see, for example, Brian McHale, *Postmodernist Fiction* (1987); Patricia Waugh, *Feminine Fictions. Revisiting the Postmodern* (1989); and Mar-guerite Alexander, *Flights from Realism;* (1990). Alison Lee's *Realism and Power. Postmodern British Fiction* (1990) shares Hutcheon's concep-tion of postmodernism.

* Reprinted from *The Politics of Postmodernism* (London and New York: Routledge, 1989), pp. 47–61.

In *Postmodernist Fiction*, Brian McHale has noted that both modernist and postmodernist fiction show an affinity for cinematic models, and certainly the work of Manuel Puig or Salman Rushdie would support such a claim. But historiographic metafiction, obsessed with the question of how we can come to know the past today, also shows an attraction to photographic models – and to photographs – either as physically present (in Michael Ondaatje's *Coming Through Slaughter*) or as the narrativised trappings of the historical archive (in Timothy Findley's *The Wars*, Maxine Hong Kingston's *China Men*, or Gayl Jones's *Corregidora*). In raising (and making problematic) the issue of photographic representation, postmodern fiction often points metaphorically to the related issue of narrative representation – its powers and its limitations. Here, too, there is no transparency, only opacity. The narrator in John Berger's novel G. tries to describe an actual historical and political event, but ends up in despair: 'Write anything. Truth or untruth, it is unimportant. Speak but speak with tenderness, for that is all that you can do that may help a little. Build a barricade of words, no matter what they mean' (John Berger, *G* (New York: Pantheon, 1972), p. 75). The politics of narrative representation can apparently sometimes be limited efficacy when it comes to the representation of politics.

It is not surprising that this should be the case, especially with historical representation, for the question of historiography's representational powers is a matter of current concern in a number of discourses but most obviously, perhaps, in historiographic metafiction. Roa Bastos's *I the Supreme* is a typical, if extreme, example of this. El Supremo (José Gaspar Rodríguez Francia) did exist and did rule Paraguay from 1814 to 1840, but the novel we read opens with a story about the instability of even a dictator's power over his self-representation in the documents of history: he discovers that his decrees are frequently parodied so well and so thoroughly that 'even the truth appears to be a lie' (Augusto Roa Bastos, *I the Supreme*, trans. Helen Lane (New York: Aventura, 1986), p. 5), and the competence of the scribe to whom the dictator 'dictates' his text is suspect. This novel disorients its readers on the level of its narration (Who speaks? Is the text written? Oral? Transcribed?), its plot and temporal structures, and even its material existence (parts of the text are said to have been burned): 'Forms disappear, words remain, to signify the impossible. No story can ever be told' (p. 11), especially, perhaps, the story of absolute power.

'I the Supreme' and *I the Supreme* equally distrust history's ability and will to convey 'truth': 'The words of power, of authority, words above words, will be transformed into clever words, lying words. Words below words' (Roa Bastos, *I the Supreme*, p. 29). Historians, like novelists, are said to be interested not in 'recounting the facts but [in] recounting that they are recounting them' (p. 32). Yet the text does provide a narrative of the historical past of Paraguay, albeit one recounted in anachronistic wording that underlines the present time of the recounting to the (doubly dictated-to) scribe who writes down what he is told to. Or does he? He openly admits to not understanding the meaning of what he transcribes, and, therefore, to misplacing words, to writing 'backwards' (p. 35). The text metafictionally includes even a reference to Roa Bastos and his novel: 'One or another of those *émigré*-scribblers will doubtless take advantage of the impunity of distance and be so bold as to cynically affix his signature' to the text we read (p. 35). And so he does.

I the Supreme is a novel about power, about history-writing, and about the oral tradition of story-telling. It thematises the postmodern concern with the radically indeterminate and unstable nature of textuality and subjectivity, two notions seen as inseparable: 'I must dictate/write; note it down somewhere. That is the only way I have of proving that I still exist' (*I the Supreme*, p. 45). Writing here is not 'the art of tracing flowery figures' but that of 'deflowering signs' (p. 58). Or, as the text explicitly states: 'This is representation. Literature. Representation of writing as representation' (p. 60). However, the power of literary representation is as provisional as that of historiography: 'readers do not know if they [Don Quixote and Sancho Panza] are fables, true stories, pretended truths. The same will come to pass with us. We too will pass for real-unreal beings' (p. 60).

The entire novel is full of such remarks about representation – in the narratives of both fiction and history. The 'Final Compiler's Note' states:

> The reader will already have noted that, unlike ordinary texts, this one was read first and written later. Instead of saying and writing something new, it merely faithfully copies what has already been said and composed by others . . . [T]he re-scriptor declares, in the words of a contemporary author, that the history contained in these *Notes* is reduced to the fact that the story that should have been told in them has not been told. As a consequence, the characters and facts that figure in them have earned, through the fatality of the written language, the right to a fictitious and autonomous existence in the service of the no less fictitious and autonomous reader.
>
> (*I the Supreme*, p. 435)

This is postmodern de-naturalising – the simultaneous inscribing and subverting of the conventions of narrative.

Coinciding with this kind of challenge in the novels themselves, there have been many theoretical examinations of the nature of narrative as a major human system of understanding – in fiction, but also in history, philosophy, anthropology, and so on. Peter Brooks (*Reading for the Plot* (New York: Random House, 1984), p. xii) has claimed that with the advent of romanticism, narrative became a dominant mode of representation, though one might wonder what the status of the classical epic and the Bible might be. He is likely right to say, however, that in the twentieth century there has been an increasing suspicion of narrative plot and its artifice, yet no diminishing of our reliance on plotting, however ironised or parodied (p. 7). We may no longer have recourse to the grand narratives that once made sense of life for us, but we still have recourse to narrative representations of some kind in most of our verbal discourses, and one of the reasons may be political.

Lennard Davis describes the politics of novelistic narrative representation in this way: 'Novels do not depict life, they depict life as it is represented by ideology' (Lennard Davis, *Resisting Novels: Ideology and Fiction* (New York and London: Methuen, 1987), p. 24). Ideology – how a culture represents itself to itself – 'doxifies' or naturalises narrative representation, making it appear as natural or common-sensical (p. 25); it presents what is really *constructed* meaning as something *inherent* in that which is being represented. But this is precisely what postmodern novels like Peter Ackroyd's *Chatterton* or Roa Bastos's *I the Supreme* or Graham Swift's *Waterland* are about. And in none of these cases is there ever what Jameson associates with the postmodern: 'a repudiation of representation, a "revolutionary" break with the (repressive) ideology of storytelling generally' (Fredric Jameson, (1984) p. 54). This misconception shows the danger of defining the postmodern in terms of (French or American) anti-representational late modernism, as so many do. In these novels, there is no dissolution or repudiation of representation; but there *is* a problematising of it.

Historiographic metafiction is written today in the context of a serious contemporary interrogating of the nature of representation in historiography. There has been much interest recently in narrative – its forms, its functions, its powers, and its limitations – in many fields, but especially in history. Hayden White has even asserted that the postmodern is 'informed by a programmatic, if ironic, commitment to the return to narrative as one of its enabling presuppositions' (Hayden White, *The Content of the Form: Narrative Discourse and Historical Representation*(Baltimore, Maryland and London: Johns Hopkins University Press, 1987), p. xi). If this is the case, his own work has done much to make it so. Articles like 'The value of narrativity in the representation of reality' have been influential in raising questions about narrative representation and its politics in both history and literature. From a different angle, the work of Dominick LaCapra has acted to de-naturalise notions of historical documents as representations of the past and of the way such archival traces of historical events are used within historiographic and fictive representations. Documents are not inert or innocent, but may indeed have 'critical or even potentially transformative relations to phenomena "represented" in them' (Dominick LaCapra, *History and Criticism* (Ithaca, New York: Cornell University Press, 1985) p. 38).

Of course, it is not just historiographic theory that has deconstructed narrative representation. Feminist thought, such as that of Teresa de Lauretis, has done much to deconstruct it as well. It has explored how 'narrative and narrativity . . . are mechanisms to be employed strategically and tactically in the effort to construct other forms of coherence, to shift the terms of representation, to produce the conditions of representability of another – and gendered – social subject' (Teresa de Lauretis, *Technologies of Gender. Essays on Theory, Film, and Fiction* (Bloomington, Ind.: Indiana University Press, 1987) p. 109). Narrative is indeed a 'socially symbolic act,' as Jameson claims, but it is also the outcome of social interaction. In the work of Maxine Hong Kingston or Gayl Jones, story-telling is not presented as a privatised form of experience but as asserting a communicational bond between the teller and the told within a context that is historical, social, and political, as well as intertextual.

The same is true in the postmodern fiction of Salman Rushdie or Gabriel García Márquez. It is not simply a case of novels metafictionally revelling in their own narrativity or fabulation; here narrative representation – story-telling – is a historical and a political act. Perhaps it always is. Peter Brooks argues: 'We live immersed in narrative, recounting and reassessing the meaning of our past actions, anticipating the outcome of our future projects, situating ourselves at the intersection of several stories not yet completed' (*Reading for the Plot*, p. 3). In Fowles's *The French Lieutenant's Woman* the hero does just this – at great length – and the contemporary narrator interrupts to forestall our objections in the name of a kind of postmodern mimesis of process, reminding us that we too do this constantly. While it is undoubtedly true that modernism has already challenged the conventions of what could/ should be narrated and had already explored the limits of narrative's ability to represent 'life,' it is postmodern culture at large that may have become 'novelistic.' As Stephen Heath has argued, it mass-produces narratives (for television, radio, film, video, magazines, comic books, novels), thereby creating a situation in which we must consume 'the constant narration of the social relations of individuals, the ordering of meanings for the individual in society' (Stephen Heath, *The Sexual Fix* (London: Macmillan; 1982), p. 85). Perhaps this is why story-telling has returned – but as a problem, not as a given.

It is still a truism of anti-postmodernist criticism that this return has been at the expense of a sense of history. But perhaps it just depends on your definition of history – or History. We may indeed get few postmodern narrative representations of the heroic victors who had traditionally defined who and what made it into History. Often we get instead both the story and the story-telling of the non-combatants or the losers: the Canadian Indians of Ruby Wiebe's *The Temptations of Big Bear* or Leonard Cohen's *Beautiful Losers*; the women of Troy in Christa Wolf's *Cassandra*; the blacks of South Africa or America in the work of J.M. Coetzee, André Brink, Toni Morrison, or Ishmael Reed.

Equally interesting are the postmodern attempts to go beyond the traditional representational forms of both fictional and historical narration: Patrick Süskind's *Perfume* offers the fictionalised history of eighteenth-century France in all its *olfactory* glory, though it must do so through verbal representations of the physical sense that narrative so rarely records. The novel offers the sense of smell as the vehicle not only for its historical and social contextualising but also for its metafictional commentary, since this is the tale of Jean-Baptiste Grenouille, the product of French peasant misery who is born an 'abomination' – with no bodily odor himself, but with the most discerning nose in the world. The story's narrator is omniscient and controlling, as well as being our contemporary and in complicity with us as readers. He uses this power and position to emphasise from the start the limits of his (and our) language. As a boy Grenouille has trouble learning the words of things that have no smell: 'He could not retain them, confused them with one another, and even as an adult used them unwillingly and often incorrectly: justice, conscience, God, joy, responsibiity, humility, gratitude, etc. – what these were meant to express remained a mystery to him' (Patrick Süskind, *Perfume: The Story of a Murderer*, trans. John E. Woods (New York: Knopf, 1986), p. 25). This may not be surprising, perhaps, for the protagonist of a novel subtitled: *The Story of a Murderer*.

Grenouille is constantly aware of the discrepancy between the 'richness of the world perceivable by smell' and 'the poverty of language' (Süskind, *Perfume*, p. 26). The narrator suggests that this linguistic impoverishment accounts for our normal inability to make anything other than gross distinctions in the 'smellable world' (p. 125). The text links the failure of language to Grenouille's creativity as the distiller and creator of the greatest perfumes in the world, and yet, as readers, we can never forget that we know of this only through the very language of the novel. The postmodern paradox of inscription and subversion governs the metafictive reflexivity. It also structures the plot, for this is a novel about power: the power the poor peasant was not born into; the power he acquires in serving others with his gifts (as a master of scents); the power to kill (for the perfect scent); the power that perfect scent wields over others. His executioners and the crowd gathered to witness justice done to this multiple murderer suddenly fall into an ecstatic orgy of love for their victim – when he applies the 'perfume' distilled from the murdered girl who had possessed the most powerful smell in the world:

'A power stronger than the power of money or the power of terror or the power of death: the invincible power to command the love of mankind' (p. 252).

Perfume points to the absence of the representation of the sense of smell in historical, social, or fictional narratives. The olfactory density of the novel – recounted through verbal representation, of course – is historically specific and accurate and also socially significant. This is historiographic metafiction, fictionalised history with a parodic twist. The form this twist takes may vary from novel to novel, but it is always present: Mario Vargas Llosa's *The War of the End of the World* represents the history of the 1896 Canudos War in northeastern Brazil, but its parody shows how traditional narrative models – both historiographical and fictional – that are based on European models of continuous chronology and cause-and-effect relations are utterly inadequate to the task of narrating the history of the New World.

Such a clashing of various possible discourses of narrative representation is one way of signalling the postmodern use and abuse of convention that works to 'de-doxify' any sense of the seamlessness of the join between the natural and the cultural, the world and the text, thereby making us aware of the irreducible ideological nature of every representation – of past or present. This complexity of clashing discourses can be seen in many historiographic metafictions. In Angela Carter's 'Black Venus', as we shall see in the last chapter, the discourses of male erotic representation of woman and those of female and colonial self-representations are juxtaposed with a certain political efficacy. Similarly, confrontations between contemporary narrators and their narrated historical contexts occur in novels as diverse as Banville's *Doctor Copernicus* and Fowles's *The French Lieutenant's Woman* or *A Maggot*.

In challenging the seamless quality of the history/fiction (or world/art) join implied by realist narrative, postmodern fiction does not, however, disconnect itself from history or the world. It foregrounds and thus contests the conventionality and unacknowledged ideology of that assumption of seamlessness and asks its readers to question the process by which we represent our selves and our world to ourselves and to become aware of the means by which we *make* sense of and *construct* order out of experience in our particular culture. We cannot avoid representation. We *can* try to avoid fixing our notion of it and assuming it to be transhistorical and transcultural. We can also study how representation legitimises and privileges certain kinds of knowledge – including certain kinds of historical knowledge. As *Perfume* implies, our access through narrative to the world of experience – past or present – is always mediated by the powers and limits of our representations of it. This is as true of historiographical narrative as it is of fictional.

In his review article, 'The question of narrative in contemporary historical theory', Hayden White outlines the role assigned to narrative representation in the various schools of thought about the theory of history. Given that narrative has become problematic in historiography as well as fiction, what is interesting is that the same issues arise: narrative representation as a mode of knowledge and explanation, as unavoidably ideological, as a localisable code. One way of outlining some of these parallel concerns would be to look at historiographic metafiction that directly addresses the intersection of the debates about representation in both the novel and history: Graham Swift's *Waterland*, a didactic fictive lesson or a meditation on history – or both. No historical characters populate this book, but it is a profoundly historical work none the less, in both form and content.

Its first (unattributed) epigraph conditions our entry into the novel and prepares us for the 'de-doxifying' of narrative representation that it proceeds to enact: '*Historia* ae, f. 1 inquiry, investigation, learning 2. a) a narrative of past events, history. b) any kind of narrative: account, tale, story.' The novel's action opens in the 'fairy-tale' landscape of the fen country of England, a land so flat that it drives its inhabitants either to 'unquiet' or to telling stories, especially to calm the fears of children. This is a land 'both palpable and unreal' (Graham Swift, *Waterland* (London: Heinemann, 1983) p. 6), an apt, self-reflexive setting for any fiction. The narrator, Tom Crick, comes from a family that has the 'knack for telling stories' of all kinds: true or made up, believable or unbelievable – 'stories which were neither one thing nor another' (pp. 1–2). This is a fitting description, too, of *Waterland* itself.

However, the second chapter is called 'About the end of history'. It is addressed to the second-person plural 'Children' by Crick, their history teacher, who has spent his life trying to 'unravel the mysteries of the past' (Swift, *Waterland* p. 4), but who is now to be retired because of some personal embarrassment, though the official reason is that his school is 'cutting back on history.' Crick's response is to defend his discipline – and his personal past: 'sack *me*, don't dismiss what I stand for. Don't banish my history' (p. 18). But his students seem little interested in his subject; for them history is a 'fairy tale' (p. 5) and they prefer to learn of the 'here and now' of a world threatened by nuclear annihilation. From the opening pages of the novel, both history-telling and story-telling are thus linked to fear.

They are also connected to the marshy, reclaimed land of the fen country, primarily through the major historical metaphor of the novel: 'Silt: which shapes and undermines continents; which demolishes as it builds; which is simultaneous accretion and erosion; neither progress nor decay' (*Waterland* p. 7). A more perfect image of postmodern paradox would be hard to find. In terms of history, the allegorical, slow 'process of human siltation' is contrasted with that of revolution and of 'grand metamorphoses.' To Crick, reality is what the monotonous fens provide: reality is 'that nothing happens'. Historiography's causality is only a construct: 'How many of the events of history have occurred . . . for this or for that reason, but for no other reason, fundamentally, than the desire to make things happen? I present to you History, the fabrication, the diversion, the reality-obscuring drama. History, and its near relative, Histrionics' (p. 34). He would like to replace the heroes of history with the silenced crowds who do the 'donkey-work of coping with reality' (p. 34).

Nevertheless, Crick realises that we all imitate 'the grand repertoire of history' in miniature and endorse 'its longing for presence, for feature, for purpose, for content' (*Waterland* pp. 34–5) in order to convince ourselves that reality means something. He himself attributes his becoming a history teacher to the tales his mother told him when he was afraid of the dark as a child. Later, when he wanted 'an Explanation', he studied history as an academic discipline, only to 'uncover in this dedicated search more mysteries, more fantasticalities, more wonders and grounds for astonishment' (p. 53). In other words, as it had begun for him, history continues to be 'a yarn': 'History itself, the Grand Narrative, the filler of vacuums, the dispeller of fears of the dark' (p. 53).

The story Crick actually tells us and the 'Children' is one that is overtly fictive history, and we get to watch the fictionalising process at work. At one point we are told: 'History does not record whether the day of Thomas's funeral was one of those dazzling mid-winter Fenland days' (*Waterland* p. 70), but fourteen pages later, Thomas's funeral takes place under a definitely dazzling sky. Crick is aware of this creative, constructive process. At one point he stops: 'Children, you are right. There are times when we have to disentangle history from fairy-tale . . . History, being an accredited sub-science, only wants to know facts. History, if it is to keep on constructing its road into the future, must do so on solid ground' (p. 74) – something his slippery fen-country tale often seems to lack. Swift manages to raise the issue of narrative emplotment and its relation to both fictionality and historiography at the same time as he begins his problematisation of the notion of historical knowledge. Crick tells his students: 'When you asked, as all history classes ask, as all history classes should ask, what is the point of history? Why history? Why the past?' he feels he can reply: 'Isn't this seeking of reasons itself inevitably an historical process, since it must always work backwards from what came after to what came before?' (p. 92).

The study of history – that 'cumbersome but precious bag of clues' – involves inquiry that attempts to 'uncover the mysteries of cause and effect' (*Waterland* p. 92), but most of all it teaches us 'to accept the burden of our need to ask why' (p. 93). That process of asking becomes more important than the details of historiography: 'the attempt to give an account, with incomplete knowledge, of actions themselves undertaken with incomplete knowledge' (p. 94). As he later says, 'History: a lucky dip of meanings. Events elude meaning, but we look for meanings' (p. 122) and we create them.

Tom Crick is in some ways an allegorical representation of the postmodern historian who might well have read, not just Collingwood, with his view of the historian as storyteller and detective, but also Hayden White, Dominick LaCapra, Raymond Williams, Michel Foucault and Jean-François Lyotard. The debates about the nature and status of narrative representation in historical discourse coincide and are inextricably intertwined with the challenges offered by historiographic metafiction. Yet we have seen that postmodern fiction is typically denounced as dehistoricised, if not ahistorical, especially by Marxist critics. In the light of fiction like *Waterland* or *Midnight's Children* or *Ragtime* this position would seem difficult to maintain. Of course, the problematised histories of postmodernism have little to do with the single totalising History of Marxism, but they cannot be accused of neglecting or refusing engagement with the issues of historical representation and knowledge.

Among the consequences of the postmodern desire to denaturalise history is a new self-consciousness about the distinction between the brute *events* of the past and the historial *facts* we construct out of them. Facts are events to which we have given meaning. Different historical perspectives therefore derive different facts from the same events. Take Paul Veyne's example of Louis XIV's cold: even though the cold was a royal one, it was not a political event and therefore it would be of no interest to a history of politics, but it could be of considerable interest for a history of health and sanitation in France (Paul Veyne, *Comment on écrit l'histoire* (Paris: Seuil, 1971) p. 35). Postmodern fiction often thematises this process of turning events into facts through the filtering and interpreting of archival documents. Roa Bastos's *I the Supreme* presents a narrator who admits to being a compiler of discourses and whose text is woven out of thousands of documents researched by the author. Of course, documents have always functioned in this way in historical fiction of any kind. But in historiographic metafiction the very process of turning events into facts through the interpretation of archival evidence is shown to be a process of turning the traces of the past (our only access to those events today) into historical representation. In so doing, such postmodern fiction underlines the realisation that 'the past is not an "it" in the sense of an objectified entity that may either be neutrally represented in and for itself or projectively reprocessed in terms of our own narrowly "presentist" interests' (Dominick LaCapra, *History, Politics and the Novel* (Ithaca, New York: Cornell University Press, 1987), p. 10). While these are the words of a historian writing about historical representation, they also describe well the postmodern lessons about fictionalised historical representation.

The issue of representation in both fiction and history has usually been dealt with in epistemological terms, in terms of how we know the past. The past is not something to be escaped, avoided, or controlled – as various forms of modernist art suggest through their implicit view of the 'nightmare' of history. The past is something with which we must come to terms and such a confrontation involves an acknowledgement of limitation as well as power. We only have access to the past today through its traces – its documents, the testimony of witnesses, and other archival materials. In other words, we only have representations of the past from which to construct our narratives or explanations. In a very real sense, postmodernism reveals a desire to understand present culture as the product of previous representations. The representation of history becomes the history of representation. What this means is that postmodern art acknowledges and accepts the challenge of tradition: the history of representation cannot be escaped but it can be both exploited and commented on critically through irony and parody. The forms of representation used and abused by this paradoxical postmodern strategy can vary – from the parodic and historic architectural forms in Peter Ackroyd's *Hawksmoor* that mirror and structure the novel's intricate narrative representation (itself parodic and historic) to the strangely transcribed oral histories of the post-nuclear-holocaust world of Russell Hoban's *Riddley Walker*, where the narratives of the past exist but are, in the text's words, 'changet so much thru the years theyre all bits and blips and all mixt up' (Russell Hoban, *Riddley Walker* (London: Picador, 1980), p. 20).

As this kind of novel makes clear, there are important parallels between the processes of history-writing and fiction-writing and among the most problematic of these are their common assumptions about narrative and about the nature of mimetic representation. The postmodern situation is that a 'truth is being told, with "facts" to back it up, but a teller constructs that truth and chooses those facts' (Barbara Foley, *Telling the Truth: The Theory and Practice of Documentary Fiction* (Ithaca, New York and London: Cornell University Press, 1986), p. 67). In fact, that teller – of story or history – also constructs those very facts by giving a particular meaning to events. Facts do not speak for themselves in either form of narrative: the tellers speak for them, making these fragments of the past into a discursive whole. The 'true' story of the historical gangster, Jack Diamond, that we read in William Kennedy's *Legs* is shown to be a postmodern compromised one from its very title: 'Legs' is the protagonist's public label, the name the newspapers give him. In Jack's words: 'All the garbage they ever wrote about me is true to people who don't know me' (William Kennedy, *Legs* (Harmondsworth:

Penguin, 1975), p. 245) – that is to say, to people like us. Brian McHale calls this kind of work a 'revisionist historical novel' (Brian McHale, *Postmodernist Fiction* (London and New York: Methuen, 1987), P. 90) because he feels it revises and reinterprets the official historical record and transforms the conventions of historical fiction. I would rather put this challenge in terms of a de-naturalising of the conventions of representing the past in narrative – historical and fictional – that is done in such a way that the politics of the act of representing are made manifest.

One of the clearest examples of this process self-consciously at work is (ironically) a novel by a Marxist critic who has accused postmodern fiction of being ahistorical: Terry Eagleton's *Saints and Scholars*. The introductory note to the novel asserts that the story is 'not entirely fantasy'. Some of the characters are real, as are some of the events, but most of the rest is invented. This becomes evident in the first chapter, a fictionalised historical account of the last hours of Irish revolutionary James Connolly before he is executed in Kilmainham gaol on 12 May 1916. But the account ends with a remark that engenders the rest of the fiction to follow:

> But history does not always get the facts in the most significant order, or arrange them in the most aesthetically pleasing pattern. Napoleon survived the battle of Waterloo, but it would have been symbolically appropriate if he had been killed there. Florence Nightingale lingered on until 1910, but this was an oversight on history's part.
>
> (Terry Eagleton, *Saints and Scholars* (London and New York: Verso, 1987) p. 10)

So the narrator arrests the bullets of the firing squad in mid-air in order to 'prise open a space in these close-packed events through which Jimmy may scamper, blast him out of the dreary continuum of history into a different place altogether' (p. 10).

The plot action eventually comes to settle around a cottage on the west coast of Ireland where gather, thanks to irony and chance, a wondrous collection of historical and fictional eccentrics: 'A Scottish Irishman [Connolly], an Irish Hungarian [Leopold Bloom], an anglicised Austrian [Ludwig Wittgenstein], and a Russian [Nicolai Bakhtin, Mikhail's brother], (*Saints and Scholars*, pp. 131–2). Though some are real and others fictional, all characters work to problematise the very distinction: Nicolai Bakhtin is said to be exceedingly extravagant but nevertheless historically real, and the others think he is 'an entirely fictional character, and the only real thing about him was that he knew it' (p. 30). When he later tells the fictive Leopold Bloom that the notion of individuality is a 'supreme fiction', Joyce's character replies: 'You might be a bleeding fiction . . . You look pretty much like one to me. I happen to be real. I think I'm just about the only real person here' (p. 135).

The novel's metafictionality operates through many such parodic intertextual echoes. To offer another instance: Bakhtin asks Connolly about the success of the Easter Rising because he is eager to know whether he is 'in the presence of a world-historical figure' (*Saints and Scholars*, p. 94) – Lukács's term for the real personages found within historical fiction. The text's self-reflexivity also functions on the level of language and this is where Wittgenstein fits in. But what is also made clear is that Wittgenstein's famous linguistic theories are the direct product of his personal history, and particularly of his national history as a Viennese and his racial history as a Jew. When he (characteristically) tries to convince Connolly that the limits of his language are the limits of his world, the orator and man of action replies: 'What do you propose instead? That we should languish in the prison-house of language . . .?' (p. 114). The echo of the title of Jameson's book, *The Prison-House of Language*, is not just a clever move in some literary-critical recognition game: it invokes the entire context of Marxist criticism's (and Eagleton's own) stand against the reflexivity of language and narrative in the name of politics. This is important because *Saints and Scholars* attempts to reconcile these seemingly opposing positions – as indeed does much historiographic metafiction.

Eagleton's novel ends with another deferral of those firing-squad bullets heading for Connolly's body: 'When the bullets reached him he would disappear entirely into myth, his body nothing but a piece of language, the first cry of the new republic' (*Saints and Scholars*, p. 145). Of course, we *do* only know Connolly today primarily from pieces of language, the traces and texts of the past. Eagleton wants to do more than problematise this epistemological reality, though. He offers as well a new way of representing history – not derived from the official accounts of the victors, but taken from the unofficial, usually unrecorded perspective of the victims of history. The novel's densely detailed descriptions of the life of the poor and the working class in Dublin are accompanied by analyses of the causes of the misery: the economic and political maneuverings of imperialist Britain. The plot contrasts a Viennese Jew's desire to be 'hiding from history' (p. 84) with an Irish revolutionary leader's view that to be free 'you have to remember' (p. 128), tell your own story, and represent yourself: 'A colonial territory was a land where nothing happened, where you reacted to the narrative of your rulers rather than created one of your own' (p. 104). Talk is all that is left to 'a race bereft of its history' (p. 104) but talk – discourse – is a kind of action: 'Discourse was something you did . . . The Irish had never fallen for the English myth that language was a second-hand reflection of reality' (p. 105). Obviously, neither did the postmodern.

This is the kind of novel that works towards a critical return to history and politics *through* – not despite – metafictional self-consciousness and parodic intertextuality. This is the postmodernist paradox, a 'use and abuse' of history that Nietzsche, when considering that subject, never contemplated. In Roland Barthes's terms, we are shown that there is 'nothing natural anywhere, nothing but the historical' anywhere (Barthes 1977, p. 139).

21 Carlos Fuentes, 'Words Apart'*

Salman Rushdie's *The Satanic Verses* has met with the most extra-ordinary response of any twentieth-century fiction in English. This has included demonstrations, riots, book-burning, an appeal to the laws of blasphemy, and the unprecedented mobilisation of the Western literary and artistic community in the book and author's defence. The death threat pronounced by the Ayatollah Khomeini in February 1989, which forced Rushdie into an extended period of hiding, is grotesque proof of the real risks and dangers postmodernist fiction might run. The later claim that in rejecting 'Westernisation', or modernity, Islamic society is itself 'postmodernist' (Akbar Ahmed, *The Guardian* 5 July, 1990, pp. 21–2) only served to expose further the bizarre gulf in understanding and beliefs this episode revealed.

Censorship, book-burning and murder all occur in Umberto Eco's *The Name of the Rose*. His detective, William of Baskerville, stands for a broad tolerance which would allow sacred and subversive texts to coexist: a triumph for modern humanism over medieval superstition and dogma. The 'Rushdie affair' may yet follow a similar course. It began however by jolting the methods of critique and satire into dramatic conflict with a fundamentalism worthy of Eco's Inquisition. Carlos Fuentes writing shortly after the issue of the *fatwa* drew on the Russian linguist and critic Mikhail Bakhtin's concept of 'dialogics' to describe this situation, invoking a model which recognises that moments of crisis stretch beyond tolerance to stark opposition. Rushdie's decision to seek a more flexible 'dialogue', within Islam, takes the issues, one might think, finally beyond matters of mere fiction or intertextuality. Fuentes had suggested otherwise, however. For this episode, he says, proved the continuing influence of words

---

* Reprinted from *The Guardian*, 24 February 1989, and included in *The Rushdie File*, ed. Lisa Appignanesi and Sara Maitland (London: ICA Fourth Estate Ltd., 1989), pp. 245–9.

not their impotence, confirming the human need for a literature of paradox, doubt and complexity.

In addition to the documentation and essays in *The Rushdie File*, see 'Beyond the Rushdie Affair', *Third Text*, 11 (Summer 1990). Marguerite Alexander's *Flights from Realism* (1990) contains some discussion of the destabilising ironies in the text of Rushdie's novel as well as in surrounding events in the West and Islam (pp. 200–6).

Mikhail Bakhtin was, probably, the greatest theorist of the novel in our century. His life, in a way, is as exemplary as his books. Shunted off to remote areas of the Soviet Union by the minions of Stalinism for his unorthodox ideas, Bakhtin could not profit from rehabilitation when it came under Brezhnev, simply because he had never been accused of anything. A victim of faceless intolerance, his political nemesis was Stalin, but his literary symbol was Kafka.

His case was and is not unique. I have thought a lot about Bakhtin while thinking about Salman Rushdie during these past few weeks. Rushdie's work perfectly fits the Bakhtinian contention that ours is an age of competitive languages. The novel is the privileged arena where languages in conflict can meet, bringing together, in tension and dialogue, not only opposing characters, but also different historical ages, social levels, civilisation and other, dawning realities of human life. In the novel, realities that are normally separated can meet, establishing a dialogic encounter, a meeting with the other.

This is no gratuitous exercise. It reveals a number of things. The first is that, in dialogue, no one is absolutely right; neither speaker holds an absolute truth or, indeed, has an absolute hold over history. Myself and the other, as well as the history that both of us are making, still are not. Both are unfinished and so can only continue to be. By its very nature, the novel indicates that we are becoming. There is no final solution. There is no last word.

This is what Milan Kundera means when he proposes that the novel is a constant redefinition of men and women as problems, never as sealed, concluded truths. But this is precisely what the Ayatollahs of this world cannot suffer. For the Ayatollahs reality is dogmatically defined once and for all in a sacred text. But a sacred text is, by definition, a completed and exclusive text. You can add nothing to it. It does not converse with anyone. It is its own loudspeaker. It offers perfect refuge for the insecure who then, having the protection of a dogmatic text over their heads, proceed to excommunicate those whose security lies in search for the truth. I remember Luis Buñuel constantly saying: 'I would give my life for a man who is looking for the truth. But I would gladly kill a man who thinks that he has found the truth.'

This Buñuelian, surrealist sally is now being dramatically acted out in reversal. An author who is looking for the truth, has been condemned to death by a priestly hierarchy, whose deep insecurity is disguised by their pretension to holding the truth. The Ayatollahs, nevertheless, have done a great service to literature, if not to Islam. They have debased and caricatured their own faith. But they have shifted the wandering attention of the world to the power of words, literature and the imagination, in ways totally unforeseen in their philosophy.

For the intolerance of the Ayatollahs not only sheds light on Salman Rushdie and his uses of the literary imagination. By making this imagination so dangerous that it deserves capital punishment, the sectarians have made people everywhere wonder what it is that literature can say that can be so powerful and, indeed, so dangerous.

In a deservedly famous commentary, Philip Roth once distinguished between reactions to literature East and West. In totalitarian regimes, Roth said, everything matters and nothing goes. In the liberal democracies, nothing matters and everything goes. Suddenly, *The Satanic Verses* have pushed the 'nothing goes' of intolerance right out into the public squares of indifference. Suddenly, we all realise that everything matters, whether it goes or not.

I do not truly believe that there is a single intelligent writer in either Europe, both Americas, Africa, Asia or Down Under, who does not feel threatened by the possibilities so melodramatically opened by the Ayatollah's crusade against the freedom of the imagination. It can't happen here? You can bet your bottom dollar, peso, franc or pound that it can.

Saying the same thing as Roth, Italo Calvino once wrote that when politics pays too much attention to literature, this is a bad sign, mostly for literature. But, he added, it is also a bad sign when politics doesn't want to hear the word 'literature' mentioned. It means that the society has become afraid of any use of language that calls into question the certitudes it holds about itself.

I have always conceived the novel (at least those I try to write) as a crossroads between the individual and the collective destinies of men and women. Both tentative, both unfinished, but both only sayable and minimally understandable if it is previously said and understood that, in fiction, truth is the search for truth, nothing is pre-established and knowledge is only what both of us – reader and writer – can imagine.

There is no other way to freely and fruitfully explore the possibilities of our unfinished humanity. No other way to refuse the death of the past, making it present through memory. No other way of effectively giving life to the future, through the manifestation of our desire.

That these essential activities of the human spirit should be denied in the name of a blind yet omniscient, paralytical yet actively homicidal dogmatism is both a farce and a crime in itself. Salman Rushdie has done the true religious spirit a service by brilliantly imagining the tensions and compliments that it establishes with the secular spirit. Humour, certainly, cannot be absent, since there is no contemporary language that can utter itself without a sense of the diversification of that same language. When we all understood everything, the epic was possible. But not fiction. The novel is born from the very fact that we do not understand one another any longer, because unitary, orthodox language has broken down. Quixote and Sancho, the Shandy brothers, Mr and Mrs Karenin: their novels are the comedy (or the drama) of their misunderstandings. Impose a unitary language: you kill the novel, but you also kill the society.

I hope that everyone, after what has happened to Salman Rushdie and *The Satanic Verses*, now understands this. Fiction is not a joke. It is but an expression of the cultural, personal and spiritual diversity of mankind.

Fiction is a harbinger of a multipolar and multicultural world, where no single philosophy, no single belief, no single solution, can shunt aside the extreme wealth of mankind's cultural heritage. Our future depends on the enlarged freedom for the multiracial and the polycultural to express itself in a world of shifting, decaying and emerging power centres.

Salman Rushdie has given form to a dilemma previously embodied, at diverse levels, in the West, by the novels of Hernarus, Mauriac and Camus, as well as the films of Bergman, Fellini and Buñuel. And that is: Can the religious mentality thrive outside of religious dogma and hierarchy? These are questions essential to any ideas of freedom. But the burdens of freedom, as Dostoyevsky's Grand Inquisitor well knew, can be heavier than the chains of liberty. 'Long live my chains!' exclaimed the Spanish patriots painted by Goya as their revolutionary liberators, the Napoleonic troops, mowed them down. And, in another direction, Georg Buckner proclaimed, in *Danton's Death*, that since God no longer existed, mankind was now responsible for its own destiny and could not shift the blame any more.

The modern age, by liberating both the freedom for good and the freedom for evil, has placed upon us all the obligation to relativise both. Absolute good is called polyanna. Absolute evil is called Hitler. Relative good is called Simone Weil. Relative evil is called de Sade. But the name of relativity is no longer virtue; it is value. Bad literature stays at the level of virtue; it pits good guys against bad boys. Good literature rises to the level of values in conflict with one another. This is what Salman Rushdie has done in all of his novels.

That he has dramtised the conflict within Islam does not, however, exempt the rest of us, within the Judeo-Christian tradition, from looking at our own sources of intolerance or at our own limits when our own symbols are set into conflictive motion. Artists have been silenced or 'disappeared' in Latin America for not spouting the official truth of our local, mostly military, Ayatollahs. Jean-Luc Godard in Europe and Martin Scorsese in the United States have been attacked for seriously exploring in the Catholic faith what Rushdie is exploring in the Islamic faith, that is, the combinations, the possibilities, the ghosts beyond the dogmas. A number of Jewish writers and comedians have poked fun at Judaism. What are the limits? What if a Jewish writer imagined Anne Frank as a young whore? What if a Catholic writer depicted Joseph, the jealous philicide, as the true betrayer of Christ?

The alarming thing about Salman Rushdie's experience in intolerance is that it has revealed a seething alliance of commerical cowardice and fundamentalist intolerance surrounding the self-proclaimed island of rationality in any given society. Sects coexist with commericalism in Georgia and Guatemala. Allow these two factors – booksellers and publishers succumbing to terrorist threats, and zealots of all faiths discovering their sectarian brotherhood, be it Muslim, Christian or Jewish – and the margins of freedom in our world will quickly and frighteningly shrink.

The defence of Salman Rushdie is a defence of ourselves. It is a matter of pride to say that Rushdie has given us all a better reason to understand and protect the profession of letters at the highest level of creativity, imagination, intelligence and social responsibility.

Notes on Authors

(Full publication details are not given where texts also appear under Further Reading.)

THEODOR WIESENGRUND ADORNO (1903–69) was born in Frankfurt of Jewish-Italian parents. He studied philosophy and music in Vienna and taught briefly at Oxford before departing for the United States in 1938. There he became a leading member of the Institute for Social Research in New York. In 1950 he returned to the University of Frankfurt to re-establish the Institute there with Max Horkheimer. His works in translation include *Prisms* (1967); *The Dialectic of Enlightenment*, with Max Horkheimer, 1972); *The Philosophy of Modern Music* (1973); *Negative Dialectics* (New York: Seabury Press, 1973); and *Aesthetic Theory* (1984).

JEAN BAUDRILLARD (1929–) is a leading and controversial commentator on postmodernism, both an undoubted influence and the subject of severe critique. His extensive writings, many now in translation, include *The Mirror of Production* (1975); *Simulations* (1983); *America* (1988); and *Fatal Strategies* (1990). A volume of *Selected Writings* (ed. Mark Poster) appeared in 1988. Baudrillard was Professor of Sociology at the University of Paris, X, Nanterre, between 1966 and 1988.

HOUSTON A. BAKER JR. (1943–) is the Albert M. Greenfield Professor of Human Relations and Director of the Center for the Study of Black Literature and Culture at the University of Pennsylvania. He has written widely in the area of Afro-American literary and cultural study, and is also a poet. In addition to the volume *Modernism and the Harlem Renaissance* (1987), his publications include *Long Black Song: Essays in Black American Literature and Culture* (Virginia: University Press of Virginia, 1972); and *Blues, Ideology and Afro-American Literature* (Chicago: University of Chicago Press, 1987).

WALTER BENJAMIN (1892–1940), studied philosophy and literature in Germany and Switzerland before the First World War, and was then employed as a journalist and translator, working intermittently from 1928 on his 'Arcades' project, a prospective major work on Charles Baudelaire and modernity. In the twenties he met Adorno and Brecht, the main but contradictory influences on his own highly original Marxism. He left Germany for Paris after 1933 and received a stipend from the Institute for Social Research which published some of his essays. In September 1940, confronted by the Gestapo at Port Bou on his way to the United States, he committed suicide. Benjamin's reputation is almost entirely posthumous, gained by the essays collected in translation as *Illuminations* (1970); *Understanding Brecht* (1973); and the study *Charles Baudelaire: A Lyric Poet in the Era of High Capitalism* (1973).

MARSHALL BERMAN has worked as a freelance writer and critic, and taught at the Universities of Stanford and New Mexico, and at the City College and City

248

University of New York. He is the author of *The Politics of Authenticity, Radical Individualism and the Emergence of Modern Society* (New York: Atheneum, 1970).

BERTOLT BRECHT (1896–1956) poet, playwright and theatre director was born in Augsburg and, after early success, moved to Berlin and there staged the celebrated *Threepenny Opera* (1928). In the late twenties, Marxist theory, Soviet revolutionary art, Noh theatre, music hall and cabaret combined to influence Brecht's conception of an anti-illusionist 'epic theatre' and its allied 'alienation effects'. After 1933 he lived in Scandinavia and in 1941 travelled to the United States to work in Hollywood. The plays *Galileo, The Caucasian Chalk Circle* and *Mother Courage* belong to this period. After an appearance before the House UnAmerican Activities Committee in 1947, Brecht returned to Europe and to East Berlin where he established the Berliner Ensemble. Brecht's plays are available in translation in Britain by Eyre Methuen, as are *Poems 1913–1956* (ed. John Willett and Ralph Manheim, 1979); and *Brecht on Theatre* (ed. and trans. John Willett, 1964).

PETER BÜRGER is Professor of French and Comparative Literature at the University of Bremen. He has written on French surrealism and the French Enlightenment and is author of a collection of theoretical essays *Vermittlung – Rezeption – Funktion* (Frankfurt: Suhrkamp, 1983) and editor of the series *Heute für kritische Literaturwissenschaft*. A collection of essays, *The Decline of Modernism*, trans. Nicholas Walker (Cambridge: Polity Press, 1992).

IAIN CHAMBERS (1949–) is Professor in the Department for the Study of Literature and Language, the Oriental Institute, the University of Naples. He is the author of *Urban Rhythms: Pop Music and Popular Culture* (London: Macmillan; New York: St Martin's Press, 1985); *Popular Culture. The Metropolitan Experience* (1986); and *Border Dialogues: Journeys in Postmodernity* (1990).

UMBERTO ECO (1929–) is a distinguished semiotician, cultural critic and novelist. Eco's works include *A Theory of Semiotics* (Bloomington, Indiana: Indiana University Press, 1976); *The Role of the Reader* (London: Hutchinson, 1981); *Faith in Fakes*, also published as *Travels in Hyperreality* (1987); and the best selling novels *The Name of the Rose* (1980, London: Secker and Warburg, 1983; Pan 1984); and *Foucault's Pendulum* (London: Secker and Warburg, 1989; Pan 1990). Eco is Professor of Semiotics at the University of Bologna and Visiting Professor at Columbia University, USA.

CARLOS FUENTES (1929–) is a Mexican novelist, diplomat and political essayist. Fuentes was Mexican Ambassador to Paris in 1975 and held professorships at Harvard and Cambridge in 1986–87. His novels include *The Death of Artemio Cruz* (New York: Farrar, Straus & Giroux, (1964); *Terra Nostra* (New York: Farrar, Straus & Giroux, 1976); and *The Old Gringo* (New York: Farrar, Straus & Giroux, 1985). As well as articles and essays on Latin American fiction he has published the study *Gabriel García Márquez and the Invention of America* (Liverpool: Liverpool University Press, 1987).

JÜRGEN HABERMAS (1929–) is a widely esteemed social theorist, whose sustained defence of rationality and the Enlightenment project has significantly shaped debates on modernity and postmodernity. Habermas was appointed assistant to Adorno at the Frankfurt Institute of Social Research in 1956, and later became Director of the Max Planck Institute. He is currently Professor of Sociology and Philosophy at the Johann Wolfgang Goethe University in Frankfurt. His works in translation include *Legitimation Crisis* (1976); *The Philosophical Discourse of Modernity* (1988); and *The Structural Transformation of the Public Sphere* (1989).

DAVID HARVEY (1935–) has taught at Johns Hopkins University and since 1987 at the University of Oxford, where he is Halford Mackinder Professor of Geography. He is the author of *The Limits to Capital* (Oxford: Basil Blackwell, 1982); *The Urban*

Modernism/Postmodernism

Experience (Oxford: Basil Blackwell, 1985); and *Social Justice and the City* (Oxford: Basil Blackwell). A volume entitled *Postmodernism and the City* is forthcoming.

LINDA HUTCHEON (1947–) is Professor of English and Comparative Literature at the University of Toronto. She is the author of a series of studies of postmodernist fiction, including *Narcissistic Narrative: the Metafictional Paradox* (1980); *A Poetics of Postmodernism* (1988); and *The Politics of Postmodernism* (1989). A new study, *Irony and the Power of the Unsaid*, is forthcoming.

FREDRIC JAMESON (1934–) is an American Marxist critic, whose interpretation of developments in European theory and contemporary culture have made his writings of central importance to literary and cultural studies. His publications include *Marxism and Form* (1971); *The Prison House of Language* (Princeton, New Jersey: Princeton University Press, 1972); and *The Political Unconscious. Narrative as a Socially Symbolic Act* (New York and London: Methuen, 1981). His most recent works are *Late Marxism: Adorno or the Persistence of the Dialectic* (1990); *Postmodernism, Or the Cultural Logic of Late Capitalism* (1991); and a study on film, *Signatures of the Visible* (New York and London: Routledge, 1991). Jameson has taught at several American Universities and is at present Professor of Comparative Literature and Director of the Graduate Program in literature and theory at Duke University. He is a co-founder of the journal *Social Text*.

GEETA KAPUR is a prominent art historian and critic. She is Senior Fellow at the Nehru Memorial Museum and Library in New Delhi and author of *Contemporary Indian Artists* (Villas, India and London: Vikas/Sangam Books, 1978). She is a regular contributor to the journal *Third Text*, and a member of its International Council.

LAURA KIPNIS (1956–) is a video artist and Assistant Professor in the Department of Radio, TV and Film at Northwestern University. Her video tapes include *A Man's Woman*, produced in association with Channel Four Television, and most recently 'Marx: the Video'. A collection of essays and videoscripts, *Symptoms*, is forthcoming from the University of Minnesota Press.

JULIA KRISTEVA (1941–) was born in Bulgaria, and gained a distinguished reputation as a linguist and semiotician in association with the *Tel Quel* group in Paris in the late sixties and seventies. Her work on language, subjectivity and sexuality, drawing especially upon Lacanian psychoanalysis, has been at the centre of contemporary feminist debate. Kristeva is Professor of Linguistics at the University of Paris VIII, and a psychoanalyst. Her works in translation include *Revolution in Poetic Language* (1984); *Desire in Language* (Oxford: Basil Blackwell; New York; Columbia University Press, 1980); and, most recently, *Black Sun. Depression and Melancholia* (New York: Columbia University Press, 1989); and the award-winning *Strangers to Ourselves* (Brighton: Harvester Wheatsheaf, 1991). *The Kristeva Reader*, ed. Toril Moi (Oxford: Basil Blackwell) was published in 1986).

GEORG LUKÁCS (1885–1971) the Hungarian-born Marxist philosopher and critic, is best known for his defence of 'critical realism' and his strictures against literary modernism. Lukács studied in Germany and later settled in Vienna (1919–29), where he wrote *History and Class Consciousness* (1923, London: Merlin, 1971), a major exposition of Marxist dialectic from a Hegelian perspective. He worked at the Soviet Academy of Science in Moscow and after Stalin's death was appointed Hungarian Minister of Culture but deported at the time of the Soviet invasion and only readmitted to the Communist Party in 1967. His wide influence can be detected in the work of the Frankfurt School, the criticism of Lucian Goldmann, Raymond Williams and Fredric Jameson. Other works include *The Theory of the Novel* (1916; London: Merlin, 1971); *The Historical Novel* (first published 1947; London: Merlin Press, 1962); and *The Meaning of Contemporary Realism* (1963).

250

JEAN-FRANÇOIS LYOTARD was for fifteen years a member of the revolutionary Marxist group 'Socialisme ou Barbarie'. In the sixties he came to question Marxist explanation and began his alternative 'post-Marxist' investigations in philosophy, language, and the arts; a development recounted in *Peregrinations* (New York: Columbia University Press, 1988). In addition to *The Postmodern Condition* (1984), Lyotard's writings in translation include, *Just Gaming* (1985) and *The 'Differend'* (1988). Lyotard is Professor Emeritus of Philosophy at the University of Paris VIII and Professor at the University of California, Irvine.

JEAN RADFORD is Senior Lecturer in Humanities at Hatfield Polytechnic and author of *Norman Mailer: a Critical Study* (London: Macmillan, 1976) and *Dorothy Richardson* (Brighton: Harvester Wheatsheaf, 1991). She has also edited *The Progress of Romance* (London: Routledge & Kegan Paul, 1986) and written introductions to three novels by May Sinclair.

YVONNE RAINER (1934-) is an American dancer, choreographer and film-maker who teaches on the Independent Study Program at the Whitney Museum of Modern Art, New York. A founder member of the experimental Judson Dance Theatre she began exploring subjectivity and sexuality in short non-realist films in the late sixties. Her choreographic work includes *My Body's House* (1964); *The Mind is a Muscle* (1966–68); and her films, *Journeys from Berlin* (1971); *Lives of Performers* (1972); *Kristina Talking Pictures* (1976); and *The Man Who Envied Women (1985)*. *The Films of Yvonne Rainer* (Bloomington: Indiana University Press, 1989) contains film scripts, interviews and critical essays.

CORNEL WEST (1953-) is Professor of Religion and Director of the Afro-American Studies Programme at Princeton University. In 1989 he was Visiting Fellow at the British Film Institute, London. His writings include *Prophetic Fragments* (Grand Rapids, Michigan: Eerdmans, 1988); *The American Evasion of Philosophy. A Genealogy of Pragmatism* (Madison: University of Wisconsin Press, 1989); and *The Ethical Dimensions of Marxist Thought* (New York: Monthly Review Press, 1991). He is co-editor of *Out There: Marginalisation and Contemporary Cultures* (Cambridge, Mass.: MIT Press, 1990) and a member of the editorial board of the journal *Social Text*.

RAYMOND WILLIAMS (1921–88) was born in Pandy, Abergavenny, Gwent, and educated at Cambridge, where he was later Lecturer in English and Professor of Drama (1974–83). He has had an enormous international influence upon literary criticism, media studies and Left cultural politics. His numerous writings include *Culture and Society* (London: Chatto and Windus, 1958); *The Country and The City* (London: Chatto and Windus, 1973); *Problems in Materialism and Culture* (London: Verso, 1980) and *Resources of Hope* (London and New York: Verso, 1989). Williams is also the author of half a dozen novels, including the posthumously published *People of the Black Mountains*. Perhaps the best introduction to his work and thinking remains the interviews collected as *Politics and Letters* (London: Verso, 1979).

LALEEN YAYAMANNE (1947-) is a Sri Lankan-born film-maker and film-lecturer who teaches at the Power Institute of Fine Arts, The University of Sydney, Australia. She has directed *A Song of Ceylon* (1985) and written essays on '"Ceylon", a clash of cultures' and 'Myths of femininity in Sri Lankan cinema'.

Further Reading

The following are select bibliographies of theoretical and general critical studies. The reader will find additional reading in the Headnotes to relevant sections, as well as in the Notes on Authors. For more extensive bibliographies on modernism see Bradbury and McFarlane (eds), *Modernism* (1976) and Eugene Lunn, *Marxism and Modernism* (1985). For fuller bibliographies on postmodernism see Steven Connor, *Postmodernist Culture* (1989) and Linda Hutcheon, *The Politics of Postmodernism* (1989). Where books and articles discuss both modernism and postmodernism they have generally been included under the latter.

Modernity and Modernism

ADORNO, THEODOR and MAX HORKHEIMER *Dialectic of Enlightenment*, trans. John Cumming (London: Allen Lane, 1972).

ANDERSON, PERRY 'Modernity and Revolution' in *Marxism and the Interpretation of Culture*, ed. Nelson and Grossberg (London: Macmillan, 1988), pp. 317–33.

BENJAMIN, ANDREW (ed.) *The Problems of Modernity. Adorno and Benjamin* (London and New York: Routledge, 1989).

BENJAMIN, WALTER *Illuminations*, ed. Hannah Arendt (London: Collins/Fontana, 1973).

BERMAN, MARSHALL *All That is Solid Melts Into Air. The Experience of Modernity* (London: Verso, 1983).

BENSTOCK, SHARI *Women of the Left Bank. Paris 1900–1940* (London: Virago, 1987).

BLOCH, ERNST *Heritage of Our Times*, (1935) trans. Neville Plaice and Stephen Plaice (Berkeley: University of California Press, 1991).

BLOCH, ERNST et al. *Aesthetics and Politics* (London: Verso, 1977).

BRADBURY, MALCOLM *The Social Context of Modern English Literature* (New York: Schocken, 1971).

BRADBURY, MALCOLM and JAMES McFARLANE (eds), *Modernism 1890–1930* (Harmondsworth: Penguin, 1976).

BRONNER, STEVEN and DOUGLAS KELLNER (eds), *Critical Theory and Society: a Reader* (London: Routledge, 1989).

FRISBY, DAVID *Fragments of Modernity. Theories of Modernity in the Work of Simmel, Kracauer and Benjamin* (Cambridge: Polity Press/Basil Blackwell, 1988).

JAMESON, FREDRIC *Marxism and Form* (Princeton, New Jersey: Princeton University Press, 1971).
—— *Late Marxism: Adorno or the Persistence of the Dialectic* (London and New York: Verso, 1990).
LUNN, EUGENE *Marxism and Modernism* (Berkeley: University of California Press, 1982, London: Verso, 1985).
MORETTI, FRANCO 'The Spell of Indecision' in *Marxism and the Interpretation of Culture*, ed. Nelson and Grossberg (London: Macmillan, 1988), pp. 339–46.
ROBINSON, LILLIAN and LISA VOGEL, 'Modernism and History', *New Literary History*, 3, 1 (Autumn 1971): 177–99.
STEINER, GEORGE *In Bluebeard's Castle: Some Notes Towards the Redefinition of Culture* (London: Faber and Faber; New Haven: Yale University Press, 1971).
WILLETT, JOHN *The New Sobriety. Art and Politics in the Weimar Period, 1917–1933* (London: Thames and Hudson, 1978).
—— *The Weimar Years. A Culture Cut Short* (London: Thames and Hudson, 1984).

Modernism, Literature and Culture

ADORNO, THEODOR *Prisms*, trans. S and S. Weber (London: Neville Spearman, 1967).
—— *Aesthetic Theory*, trans. C. Lenhardt, ed. G. Adorno and R. Tiedmann (London: Routledge, 1984).
ANTIN, DAVID 'Some Questions About Modernism', *Occident*, 8 (Spring 1974): 7–38.
BAKER, HOUSTON A. *Modernism and the Harlem Renaissance* (Chicago and London: University of Chicago Press, 1987).
BAKHTIN, MIKHAIL *The Dialogic Imagination*, ed. M. Holquist, trans. C. Emerson and M. Holquist (Austin: University of Texas Press, 1981).
BEEBE, MAURICE 'What Modernism Was' *Journal of Modern Literature*, 3 (1974): 1065–84.
BELL, MICHAEL *The Context of English Literature 1900–1930* (London: Methuen, 1980).
BENJAMIN, WALTER *Understanding Brecht*, trans. Anna Bostock, Introduction by Stanley Mitchell (London: New Left Books, 1973).
—— *Charles Baudelaire: a Lyric Poet in the Era of High Capitalism* trans. Harry Zohn (London: New Left Books, 1973).
BERGONZI, BERNARD 'The Advent of Modernism 1900–1920', in *The Twentieth Century*, ed. B. Bergonzi (London: Barrie and Jenkins, 1970), pp. 17–48.
—— *The Myth of Modernism and Twentieth-Century Literature* (New York: St Martin's Press, 1988).
BRECHT, BERTOLT *Brecht on Theatre*, ed. and trans. John Willett (New York: Hill and Wang; London: Eyre Methuen, 1964).
BROWN, DENNIS *The Modernist Self in Twentieth-Century English Literature* (London: Macmillan, 1989).
CHIARI, JOSEPH *The Aesthetics of Modernism* (London: Vision Press, 1970).
COLLIER, PETER and JUDY DAVIES (eds) *Modernism and the European Unconscious* (New York: St Martins Press; Cambridge: Polity Press/Basil Blackwell, 1990).
CRAIG, DAVID 'Loneliness and Anarchy: Aspects of Modernism' in *The Real Foundations. Literature and Social Change* (London: Oxford University Press, 1974), pp. 171–94.
CRONIN, ANTHONY *A Question of Modernity* (London: Secker and Warburg, 1966).

253

DE JONGH, JAMES *Vicious Modernism: Black Harlem and the Literary Imagination* (Cambridge: Cambridge University Press, 1990).

DE MAN, PAUL 'Literary History and Literary Modernity' and 'Lyric and Modernity' in *Blindness and Insight* (New York and London: Oxford University Press, 1971), pp. 142–86.

EAGLETON, TERRY *Exiles and Emigrés: Studies in Modern Literature* (London: Chatto and Windus, 1970).

—— *Walter Benjamin. Or Towards a Revolutionary Criticism* (London: Verso, 1981).

—— *Against The Grain. Essays 1975–1985* (London: Verso, 1986).

ELLMAN, RICHARD and CHARLES FEIDELSON JR (eds) *The Modern Tradition, Backgrounds of Modern Literature* (New York and London: Oxford University Press, 1965).

FAULKNER, PETER *Modernism* (London: Methuen, 1977).

—— (ed.) *A Modernist Reader. Modernism in England 1910–1930* (London: Batsford, 1986).

GARVIN, HARRY R. (ed.) *Romanticism, Modernism, Postmodernism* (Lewisburg, Ohio: Bucknell University Press, 1980).

GILBERT, SANDRA and SUSAN GUBAR *No Man's Land. The Place of the Woman Writer in the Twentieth Century* 2 vols (New Haven and London: Yale University Press, 1988, 1989).

GRAVES, ROBERT and LAURA RIDING *A Survey of Modernist Poetry* (1927; repr. Michigan: Scholarly Press, 1972).

HAMBURGER, MICHAEL *The Truth of Poetry* (London: Weidenfeld and Nicolson, 1969; Harmondsworth: Penguin, 1972).

HANSCOMBE, GILLIAN and VIRGINIA L. SMYERS *Writing For Their Lives. The Modernist Women 1910–1940* (London: The Women's Press, 1987).

HASTY, OLGA PETERS and SUSANNE FUSSO *America Through Russian Eyes, 1874–1926* (New Haven: Yale University Press, 1988).

HOFFMAN, GERHARD, ALFRED HORNUNG and RÜDIGER KUNOW '"Modern", "Postmodern" and "Contemporary" as Criteria for Analysis of 20th-Century Literature', *Amerikastudien*, **22** (1977): 19–46.

HOWE, IRVING (ed.)*Literary Modernism* (Greenwich, Connecticut: Fawcett Publications Inc., 1967).

—— *The Decline of the New* (New York: Harcourt Brace; London: Victor Gollancz, 1971).

HUYSSEN, ANDREAS and DAVID BATHRICK (eds) *Modernity and the Text. Revisions of German Modernism* (New York: Columbia University Press, 1989).

JAMESON, FREDRIC *Fables of Aggression: Wyndham Lewis, the Modernist as Fascist* (Berkeley, California and London: University of California Press, 1979).

JOSOPOVICI, GABRIEL *The Lessons of Modernism and Other Essays* (London: Macmillan, 1977).

KAMPF, LOUIS *On Modernism: the Prospects for Literature and Freedom* (Cambridge, Mass: MIT Press, 1967).

KAZIN, ALFRED 'On Modernism', *New Republic* (17 January 1976): 29–31.

KENNER, HUGH *The Pound Era* (London: Faber and Faber, 1972).

—— *A Homemade World: the American Modernist Writers* (New York: Alfred A. Knopf, 1975; London: Marion Boyars, 1977).

KERMODE, FRANK *The Sense of An Ending: Studies in the Theory of Fiction* (London and New York: Oxford University Press, 1967).

—— *Continuities* (London: Routledge & Kegan Paul; New York: Random House, 1968).

KRISTEVA, JULIA *Revolution in Poetic Language* (1974), trans. Margaret Waller, (New York: Columbia University Press, 1984).

KRUTCH, JOSEPH WOOD 'Modernism' in Modern Drama: a Definition and an Estimate* (Ithaca: Cornell University Press, 1953).

Further Reading

LANGBAUM, ROBERT *The Modern Spirit: Essays on the Continuity of Nineteenth- and Twentieth-Century Literature*) New York: Oxford University Press; London: Chatto and Windus, 1970).

LEVIN, HARRY 'What was Modernism' in *Refractions: Essays in Comparative Literature* (New York: Oxford University Press, 1966) pp. 271–95.

—— *Memories of the Moderns* (New York: New Directions, 1980).

LODGE, DAVID *The Modes of Modern Writing* (London: Edward Arnold, 1977).

LUKÁCS, GEORG *The Meaning of Contemporary Realism* trans. John and Necke Mander (London: Merlin Press, 1963).

MURDOCH, IRIS 'Against Dryness', *Encounter*, **16**, 1 (January, 1961): 16–20.

NICHOLLS, PETER *Modernisms. A Literary Guide* (London: Macmillan, 1991).

PERKINS, DAVID *A History of Modern Poetry from the 1890s to the High Modernist Mode* (Cambridge, Mass.; and London: Belknap Press/Harvard University Press, 1976).

PERLOFF, MARJORIE *The Dance of the Intellect. Studies in the Poetry of the Pound Tradition* (Cambridge: Cambridge University Press, 1985).

ROSENBERG, HAROLD *The Tradition of the New* (New York: McGraw-Hill, 1965).

SPENDER, STEPHEN *The Struggle of the Modern* (London: Hamish Hamilton; Berkeley: University of California Press, 1963).

STEAD, C. K. *The New Poetic* (London: Hutchinson, 1964; Harmondsworth: Penguin, 1979).

STEINMAN, LISA M. *Made in America. Science, Technology and Modern American Poets* (New Haven: Yale University Press, 1987).

SVARNY, ERIK *'The Men of 1914': T. S. Eliot and Early Modernism* (Milton Keynes: Open University Press, 1989).

SYMONS, JULIAN *Makers of the New. The Revolution in Literature 1912–1939* (London: André Deutsch, 1987).

TRILLING, LIONEL 'On the Modern Element in Literature', 1961, reprinted as 'On the Teaching of Modern Literature' in *Beyond Culture: Essays on Literature and Learning* (New York: Viking, 1965; London: Secker and Warburg, 1966).

WILLIAMS, RAYMOND *Drama From Ibsen to Brecht* (London: Chatto and Windus, 1969).

—— *The Politics of Modernism*, ed. and with Introduction by Tony Pinkney (London and New York: Verso, 1989).

WILSON, EDMUND *Axel's Castle. A Study in the Imaginative Literature of 1870–1930* (New York: Charles Scribner's Sons, 1931).

Modernism and the other arts (including studies of the avant-garde)

ADORNO, THEODOR *The Philosophy of Modern Music* (London: Sheed and Ward, 1973).

BAUDELAIRE, CHARLES *The Painter of Modern Life and Other Essays*, trans. and ed. Jonathan Mayne (London: Phaidon, 1964).

BÜRGER, PETER *The Theory of the Avant-Garde* trans. M. Shaw (Minneapolis: University of Minnesota; Manchester: University Press, 1984).

—— *The Decline of Modernism*, trans. Nicholas Walker (Cambridge: Basil Blackwell/ Polity Press, 1992).

BÜRGER, PETER and CHRISTA BÜRGER (eds) *Postmoderne: Alltag, Allegorie und Avantgarde* (Frankfurt am Main: Suhrkamp, 1987).

BUTLER, CHRISTOPHER *After the Wake: an Essay on the Contemporary Avant-Garde* (Oxford and New York: Oxford University Press, 1980).

CALINESCU, MATEI *Five Faces of Modernity: Modernism, Avant-Garde, Decadence, Kitsch, Postmodernism* (Durham, North Carolina: Duke University Press, 1987).

CHÉNIEUX-GENDRON, JACQUELINE *Surrealism* (New York: Columbia University Press, 1990).

CHRISTIE, IAN and RICHARD TAYLOR (eds) *Film Factory. Russian and Soviet Cinema in Documents* (London and New York: Routledge, 1988).

ELLIOT, DAVID *New Worlds, Russian Art and Society 1900–1937* (London: Thames and Hudson, 1986).

FRASCINA, FRANCIS and CHARLES HARRISON (eds) *Modern Art and Modernism. A Critical Anthology* (London: The Open University/Paul Chapman Publishing Ltd, 1982).

GREENBERG, CLEMENT 'Modernist Painting' (1965) in Frascina and Harrison (eds) ibid., pp. 5–10.

KELLY, MARY 'Re-viewing Modernist Criticism', *Screen* **22**, 3 (1981): 41–62.

KRAMER, HILTON *The Age of the Avant-Garde. An Art Chronicle of 1956–1972* (New York: Farrar, Strauss and Giroux, 1973).

KRAUSS, ROSALIND E. *The Originality of the Avant-Garde and Other Modernist Myths* (Cambridge Mass.: MIT Press, 1985).

LODDER, CHRISTINA *Russian Constructivism* (New Haven and London: Yale University Press, 1983).

PERLOFF, MARJORIE *The Futurist Moment. Avant-Garde, Avant Guerre, and the Language of Rupture* (Chicago and London: University of Chicago Press, 1986).

POGGIOLI, RENATO *The Theory of the Avant Garde*, trans. G. Fitzgerald (Cambridge, Mass.: Belknap Press/Harvard University Press, 1968).

RUSSELL, CHARLES (ed.) *The Avant-Garde Today. An International Anthology* (Urbana: University of Illinois Press, 1981).

—— *Poets, Prophets and Revolutionaries. The Literary Avant-Garde from Rimbaud through Postmodernism* (New York: Oxford University Press, 1985).

SCOTT, BONNIE KIME (ed.) *The Gender of Modernism* (Bloomington: Indiana University Press, 1990).

SHATTUCK, ROGER *The Banquet Years. The Origins of the Avant-Garde in France, 1885 to World War One: Alfred Jarry, Henri Rousseau, Erik Satie, Guillaume Apollinaire* rev. ed. (New York: Random House, 1968).

SULEIMAN, SUSAN RUBIN *Subversive Intent. Gender, Politics and the Avant-Garde* Cambridge, Mass.: Harvard University Press, 1990).

TASHJIAN, DICKRAN *William Carlos Williams and the American Scene 1920–1940* (New York: Whitney Museum of Modern Art/University of California Press, 1978).

TILLYARD, S. K. *The Impact of Modernism. The Visual Arts in Edwardian England* London: Routledge, 1988).

TIMMS, EDWARD and DAVID KELLEY (eds) *Unreal City: Urban Experience in Modern European Literature and Art* (New York: St Martin's Press; Manchester: University of Manchester Press, 1985).

TIMMS, EDWARD and PETER COLLIER (eds) *Visions and Blueprints. Avant-Garde Culture and Radical Politics in Early Twentieth-Century Europe* (New York: St Martin's Press; Manchester: University of Manchester Press, 1988).

WALSH, MARTIN *The Brechtian Aspect of Radical Cinema*, ed. Keith M. Richard (London: BFI, 1981).

WEES, WILLIAM C. *Vorticism and the English Avant-Garde* (Toronto: University of Toronto Press; Manchester: University of Manchester Press, 1972).

WEIGHTMAN, JOHN *The Concept of the Avant-Garde: Explorations in Modernism* (New York: Library Press; London: Alcove Press 1973).

WHITE, JOHN J. *Literary Futurism. Aspects of the First Avant-Garde* (Oxford: Clarendon Press, 1990).

YOUNG, ALAN *Dada and After* (Manchester: University of Manchester Press, 1983).

Postmodernity and Postmodernism

ADAM, IAN and HELEN TIFFIN, *Past the Last Post. Theorizing Post-Colonialism and Post-Modernism* (London: Harvester Wheatsheaf, 1991).

ARAC, JONATHAN (ed.) *Postmodernism and Politics* (Manchester: Manchester University Press, 1986).

BAUDRILLARD, JEAN *The Mirror of Production* (1973) trans. Mark Poster (St Louis: Telos Press, 1975).

—— *For A Critique of the Political Economy Of the Sign* (1976), trans. Charles Levin (St Louis: Telos Press, 1981).

—— *Forget Foucault* (1977), trans. Nicole Dufresne (New York: Semiotext(e), 1987).

—— *Seduction* (1979) trans. Brian Singer (London: Macmillan, 1990).

—— *Simulations* (1981) trans. Paul Foss, Paul Patton and Philip Beitchman (New York: Semiotext(e), 1983).

—— *In the Shadow of the Silent Majorities . . .* (1983) trans. Paul Foss, Paul Patton and John Johnston (New York: Semiotext(e), 1983).

—— *America* (1986) trans. Chris Turner (London and New York: Verso, 1988).

—— *Selected Writings*, ed. Mark Poster (Oxford: Polity Press, 1988).

—— *Cool Memories* (1987), trans. Chris Turner (London and New York: Verso, 1990).

—— *Fatal Strategies* (1983), trans. Philip Beitchman and W. G. J. Nieluchowsksi, ed. Jim Fleming (New York: Semiotext(e); London: Pluto, 1990).

BAUMAN, ZYGMUNT *Legislators and Interpreters: On Modernity, Post-Modernity and Intellectuals* (Ithaca: Cornell University Press, 1987).

BELL, DANIEL *The Coming of Post-Industrial Society* New York: Basic Books, 1973).

BELL, DAVID *The Cultural Contradictions of Capitalism* (New York: Basic Books, 1976).

BENNINGTON, GEOFF *Lyotard: Writing the Event* (Manchester: Manchester University Press, 1988).

BERMAN, R. A. 'The Routinization of Charismatic Modernism and the Problem of Postmodernity' *Cultural Critique*, 5 (1987): 49–68.

BERNSTEIN, RICHARD J. (ed.) *Habermas and Modernity* (Cambridge: Polity Press/Basil Blackwell 1985).

BOYNE, ROY and ALI RATTANSI (eds) *Postmodernism and Society* (London: Macmillan, 1990).

BROOKEMAN, CHRISTOPHER *American Society and Culture Since the 1930s* (London: Macmillan, 1984).

CALLINICOS, ALEX *Against Postmodernism* (Cambridge: Polity/Basil Blackwell, 1989).

CONNOR, STEVEN *Postmodernist Culture. An Introduction to Theories of the Contemporary* (Oxford: Basil Blackwell, 1989).

COOK, DAVID and ARTHUR KROKER *The Postmodern Scene, Excremental Culture and Hyper-Aesthetics* (New York: St Martins Press, 1986); London: Macmillan, 1988).

COOKE, PHILIP *Back to the Future, Modernity, Postmodernity and Locality* (London: Unwin Hyman, 1990).

DEBORD, GUY *Society of the Spectacle* (1967, Detroit: Black and Red, 1977).

DEWS, PETER *Logics of Disintegration* (London: Verso, 1987).

DOCHERTY, THOMAS *After Theory, Post Modernism/Post Marxism* (London and New York: Routledge, 1990).

DURING, SIMON 'Postmodernism or Post-Colonialism Today' *Textual Practice*, 1, 1 (1987): 32–47.

EAGLETON, TERRY 'Capitalism, Modernism and Postmodernism' in *Against The Grain* (London: Verso, 1986), pp. 131–48.

FEATHERSTONE, MIKE *Postmodernism – A Theory and Society special double issue* (London: Sage, 1988).

FEKETE, JOHN (ed.) *Life After Postmodernism. Essays on Value and Culture* (London: Macmillan, 1988).

257

FLAX, JANE *Thinking Fragments, Psychoanalysis, Feminism and Postmodernism in the Contemporary West* (Berkeley: University of California Press, 1990).

FOSTER, HAL (ed.) *The Anti-Aesthetic: Essays on Postmodern Culture* (Port Townsend: Bay Press, 1985; reprinted as *Postmodern Culture* (London and Sydney: Pluto Press, 1985).

FRANKOVITS ANDRÉ (ed.) *Seduced and Abandoned: the Baudrillard Scene* (Glebe, Australia: Stonemoss Services; New York: Semiotext(e), 1984).

FRAZER, NANCY 'The French Derrideans: Politicising Deconstruction or Deconstructing Politics', *New German Critique* 33 (1984): 127–54.

GIDDENS, ANTHONY 'Modernism and Post-Modernism', *New German Critique* 22 (1981): 15–18.

GROSZ E. A. et al. (eds) *Futur*fall: Excursions into Postmodernity* (Sydney: Power Institute of Fine Art, 1986).

HABERMAS, JÜRGEN *Legitimation Crisis*, trans. Thomas McCarthy (London: Heinemann, 1976).

—— *The Theory of Communicative Action*, 2 vols (Cambridge: Polity/Blackwell, 1985, 1988).

—— *The Philosophical Discourse of Modernity*, trans. Frederick Lawrence (Cambridge: Polity/Blackwell, 1988).

—— *The Structural Transformation of the Public Sphere*, trans. Thomas Burger in association with Frederick Lawrence (Cambridge: Polity/Blackwell, 1989).

HARVEY, DAVID *The Condition of Postmodernity* (Oxford: Basil Blackwell, 1989).

HASSAN, IHAB *The Right Promethean Fire: Imagination, Science and Cultural Change* (Urbana, Illinois: University of Illinois Press, 1980).

—— *The Postmodern Turn. Essays in Postmodern Theory and Culture* (Columbus: Ohio State University Press, 1987).

HASSAN, IHAB and SALLY HASSAN (eds) *Innovation/Renovation: New Perspectives on the Humanities* (Madison: University of Wisconsin Press, 1983).

HONNETH, AXEL 'An Aversion Against the Universal: a Commentary on Lyotard's Postmodern Condition' in *Theory, Culture and Society*, 2, 3 (1985): 147–157.

HUYSSEN, ANDREAS *After The Great Divide: Modernism, Mass Culture, Postmodernism* (Bloomington: Indiana University Press 1986; London: Macmillan, 1988).

JACOBS, JANE *Death and Life of Great American Cities* (New York: Vintage, 1961).

JAMESON, FREDRIC 'Postmodernism, or the Cultural Logic of Late Capitalism', *New Left Review*, 146 (1984): 53–92, in *Postmodernism or the Cultural Logic of Late Capitalism* (London: Verso, 1991).

—— 'The Politics of Theory: Ideological Positions in the Postmodernism Debate', *New German Critique*, 33 (1984): 55–66; reprinted in *Modern Criticism and Theory; a Reader*, ed. David Lodge (London and New York: Longman, 1988), pp. 373–83.

—— 'Postmodernism and Consumer Society' in *Postmodern Culture*. ed. Hal Foster (London and Sydney: Pluto, 1985), pp. 111–25.

—— *Postmodernism or the Cultural Logic of Late Capitalism* (London: Verso, 1991).

JARDINE, ALICE *Gynesis: Configurations of Woman and Modernity* (Ithaca and London: Cornell University Press, 1985).

KAPLAN, E. AANN (ed.) *Postmodernism and its Discontents: Theories, Practices* (London and New York, 1988).

KELLNER, DOUGLAS *Jean Baudrillard, From Marxism to Postmodernism and Beyond* (Cambridge: Polity Press/Basil Blackwell, 1988).

—— *Postmodernism/Jameson/Critique* (Washington: Maisonneuve Press, 1990).

KROKER, ARTHUR and MARILOUISE KROKER (eds) *Body Invaders: Sexuality and the Postmodern Condition* (London: Macmillan, 1988).

LACLAU, ERNESTO *New Reflections on the Revolution of Our Time* (London and New York: Verso, 1990).

LACLAU, ERNESTO and CHANTAL MOUFFE, *Hegemony and Socialist Strategy. Towards a Radical Democratic Politics* (London and New York: Verso, 1985).

LASH, SCOTT *Sociology of Postmodernism* (London: Routledge, 1990).

LOVIBOND, SARAH 'Feminism and Postmodernism' in *Postmodernism and Society* ed. Roy Boyne and Ali Rattansi (London: Macmillan, 1990). pp. 154–86.

LYOTARD, JEAN-FRANÇOIS *Just Gaming*, trans. Wlad Godzich and Brian Massumi (Minneapolis: University of Minnesota Press, 1985).

—— *The Postmodern Condition: a Report on Knowledge* (1979), trans. Geoff Bennington and Brian Massumi, foreword by Fredric Jameson (Minneapolis: University of Minnesota Press; Manchester: University of Manchester Press, 1984).

—— *Le Postmoderne expliqué aux enfants* (Paris: Galilée, 1986).

—— *The 'Différend', Phrases in Dispute* (1983), trans. G. Van Den Abbeele (Manchester: University of Manchester Press, 1988).

—— *Peregrinations. Law, Form, Event* (New York and Oxford: Columbia University Press, 1988).

—— *Inhuman*, trans. G. Bennington and Rachel Bowlby (Cambridge: Blackwell/ Polity Press, 1991).

MANDEL, ERNEST *Late Capitalism* (London: Verso, 1975).

MELVILLE, STEPHEN *Philosophy Beside Itself. On Deconstruction and Modernism* (Manchester: Manchester University Press, 1986).

MOI, TORIL 'Feminism, Postmodernism and Style: Recent Feminist Criticism in the United States', *Cultural Critique*, 9 (1988): 3–22.

MOUZELIS, NICOS *Post-Marxist Alternatives* (London: Macmillan, 1990).

NELSON, CARY and LAWRENCE GROSSBERG, *Marxism and the Interpretation of Culture* (London: Macmillan, 1988).

NICHOLSON, LINDA J. (ed.) *Feminism/Postmodernism* (London and New York: Routledge, 1990).

NORRIS, CHRISTOPHER *What's Wrong with Postmodernism. Critical Theory and the Ends of Philosophy* (Toronto: Harvester Wheatsheaf, 1990).

OWENS, CRAIG 'Feminism and Postmodernism' in *Postmodern Culture*, ed. Hal Foster (London and Sydney: Pluto, 1985), pp. 57–82.

RORTY, RICHARD 'Habermas and Lyotard on Postmodernity' in *Habermas and Modernity* ed. Richard Bernstein (Cambridge: Polity/Blackwell, 1985, pp. 161–76.

ROSS, ANDREW (ed.) *Universal Abandon? The Politics of Postmodernism* (Edinburgh: The University of Edinburgh Press, 1988).

RYAN, MICHAEL 'Postmodern Politics' *Theory, Culture and Society* 5, 2–3 (1988): 559–76.

SARUP, MADAN *An Introductory Guide to Post-Structuralism and Postmodernism* (London: Harvester Wheatsheaf, 1988).

SCHULTE-SASSE, JOCHEN 'Modernity and Postmodernism: Framing the Issue', *Cultural Critique*, 5 (1987): 5–22.

Second of January Group, *After Truth. A Post-Modern Manifesto* (London; Inventions Press, 1986).

SHEVTSOVA, MARIA 'Intellectuals, Commitment and Political Power: Interview with Jean Baudrillard', *Thesis Eleven*, 10–11 (1984/5): 166–75.

SILVERMAN, HUGH J. (ed.) *Postmodernism – Philosophy and the Arts* (New York and London: Routledge, 1990).

SIMONE MALIQALIM, TIMOTHY *About Face. Race in Postmodern America* (New York: Automedia, 1989).

TURNER, BRYAN S. (ed.) *Theories of Modernity and Postmodernity* (London: Sage, 1990).

WAKEFIELD, NEVILLE *Postmodernism: the Twilight of the Real* (London and Winchester, Mass.: Pluto Press, 1990).

WELLMER, ALBRECHT 'On the Dialectic of Modernism and Postmodernism', *Praxis International*, 4 (1985): 337–62.

—— *The Persistence of Modernity* (Cambridge, Mass.: MIT Press: Cambridge: Polity Press/Basil Blackwell, 1991).
WOLIN, RICHARD 'Modernism vs Postmodernism', *Telos*, **62** (1984/5): 9–29.

Postmodernism and Literature

ALEXANDER, MARGUERITE *Flights from Realism. Themes and Strategies in Postmodernist British and American Fiction* (London: Edward Arnold, 1990).
ALLEN, DONALD and GEORGE BUTTERICK *The Postmoderns: the New American Poetry Revised* (New York: Grove Press, 1982).
ALTIERI, CHARLES 'From Symbolist Thought to Immanence: the Ground of Postmodern American Poetics' *Boundary* 2, **1** (1973): 605–41.
—— 'Postmodernism: a Question of Definition', *Par Rapport*, **2** (1979): 87–100.
ANDREWS, BRUCE and CHARLES BERNSTEIN (eds) The L=A=N=G=U=A=G=E Book (Carbondale and Edwardville, Southern Illinois Press, 1984).
ANTIN, DAVID 'Modernism and Postmodernism. Approaching the Present in American Poetry', *Boundary* 2, **1** (Fall, 1972) 98–133.
ARAC, JONATHAN *Critical Genealogies. Historical Situations for Postmodern Literary Studies* (New York: Columbia University Press, 1987).
BARTH, JOHN 'The Literature of Exhaustion' (1966) in *The Novel Today: Contemporary Writers on Modern Fiction*, ed. Malcolm Bradbury (Glasgow: Collins/Fontana, 1977), pp. 70–83.
—— 'The Literature of Replenishment: Postmodernist Fiction', *Atlantic Monthly*, **245**, 1 (1980): 65–71.
BERTENS, HANS 'The Postmodern *Weltanschaung* and its Relation with Modernism: an Introductory Survey' in *Approaching Postmodernism*, ed. Fokkema and Bertens (1986), pp. 9–51.
BRADBURY, MALCOLM, 'Modernisms/Postmodernisms' in *Innovation/Renovation*, ed. Hassan and Hassan (1983), pp. 311–28.
ENZENSBERGER, HANS MAGNUS *The Consciousness Industry: On Literature, Politics and the Media* (New York: Seabury Press, 1974).
FEDERMAN, RAYMOND (ed.) *Surfiction: Fiction Now and Tomorrow* (Chicago: Swallow Press 1975, 2nd edn, 1981).
FIEDLER, LESLIE 'The New Mutants' and 'Cross the Border, Close the Gap' in *The Collected Essays of Leslie Fiedler*, Vol. 2 (New York: Stein and Day, 1971), pp. 379–400, 461–85.
—— 'The Death and Rebirths of the Novel: the View from '82' in Ihab and Sally Hassan (eds) op. cit., pp. 225–42.
FOKKEMA, DOUWE and HANS BERTENS (eds) *Approaching Postmodernism* (Amsterdam and Philadelphia: John Benjamins, 1986).
FOKKEMA, DOUWE and MATEI CALINESCU (eds) *Exploring Postmodernism* (Amsterdam: John Benjamins, 1988).
GRAFF, GERALD 'The Myth of the Postmodernist Breakthrough' in *The Novel Today*, ed. Malcolm Bradbury (Glasgow: Collins/Fontana, 1977) pp. 217–49.
HASSAN, IHAB *Paracriticisms: Seven Speculations of the Times* (Urbana: University of Illinois Press, 1975).
—— *The Dismemberment of Orpheus. Toward a Postmodern Literature* (New York: Oxford University Press, 1982).
HUTCHEON, LINDA *Narcissistic Narrative: the Metafictional Paradox* (New York and London: Methuen, 1980).
—— *A Poetics of Postmodernism. History, Theory, Fiction* (New York and London: Routledge, 1988).

—— *The Politics of Postmodernism* (New York and London: Routledge, 1989).

KLINKOWITZ, JEROME *Literary Disruptions: the Making of a Post-Contemporary American Fiction* (Urbana: University of Illinois Press, 1975, 2nd edn, 1980).

LE CLAIR, TOM and LARRY MCCAFFERY (eds) *Anything Can Happen. Interviews with American Novelists* (Urbana: University of Illinois Press, 1983).

LEE, ALISON *Realism and Power. Postmodern British Fiction* (London and New York: Routledge, 1990).

LODGE, DAVID 'Modernism, Anti-Modernism, Postmodernism' in *Working With Structuralism* (London: Routledge, 1981), pp. 3–16.

MALMGREN, CARL DARRYL *Fictional Space in the Modernist and Postmodernist American Novel* (Lewisburg, Pennsylvania: Bucknell University Press, 1985).

MAZZARO, JEROME *Postmodern American Poetry* (Urbana: University of Illinois Press, 1980).

MCCAFFERY, LARRY (ed.) *Postmodern Fiction: a Bio-Bibliography* (Westport, Connecticut: Greenwood Press, 1986).

MCHALE, BRIAN *Postmodernist Fiction* (London and New York: Methuen, 1987).

NEWMAN, CHARLES *The Postmodern Aura: the Act of Fiction in an Age of Inflation* (Evanston, Illinois: Northwestern University Press, 1985).

OLSON, CHARLES *Additional Prose* (Bolinas, California: Four Seasons Foundation, 1974).

—— 'The Act of Writing in the Context of Post-Modern Man' in *Olson: the Journal of the Charles Olson Archives*, **2** (1974): 28.

PÜTZ, MANFRED and PETER FREESE (eds) *Postmodernism in American Literature: a Critical Anthology* (Darmstadt: Thesen, 1984).

SCHOLES, ROBERT *Structural Fabulation: an Essay on the Fiction of the Future* (Notre Dame, Indiana: University of Notre Dame Press, 1975).

—— *Fabulation and Metafiction* (Urbana: University of Illinois Press, 1979).

SILLIMAN, RON '"Postmodernism": Sign for a Struggle, the Struggle for the Sign', *Poetics Journal* **7** (1987): 18–39.

SONTAG, SUSAN *Against Interpretation* (New York: Dell, 1967).

—— *A Susan Sontag Reader*, Introduction by Elizabeth Hardwick (Harmondsworth: Penguin, 1983).

SPANOS, WILLIAM V. (ed.) *Martin Heidegger and the Question of Literature. Toward a Postmodern Literary Hermeneutics* (Bloomington: Indiana University Press, 1979).

—— *Repetitions: The Postmodern Occasion in Literature and Culture* (Baton Rouge: Louisiana State University Press, 1987).

SUKENICK, RONALD *In Form: Digressions on the Art of Fiction* (Carbondale and Edwardsville, Illinois: Southern Illinois University Press, 1985).

WAUGH, PATRICIA *Metafiction: the Theory and Practice of Self-Conscious Fiction* (London and New York: Methuen, 1984).

—— *Feminine Fictions, Revisiting the Postmodern* (London and New York: Routledge, 1989).

WILDE, ALAN *Horizons of Assent: Modernism, Postmodernism and the Ironic Imagination* (Baltimore and London: Johns Hopkins University Press, 1981).

Postmodernism, Popular Culture and the Other Arts

APPIGNANESI, LISA (ed.) *Postmodernism. ICA Documents* 4 (London: Institute of Contemporary Arts, 1986).

BANES, SALLY *Terpsichore in Sneakers: Postmodern Dance* (Middletown, Connecticut: Wesleyan University Press, 1986).

BLAU, HERBERT *The Eye of the Prey: Subversions of the Postmodern* (Bloomington: Indiana University Press, 1987).

BURGIN, VICTOR (ed.) *Thinking Photography* (London: Macmillan, 1982).

—— *The End of Art Theory: Criticism and Postmodernity* (London: Macmillan, 1986).

CHAMBERS IAIN *Popular Culture: The Metropolitan Experience* (London and New York: Methuen, 1986).

—— *Border Dialogues. Journeys in Postmodernity* (London and New York: Comedia/Routledge, 1990).

COLLINS, JIM *Uncommon Cultures. Popular Culture and Postmodernism* (London and New York: Routledge, 1989).

COLLINS, MICHAEL *Towards Post-Modernism. Design since 1851* (London: British Museum, 1987).

CREED, BARBARA 'From Here to Modernity: Feminism and Postmodernism', *Screen*, **28**, 2 (1987): 47–68.

DAVIS, MIKE *City of Quartz. Evacuating the Future of Los Angeles* (New York and London: Verso, 1990).

DAVIS, MIKE, MICHAEL SPRINKER and FRED PFEIL, *The Year Left* (London: Verso, 1985).

DERRIDA, JACQUES 'The Theatre of Cruelty and the Closure of Representation' in *Writing and Difference*, trans. Alan Bass (London: Routledge, 1978), pp. 169–75.

—— *The Truth in Painting*, trans. Geoff Bennington and Ian McLeod (Chicago: University of Chicago Press, 1987).

DURAND, RÉGIS 'Theatre/Signs/Performance: On some Transformations of the Theatrical and the Theoretical' in *Innovation/Renovation*, ed. Ihab and Sally Hassan (Madison: University of Wisconsin Press, 1983), pp. 211–24.

ECO, UMBERTO *Travels in Hyperreality*, trans. William Weaver (London: Picador, 1987).

FERGUSON, RUSSELL et al. (eds) *Discourses. Conversations in Postmodern Art and Culture* (New York: New Museum of Modern Art/MIT Press, 1990).

FORTE JEANIE 'Women's Performance Art: Feminism and Postmodernism', *Theatre Journal* **40**, 2 (1988): 217–45.

FOSTER, HAL *Recodings: Art, Spectacle, Cultural Politics* (Port Townshend, Washington: Bay Press, 1985).

FUCHS, ELINOR 'The Theatre after Derrida' *Performing Arts Journal*, **26/7** (1985): 163–73.

GREENBERG, CLEMENT 'Modern and Postmodern', *Arts Magazine*, **54**, 6 (1980): 64–6.

HEBDIGE, DICK *Hiding in the Light* (London and New York: Routledge/Comedia, 1988).

HUGHES, ROBERT *The Shock of the New: Art and the Century of Change* (New York: Knopf, 1981).

HUTCHEON, LINDA *A Theory of Parody. The Teachings of Twentieth-Century Art Forms* (New York and London: Methuen, 1985).

JAMESON, FREDRIC 'On Magic Realism in Film', *Critical Inquiry*, **12**, 2: 301–25.

—— 'Reading Without Interpretation: Postmodernism and the Video-Text' in *The Linguistics of Writing*, ed. Derek Attridge et al. (Manchester: University of Manchester Press, 1987), pp. 199–233.

JENCKS, CHARLES *The Language of Post-Modern Architecture* 4th edn (London: Academy Editions; New York: Rizzoli, 1984).

—— *What is Postmodernism?* (London: Academy Editions; New York: St Martin's Press, 1986).

KAPLAN, E. ANN *Rocking Around the Clock: Music, Television, Post-Modernism and Consumer Culture* (London and New York: Methuen, 1987).

KRAMER, HILTON *The Revenge of the Philistines: Art and Culture, 1972–1984* (New York: Free Press, 1985).

MacCabe, Colin (ed.) *High Theory/Low Culture* (Manchester: University of Manchester Press, 1986).

McRobbie, Angela 'Postmodernism and Popular Culture' in *Postmodernism*, ed. Lisa Appignanesi, op. cit., pp. 54–8.

Morris, Meaghan *The Pirate's Fiancée* (London: Verso, 1988).

Nairne, Sandy with Geoff Dunlop and John Wyver, *State of the Art; Ideas and Images in the 1980s* (London: Chatto and Windus, 1987).

Norris, Christopher and Andrew Benjamin *What is Deconstruction?* (New York: St Martin's Press; London: Academy Editions, 1988).

Pfeil, Fred 'Postmodernism as a "Structure of Feeling"' in *Marxism and the Interpretation of Culture*, ed. Nelson and Grossberg (1988), pp. 381–403.

Roberts, David (ed.) *The Independent Group. Postwar Britain and the Aesthetics of Plenty*, Introduction by Jacquelynn Baas (Cambridge: Mass.: MIT Press, 1990).

Roberts, John *Postmodernism, Politics and Art* (Manchester: University of Manchester Press, 1990).

Simard, Rodney *Postmodern Drama. Contemporary Playwrights in America and Britain* (Landham, Maryland: University Press of America/American Theatre Association, 1984).

Portoghesi, Paolo *Postmodern: the Architecture of the Postindustrial Society*, trans. Ellen Shapiro (New York: Rizzoli, 1983).

Ulmer, Gregory *Applied Grammatology: Post(e)-Pedagogy from Jacques Derrida to Joseph Beuys* (Baltimore and London: Johns Hopkins University Press, 1985).

Venturi, Robert *Complexity and Contradiction in Architecture*, 2nd edn (New York: Museum of Modern Art and Graham Foundations, 1972).

Venturi, Robert, Denise Scott Brown and Steven Izenour *Learning from Las Vegas* (Cambridge, Mass.: MIT Press, 1977).

Wallis, Brian (ed.) *Blasted Allegories: an Anthology of Writings by Contemporary Artists* (Cambridge, Mass.: New Museum of Contemporary Art/MIT Press, 1987).

Wilson, Elizabeth *Adorned in Dreams. Fashion and Modernity* (London: Virago, 1985).

—— *Hallucinations. Life in the Post-Modern City* (London: Hutchinson Radius, 1989).

Wilcox, Leonard 'Modernism vs Postmodernism: Shepard's *The Tooth of Crime* and the Discourses of Popular Culture' *Modern Drama*, xxx no. 4 (Dec 1987): 560–73

Wright, Elizabeth *Postmodern Brecht* (London and New York: Routledge, 1988).

Wyver, John 'Television and Postmodernism' in *Postmodernism* ed. Lisa Appignanesi (London: ICA), pp. 52–4.

Special Issues on Modernity, Modernism, Postmodernism

Amerikastudien, **22**, 1 (1977), Postmodernism.

Architectural Design, **58**, 3–4 (1988), Deconstruction in Architecture.

Art and Design, **4**, 3–4 (1988), The New Modernism.

Block, **14** (Autumn, 1988), 'The Work of Art in the Electronic Age'.

Chicago Review, **33**, 2–3 (1983), Postmodernist Literature and Criticism.

Cultural Critique, **5** (Winter, 1987), 'Modernity, Modernism; Postmodernity, Postmodernism'.

The Drama Review, **19**, 1 (1975), Post-Modern Dance.

Journal of Modern Literature, **3**, 5 (1974), 'From Modernism to Postmodernism'.

Krisis, **2** (1984); 3–4 (1985), Postmodernism.

Minnesota Review, **23** (Fall, 1984), 'The Politics of Postmodernism'.

New Formations, **7** (1989), 'Modernism/Masochism'.
New Formations, **11** (1990), 'The City'.
New German Critique, **22** (1981), 'Habermas and Postmodernism'.
New German Critique, **33** (1984), 'Modernity and Postmodernity'.
New German Critique, **34** (1985); **39** (1986), On Walter Benjamin.
New Literary History, **3**, 1 (1971), Modernism and Postmodernism.
New From Nowhere, **7** (Winter, 1989), 'The Politics of Modernism'.
Par Rapport, **2**, 2 (1979), Postmodernism.
Screen, **28**, 2 (1987), Postmodern Film.
Theory, Culture and Society, **2**, 3 (1985), 'The Fate of Modernity'.
Theory Culture and Society, **5**: 2–3 (1988), Postmodernism.
Triquarterly, **26** (1973); **30** (1974); **32** (1974); **33** (1975), Postmodernism.

Relevant discussion also appears regularly in *New Left Review; October; Social Text; Textual Practice; Third Text.*

Index